Women in Citizen Advocacy

To Steve, Sam, Jacob, and Rachel and
To John and Renee

Women in
Citizen Advocacy
Stories of 28 Shapers
of Public Policy

by

Georgia Mattison
Sandra Storey

McFarland & Company, Inc., Publishers
Jefferson, North Carolina, and London

Acknowledgments: We have many people and groups to acknowledge. First we would like to thank Katherine Hanson and Barbara Burnham for talking with us in what turned out to be the motivating sessions that led to our writing this book.

Barbara and Kip Tiernan, whom we would also like to thank, let us do practice interviews with them, so we could work on the content and techniques of our later interviews.

We thank these women for agreeing to be interviewed and for supplying materials: Juanita Kennedy Morgan, Kathleen Kelley, Marlene Sciascia, Brenda LaBlanc, Lois Gibbs, Eleanor Josaitis, Stefan Harvey, Betsy Reifsnider, Janet Ferone, Carol Garvin, Diane Roach, Kattie Portis, Tish Sommers, Dorothy Ridings, Gini Laurie, Connie Spruill, Lotta Chi, Norma Wilson, Martha Cotera, Barbara Reed, Sally Mead, Charlotte Tropp, Sandra Kurjiaka, Janet Diamond, Carol Tucker Foreman, Nancy Sylvester, and Kathleen Sheekey.

We thank these organizations for contributing information, through the women we interviewed: Civil Liberties Union of Arkansas, Older Women's League, Black Women's Political Caucus, Common Cause, NETWORK, Mental Health Association, League of Women Voters, National Organization for Women, American Association of Business and Professional Women in Construction, Sierra Club, Des Moines Citizens for Community Improvement, Boston Teachers Union, St. Paul American Indian Center, Citizens Clearinghouse for Hazardous Wastes, Women, Inc., Coalition for Basic Human Needs, Ohoyo Resource Center, National Women's Employment and Education Center, Mexican American Business and Professional Women of Austin, North Pacific Rim Native American Corporation, RSVP/Share, Rehabilitation Gazette, Focus:HOPE, Interfaith, Inc., Organization of Chinese American Women, Black Hills Alliance, Center for Budget and Policy Priorities, Gray Panthers, SANE, and the New York Mayor's Office for the Handicapped.

We are especially grateful to: The Schlesinger Library on the History of Women in America at Radcliffe College; Shirley Sallet for interviewing Dorothy Ridings; Sidney Storey for interviewing Betsy Riefsnider; Helen Mattison for interviewing Charlotte Tropp; Peg Moloney, Mary Jane Storey and Dee Hopkins, for assisting us in our search for advocates to interview; Senator Tom Harkin, who led us to Brenda LaBlanc; Adrienne Cupples, who helped us design our questionnaire; Barbara Zang and Fran Froelich, whose comments on the first draft were invaluable; and Priscilla Ellis, who shared information from the realm of psychology to help us understand advocacy.

Most important, we would like to thank everyone who encouraged us by saying, "I can't wait for you to finish the book. I really need to read it."

British Library Cataloguing-in-Publication data are available

Library of Congress Cataloguing-in-Publication Data

Mattison, Georgia, 1944–
   Women in citizen advocacy : stories of 28 shapers of public policy / by Georgia Mattison [and] Sandra Storey.
      p. cm.
   Includes bibliographical references and index.
   ISBN 0-89950-770-X (library binding : 50# alkaline paper) ∞
   1. Women in politics—United States—Interviews.   2. Lobbyists—United States—Interviews.   3. Pressure groups—United States.
I. Storey, Sandra, 1946– .   II. Title.
HQ1236.5.U6M385   1992
322.4'3—dc20   91-50950
                                                   CIP

Manufactured in the United States of America

McFarland & Company, Inc., Publishers
   Box 611, Jefferson, North Carolina 28640

Contents

Introduction

A revolution has been taking place during the past decade, hidden below the surface of the daily news.

At the same time, numbers of voters have been dwindling because of what commentators say is disenchantment with electoral politics, Americans' concern about government policies that affect their lives seems to be booming.

The 1988 presidential election saw the second-lowest voter turnout this century, causing a panic among analysts about the condition of democracy. But at the same time the number of voters has shrunk, hundreds of thousands of Americans have joined groups that focus attention on public issues.

Tired of party platforms candidates ignore? How about representatives who don't come through? Care more about what's happening in the world than who's making it happen? Unsure about whether that politician on the ballot agrees with you on an issue?

It's natural that people who answer affirmatively to those questions have shifted emphasis from pulling levers in voting booths to collecting signatures at information booths to influence the world around them.

At the forefront of many groups changing public policy in cities, states and the nation's capital, women have emerged to take on roles as advocates that they say are more challenging than holding public office.

While the cult of personality dominates headlines, these advocates direct public attention to causes more than characters. If voters' apathy toward political races between individuals and parties is an indication of their dissatisfaction with politics, their growing involvement in issues shows there is hope for active democracy still. How people voice their concern is changing.

Advocates are applying an ethic of caregiving and empathy to the highly competitive world of policy-making. Having entered the win-lose arenas of legislatures, courtrooms and commission hearings, these women use their values, along with their intellects, to affect public policy directly. The gender gap—a documented distance between women's and men's opinions on issues in the early 1980s—has gradually been closed by women themselves, who use noncombative means to achieve policy victories.

This book describes the efforts of 28 women who lead efforts for change across the country. Their stories—presented in a how-to format—reveal fundamentals of advocacy that lie just beneath the surface of news stories that quote individual advocates from particular organizations on specific subjects.

Scanning a daily newspaper turns up almost a dozen policy advocates speaking in different stories on a range of topics.

On the surface, advocates in this book also seem like a dissimilar bunch. Carol Tucker Foreman is a Washington lobbyist who was working on bankruptcy law for asbestos disease victims when we interviewed her. Kattie Portis founded and still directs a drug rehabilitation program for women in Boston.

The groups vary too, from an informal collection of neighborhood residents, like Martha Cotera and her colleagues in Austin, Texas, to a huge national organization—the League of Women Voters—that works on many national, state and local issues.

Some of the advocates, like Barbara Reed, are paid; many are volunteers, like Carol Garvin. They may devote themselves to public issues full-time or ten hours a month, depending on their schedules. Advocates have a unique place in society because they hold so many different roles. Some, like Marlene Sciascia, leave non-profit groups to become affiliated with government policy-making.

Advocates in this book—of different ages, races, ethnic groups and educational backgrounds—come from all over the country. Juanita Kennedy Morgan began her fight for rights for black people during the Roosevelt administration after moving from Alabama to the capital. Environmentalist and California resident Betsy Reifsnider began her work when she was in her 20s during the Reagan administration.

The issues treated in news stories have little in common on the surface. Lois Gibbs heads an organization that helps people all over the country deal with hazardous waste problems. Nancy Sylvester focuses on national and international legislation in the U.S. Congress. Tish Sommers founded a national organization that pressed for older women's rights. Charlotte Tropp directed an aging concerns agency in northern California.

No wonder the revolution has gone unnoticed. Advocates and their activities and issues, on the surface, have so little in common, they are usually treated completely separately from one another.

But when they are interviewed in depth—not about their opinions on issues, but about what they do and how they do it—startlingly similar principles and methods emerge. Beneath the surface of the policy problems they confront, the actions they take and the principles they share are much the same:

- Public policy is not made behind closed doors when caring people are informed and involved.
- Despite the diverse interests of the American public, all issues appeal to at least one of four types of constituents.
- Policy campaigns for every kind of issue go through five identifiable steps—from identification of a problem to resolution.
- In the past, advocacy—called "community organizing"—was assumed to be for local issues only. But advocates have developed new techniques for attracting support and changing state and national policy.
- Although legislation is still the most common means of effecting change, advocates are using litigation and negotiation more often.
- Advocates realize that the forces that arbitrarily fight change put up similar, surmountable barriers.
- Although non-profit organizations' advocacy activities are regulated, these groups can and do take public policy stands and work for politicians they support.

Policy advocacy originated centuries ago. Activities today are rooted in the representative democracy created by the U.S. Constitution. Since this country was founded—granting a voice in directly choosing representatives, not positions—private citizens have formed groups, held meetings, staged demonstrations, signed petitions and much more to influence issues.

Without large amounts of money or individual clout, people have banded together to make elected government pay attention to their concerns. Elizabeth Cady Stanton, an advocate during the mid–19th century, described activities parallel to those used today.

The beauty of advocacy is that everyone can, and most everyone does, take a stand on a public issue at some time. Getting a pothole fixed takes other people and a campaign as much as getting funding for homeless shelters.

We wrote this book because we wanted to read it.

In 1981, the two of us and two friends, Barbara Burnham and Katherine Hanson, got together once a month to discuss what we called "our activism." The anecdotes and experiences we told each other over coffee in the kitchen were entertaining and educational and made us feel less isolated.

We four women lived in the same Boston neighborhood, Jamaica Plain, and we worked on different issues in different places from the neighborhood to the state house and sometimes the U.S. Congress. One person was involved in issues only several hours a month, another was a professional advocate, and the other two were somewhere in between. As the months went on, we realized we were not only feeling more secure because of talking together, but we were also learning that what we were doing was not so different.

We decided to go to the library to read more about people we had begun to call "advocates" and what they do. When we could find no such book, we decided to write one. We used the same approach that began at the kitchen table and expanded on it. We asked advocates to fill out questionnaires, and we interviewed them about their experiences. We asked for materials from their groups. We did some reading and research, especially about advocacy law.

We put together what they said in a book that we hope will inspire and inform readers the same way we were encouraged by our first friendly discussions.

—Georgia Mattison and Sandra Storey

Part One

THE ADVOCATES

Chapter One

The First Journey:
Advocates' Beginnings

*It gives me great satisfaction to see more and more people take
up a cause they believe in and work for it.*
— Brenda LaBlanc

"I was a very timid little Alabama girl, very nurtured in a segregated
fashion. Coming to Washington I thought it was going to be so very different
from Alabama, but I didn't find it all that different. In fact, in some ways I
found it worse. At that time you could ride a streetcar wherever you wanted,
but other than that, there wasn't much a black person could do."

Juanita Kennedy Morgan, executive director of the Black Women's
Political Caucus, began her story of how she became a public policy ad-
vocate. Seated in her living room surrounded by rows of family pictures,
Morgan described her 40-year fight for civil rights in vivid detail.

"I was born in Birmingham, Alabama, and I was grown up when I first
came here to Washington, D.C. I went to the Junior College at the University of Alabama, now Alabama State, and I was the valedictorian of my
class."

"In what year?"

"A year too long ago to mention," she laughed. "I won a trip from school
to Washington, D.C., in what we called 'the broken-down bus,' and I
thought Washington was the most beautiful place I'd ever seen in my life.
I knew if I ever got the opportunity I was coming here.

"A fellow who graduated at the same time as me was here, and he said
if he found any examinations, he would send them to me, and he did. So
I took an examination and passed and came here to work in the Treasury
Department. I stayed through all the segregation and everything and fought
that.

"When we started, something just got in us and we started fighting."

3

Morgan and other Treasury Department employees attacked discrimination at their place of work.

"At that time we black folks had to sit around the walls in the cafeteria. We couldn't even sit in the middle. And we fought that. One night when we were on the night shift we decided we were going to eat in the middle of the cafeteria. They took our trays, then one thing, then another. They harassed.

"But we won that, and when I tell you who we won it from, then you'll know how long I've been here. We won it from President Roosevelt—an edict from Roosevelt. Now this was before desegregation, before they desegregated the cafeterias in the street. President Roosevelt himself ordered that no government cafeterias could be segregated.

"At that time I was going to law school," Morgan continued. "I was trying to work and go to law school, and they gave me a hard way to go.

"The next thing we decided was that we didn't want to go upstairs to the bathrooms when there were bathrooms right there. So we went in there. Ultimately I was fired.

"During that period when I was out there I took a real estate exam and became a broker. That's how I survived when I was out there on the street. I don't know how in the world I did it. I could hardly tell my folks I didn't have a job. It would embarrass them."

The personal setback did not stop Juanita Kennedy Morgan. "I fought out here in the streets then for five years," she reported. "Mostly I did my own case, my own research, and I was put back on the job. I got five years' back pay, too."

Success didn't stop Morgan, either. Her experiences fighting discrimination at the workplace served to strengthen her commitment to what would be a lifetime devoted to work for civil rights in many arenas.

Private Values, Public Issues

Juanita Kennedy Morgan applied her private values to public policy issues and eventually got the policies at her workplace changed. Her motivation came from personal experience. She and her coworkers invented their own ways for solving their problems.

When individuals run into problems with government, they usually search for a personal solution. When the problem is solved, the person goes back to his or her everyday business.

Advocates are people who didn't stop when things got better for them personally. Curing their own problems was not enough. Those citizens who concentrate on solving problems for the benefit of the public have, at one time in their lives, crossed the line that separates work for personal goals from the struggle for achieving change for everybody.

Advocates have passed from the protection of their homes and the security of familiar workplaces and neighborhoods into the larger social realm. They have discovered that what's important to them as individuals is, in fact, important to everyone—that the change they want is the change everyone needs.

Advocates have run up against public policy problems in various places—at home, at work, and in the community.

They make the journey from personal to public concern in styles ranging from revolutionary to evolutionary. Some people consciously cross the border between private and public concern in one quick leap. Others are almost thrown across by events beyond their control. Still others have traveled the terrain between their own experience and public policy-making in gradual, measured steps over time.

No matter how they make the trip, it is always risky, strenuous and challenging. First comes the observation that "something's not right here." A future advocate looks at a situation and asks, like the caption under a child's puzzle, "What's wrong with this picture?"

Curiosity, combined with a desire to correct the picture, drives advocates to ask more questions. After gathering information, they devise solutions in very similar ways.

The most important point in the advocate's journey is the realization that one shares concerns with others. Future advocates notice that they could solve a problem with others' help—and what they have learned could be useful to fellow citizens. They have to make a choice.

When a person begins to take practical, purposeful steps to change the status quo, not only for himself or herself but also for strangers, that person has become an advocate.

During their journeys, advocates pick up experience and information useful for the rest of their lives. That way they construct a firm foundation in change-for-the-better on which to build their future efforts.

Although every advocate has taken this journey, each person's trip has been completely and intensely unique. Juanita Kennedy Morgan's transformation began with a real journey from Alabama to the nation's capital. Other advocates have other "travel stories" to tell.

The Union Route

Kathy Kelley, former president of the Boston Teachers Union and now a lobbyist for the state association, like Morgan, got her start as an advocate because of problems on the job.

"I came out of an Irish, male-dominated family," she said. "Most of the men are lawyers and judges. When I was growing up, the message was always, 'Be a teacher, because that's what women do.'"

Kelley got the message, but early in her teaching career she came face to face with some problems. Still a rookie teacher, she "knew then I had a choice to make. It would have been possible for me to go the political route. Or I could go the union route. I decided on the union route. I decided right then that I would work hard to build a strong, active union as the best way to clean things up for everybody.

"In the early seventies I was an untenured teacher, certified in reading and elementary education," she said. "In the seventy–seventy-one school year I applied to teach in a remedial reading program in the summer to earn some extra money. I didn't get the job, and I found out that the people who did were not really qualified to teach reading. They were math and physics teachers.

"I decided to file a grievance with the union, and I won. The next summer I didn't get the reading teacher position either, but at least a real reading teacher with twenty years of experience did.

"As I was going through this process," she explained, "I found out what a lot of people seemed to know already—that teachers were hired according to a 'code.' Next to teachers' names there would be letters sometimes, initials of their supporters on the school committee. In other words, you had to have done something special for school committee people if you wanted to get the good jobs."

Disabled People Need Autonomy

When she was 16, Marlene Sciascia of New York City got a summer job as a counselor at a camp for handicapped children. There she encountered difficulties that she did not have herself.

"Most of my duties," Sciascia remembered, "were things where I would get very close to people very quickly, because we had to provide very close personal care. That's when I started to realize what the need was for disabled people: autonomy—to be considered as an entire human being, whether physically different or not. I understood the issue of rights right away, I think from working with handicapped people on a one-to-one basis at the camp."

One recurring incident bothered her. "We used to take campers into the town very close by," she remembered. "The shopkeepers would not ask the disabled kids directly what they wanted. They asked me, 'What does she want?' It became obvious to me that people had an incorrect attitude about the handicapped and what everyone needed was more information or, essentially, more integration.

"Growing up during Vietnam was a very pivotal point, too," she reflected. "I was always on a picket line or at a demonstration then. When I was a teenager a lot of my time was spent at demonstrations. It really struck me in a way. You know, when you're really young, you don't understand completely what it is you're doing. But now I have a history in terms of world social values, and that helps."

Sciascia was so strongly influenced by her experiences that she decided to make working for the disabled her career by studying occupational therapy. After a while she changed her mind.

"The political aspects of being disabled were so important to me," she said, "but they were so missing from the program. It was all based on the medical model; it had nothing to do with the objective facts about what makes a person's life difficult when they are disabled. So I drifted away. I started a lot of women's studies and American studies then in my spare time."

Later, when she was the legislative liaison in the New York mayor's office for the handicapped, Sciascia was able to combine her interests. She found that her political work and studies "provided a very good basis" for figuring out what to do in the role of advocate for disabled rights. "I think when you work in one area of advocacy," she observed, "you realize you can use what you know for everybody else."

Dream Housing

Brenda LaBlanc worked as a clerk supervisor and systems analyst and had reared two sons with children of their own by the time she got involved with Des Moines Citizens for Community Improvement (CCI). LaBlanc's passion for housing issues started with her own home.

"I was a war bride," LaBlanc began the story of her advocacy start. "I lived in England until I was eighteen. The war was during my teen years, and I married an American from Des Moines I met then."

LeBlanc, who moved to Des Moines in 1946, attributed her interest in housing to her childhood in London. "I always lived in little apartments," she remembered, "and I always dreamed of having a house.

"When we first moved into the house we've got now, I spent the whole first day going from room to room crying, I was so emotional about having this lovely house. It's one of those old houses with walnut woodwork and oak floors. It's old, but it's beautiful!"

In 1977, she and her husband applied for a second mortgage—a simple matter, they thought. "My son was starting his own business," she explained, "and we figured a new mortgage would be the best way to get a loan. We went to the bank and applied. On the application you have to put your financial situation, to show your stability and all that. The fellow who took down the information made a comment at the time in a joking way about what a stable couple we were. He said he couldn't imagine anybody better qualified for a loan than us. So we thought we had no problem.

"But the bank took a long time to process the loan. I went to the credit union where I work and asked them for a short-term loan which they allowed me to have. Then we got a letter from the bank saying we had been turned down. I called the bank and said I wanted to talk to someone, because I was very dissatisfied. The letter that turned us down didn't give any reason. I said I wanted to know why. So he looked at the folder and said, 'We find that your house is in a state of neglect.'

"That was very insulting to me, because when you buy an old house you're working on it all the time. I said, 'That is not a fact. It is an opinion. You need facts to support an opinion.' He said then that one room needed wallpaper and the house needed paint.

"Anyway, we didn't get the loan then. We finally got the loan a year later. But we were still miffed about it, and when we saw there was going to be a meeting for people with experiences like ours to testify, we said, 'Let's go!'"

It was a long struggle, but they managed to stop red-lining in Des Moines. Now, years later, LaBlanc sits on the CCI board and "helps out with fund raising. I lend a hand whenever I can be useful to any group, as a spokesperson or to picket, demonstrate, swell the crowd or whatever. It's a great satisfaction to see more and more people take up a cause they believe in and work for it."

Leading the Fight Against Hazardous Wastes

Lois Gibbs's transformation from "sheltered housewife" with a personal problem into a nationally recognized expert and advocate for hazardous waste issues is legendary.

She wrote a book, *Lois Gibbs: My Story*, about her first experience with hazardous wastes that were harming her family and her neighbors. Then the public learned more about Gibbs from the CBS docudrama "Lois Gibbs and the Love Canal," shown in 1982. Gibbs never tires of telling of her beginnings as an advocate, because others in her situation never stop finding inspiration in the story.

The newsletter of the organization Gibbs founded, Citizens Clearinghouse for Hazardous Wastes (CCHW), is full of information about ongoing battles against wastes across the country, plus sound advice from experts on how best to conduct the effort. In the Spring 1984 issue of "Everybody's Backyard," Gibbs prefaces useful tips for new advocates with a section about her former attitudes:

"Five years ago in another lifetime I was a housewife, a homemaker and mother. My life was simple, uneventful and sheltered. I believed in the American dream and the American way. Elected officials were doing their jobs well and protecting my interests (although I had no idea what my interests were outside of my family). My taxes were being spent to build schools, roads and helping the less fortunate.

"The few laws I ever heard discussed were, to my mind, good. I had no idea they were compromised. I read about protests and huge legal suits by 'radicals' who could never be pleased no matter what was done, and people who were trying to make a quick buck.

"That was five years ago, when I trusted government, industry and institutions that said they cared. I have learned quite a bit since then, not because I wanted to, but because I was forced to. . . .

"I was shy, introverted, kept to myself. I had very few friends. My life revolved around my family," she told Steve Nearman in an interview published in the September 11, 1983, *Washington Post*.

Her first activities were "a radical change. I never would have thought," she said, "I would be doing what I'm doing now. It would have scared the shit out of me. I transcended me. And what did it was anger. My son was getting sicker and sicker. I could see him deteriorating. The motherly instinct, the anger! Somebody's gotta do something! I had no idea that somebody would be lucky me. . . .

"So I wrote up this little petition that said that I wanted to close the 99th Street School. It took me about two weeks to get the courage to knock on the first door. It was just awful. I threw up for three days before I knocked on that door. And when I got there, I was literally physically sick. Thinking back on it now, I don't know how I ever got up the nerve."

Lois Gibbs is still a mother and homemaker. But she has moved out of Love Canal to the Washington, D.C., area, and has moved out of her small world of private values and concern only for her own child's survival to become a leader in the large, sophisticated world of public policy. Although her initial struggle was personally difficult and painful, Gibbs says, "I like what it's done for me. I really do. I have a purpose in life. I have a goal."

Out of an Armchair, Onto the Streets

"My activism began suddenly," Eleanor Josaitis remembered. She too was a housewife and mother when a single event threw her from her comfortable armchair onto the streets of Detroit. Her life has not been the same since that day in the '60s.

"I was pregnant, and I was sitting in my living room in Taylor, a suburb of Detroit. I was watching the Nuremberg trials on TV, and then the news came on with these pictures of police horses riding through crowds in Selma, Alabama. The police were using cattle prods on black protesters. It hit me: My god, is this America or Nazi Germany?! I said to myself: It's nice to be an armchair liberal, but what can you *do* about it, Josaitis?"

In 1967, she and Father William Cunningham of Taylor's St. Alfred's Parish found themselves asking the same question. In the wake of Detroit's race riots they made a plan, along with Father Jerome Fraser, to recruit priests to talk from the pulpit about the causes of racial unrest.

"It was at that time, when my youngest was just a baby, that my whole family, my husband, my five children and I, moved out of the suburbs and into inner-city Detroit," Josaitis recalled. "I immediately began to be concerned with food issues in the city," she said.

The organization Josaitis and Father Cunningham founded to deal with poverty and racism in Detroit is called Focus:HOPE. Focus:HOPE, of which Josaitis is the associate director, now has to its credit more than 100 staff members, 22,000 regular volunteers and list of major public policy successes in improving people's lives throughout the city. She has been appointed to several national commissions.

Josaitis said she still carries a scrap of paper in her wallet with the message she first got decades ago while watching TV written on it — "Above all, do something."

Feeding Poor People

For more than a year in the early '70s, Stefan Harvey was forced to face the ravages of real poverty in this country. Harvey, who has been an advocate for food programs for the poor ever since, had to examine and refine her ideals first. Harvey now works for the Center for Budget and Policy Priorities in Washington, D.C.

"I think the year I spent as a VISTA volunteer in rural Alabama provided me with a set of experiences and a perception which made me feel the need to be involved in social change," Harvey says. "It wasn't as if I joined VISTA and suddenly did a one hundred eighty-degree political turn. It was part of my great liberal (with a small 'l') upbringing.

"I am convinced though," she says now, "that my experiences in Alabama changed the way I thought and the things I was interested in. It provided me with a first-hand experience of what it is like to be poor in this country. It was something very different from reading about it in books, which until then was all I had done.

"There is a cliché that Peace Corps and VISTA are good because they radicalize the people who go through the experience, and I don't think it's false. I will never deny until the day I die that I got a lot more out of that year of experience from the people I worked with than I ever gave."

Protecting the Nation's Jewels

Betsy Reifsnider, who has had wonderful experiences in the wilderness, sees nature as a gift she repays by working as conservation co-ordinator for the Sierra Club Angeles Chapter. The route Reifsnider took to becoming a full-time advocate features stops in the mountains of California, local city council offices and Japan.

"My father's side of the family had a lot of dealings with Japan," she explained. "He was born there, and I have spent time there, too. I speak Japanese. On my father's side of the family we've always had the idea of compromise and harmony. I love mountain climbing and going out into wilderness areas. How beautiful and wonderful they are! We must save them! They are America's crown jewels.

"I learned to rock climb at Stony Point in the San Fernando Valley. I read in our local Sierra Club publication in 1978 that they were going to have a housing development put in there. They said certain people in the Sierra Club wanted to stop that and make a city park instead. They said, 'If you can help, please do so.' They listed all the city council people and their phone numbers.

"I took it upon myself to go in and say, 'I am a local citizen. I learned to rock climb there, and I don't think it should become a housing development. It should become a city park.

"I relied on the Sierra Club information I had, but I went in as a private citizen. And we won! I came onto the Sierra Club staff in 1981."

Surprised and Angry About the ERA

Janet Ferone turned to the National Organization for Women (NOW) to learn more about women's rights when she was still in high school. The past president of the Greater Boston chapter, Janet traces her interest in women's issues from childhood and schools days.

"When I was in high school I became interested in the women's movement from reading some NOW literature," Ferone said of her beginnings. "When I heard about the ERA [Equal Rights Amendment] I was more surprised than angry that we didn't have it already. I thought, well, that doesn't make any sense!

"That's when I joined the local chapter of NOW, I wasn't really that involved; I just had my name on the membership list. It wasn't until I moved away from my hometown to the Boston area in 1978 that I really started thinking about the women's movement. It came from meeting other women in town who were feminists and had ideas similar to mine. Because of my job as a special education teacher I was primarily interested in the issue of women and education."

In the summer of 1981, a year before the ERA ratification deadline, NOW devised a campaign where women in favor of the ERA went door to door in Utah to talk to women about the amendment, much as Mormon missionaries do.

Ferone remembered, "When I saw the Missionary Project advertised in NOW's newsletter, the 'National Times,' I thought it would be a chance for me to really put myself into the center of the issue, rather than just doing it in my spare time. Since I worked in a school I had time off in the summer and was able to do it with a minimum of trouble."

In college Ferone designed her own major—Gender Correlates of Human Behavior—about "the differences in behavior between men and women and how stereotypes affect the way each lives."

The Right to Strike for Peace

"The beginning of empowerment" for Nancy Sylvester, who now works with NETWORK, a social justice lobby, came on a quadrangle at St. Louis University in 1971 during an anti-war demonstration.

Sylvester, who has been a member of the Sisters of Mercy since she was 17, grew up on the south side of Chicago with Catholic teachings. She set the stage for her turning point experience by saying that, "The Catholic community had just had Vatican II. Things were blossoming in philosophy and scripture. We were absolutely challenged as everything became refined and transformed."

Sylvester was doing draft counseling at the university while she worked for degrees in philosophy and political science. When an anti-war strike was called, Sylvester had to make a decision. "What going on strike meant was losing all your course credits, and I wasn't paying the tuition; the congregation was. I chose to stay in the struggle.

"At that point what became a symbol of success was the power to strike. On that campus, that was the thing we focused on. Well, we won that. We were all on this quadrangle, and when the decision came, we were almost euphoric — all of us. People were excited and jubilant. It was like a high, even though we were all very sober. It was that kind of exhilaration. A group of us together — and success!

"Being able to touch on that experience continues to provide me with hope. I know that it's possible that working together we can achieve change. We can have a success. I don't think you need many of those experiences in your life if they're deep enough."

Reaching for the Language

"I got interested in mental health in the most casual way possible," Carol Garvin recalled. "We had lived in Canada in the early seventies. My husband had been sent up there on business. When we came back it took a while to get the children settled again. I got out of things here in Aiken [South Carolina] over those years."

Garvin, president of the Mental Health Association of South Carolina and later president of the national association, remembered receiving a phone call after she returned to Aiken. "Somebody said, 'Why don't you come onto the local mental health board?'

"I said I knew nothing about mental health, and she said that nobody else did either. And it was true! Nobody on the local board knew much about it at the time. It was a gradual thing. At that time this particular chapter wasn't doing anything much. After a year or so I began to get a drift of what we might be doing.

"Then several of us, five or six of us, decided to really do something and revitalize the group. We began to get a hold of things. I think it was partially that I was interested in the opportunity created by the vacuum in leadership. I thought: we can make this more meaningful and make the group function better and *do* something.

"Going to the [mental] hospital for the first time was a little bit frightening. I don't think it would be accurate to describe me as a person who can be 'overwhelmed with compassion,' but it was a moving experience.

"I've always related to mental illness in a kind of practical way, in the sense that you can become almost immobilized by too much pity. So I have tried to be somewhat objective. It was a combination of feeling deeply about people's needs and yet also being interested in a sort of practical way — about what I could *do*. I don't think I would have wanted to see all that suffering without thinking about practical things I could do. That gradually got me involved very deeply.

"Another aspect was that I was at a stage in my life where my children didn't need me so much anymore. Looking back on it, I feel it came to me at a good time, because I had some energy to give to it.

"As I began to work in the association I became very conscious of language. When I began to assimilate some things, what the Mental Health Association does began to make sense to me. It was a combination of working in a practical way getting to know the people, working in the hospital and becoming conscious of things and learning how to express them.

"Being able to find the words to precisely describe what mental health is all about—that's what really interests me—reaching for the language."

Personal Dysfunction to Public Service

The letterhead says "St. Paul American Indian Center" in bold, italic script. The letter is addressed to the State of Minnesota, Department of Corrections:

> To Whom It May Concern:
> My name is Diane Roach. I am a recovering, dual-dependent person and I work as an Indian Child Welfare Advocate.
> I have had a good deal of experience with battered women's issues and family dysfunction because I personally had to deal with this problem. I received counseling and support for six months while in a recovery program at Jane Dykeman Halfway House. I was also involved in the Aftercare Exchange Program at Team Halfway House for six months (a support group for women).
> I feel abuse against women is a very tragic and disruptive problem facing many American Indian families and I would like to see a program for battered women at the St. Paul American Indian Center receive your support.
> Sincerely, Diane Roach, Indian Child Welfare Advocate

Diane Roach knows the intricacies of dealing with the state and local agencies that serve Native Americans in the St. Paul area. In addition, she articulates the various problems families face very clearly. The process she uses to help others, she says, mirrors the process she went through herself.

"I have taken most of my personal dysfunctions and dissected them," she said frankly. "I took a look at them, and tried to put myself back together. I think I have been through every kind of personal dysfunction there is! Whatever it is, I've been through it," she laughed softly.

"I was in limbo in the white foster care system as a youngster. I am a recovering alcoholic. I really believe I have been put here for a purpose. I didn't used to think that before, when I was chemically dependent. I didn't think I could ever change, but people kept telling me I *could* change. They said I could take the bad that I thought I was and turn it into good.

"That's what I am trying to do now, make something positive out of my experience. I began to do advocacy work through a healing process within myself."

Diane Roach is one of many advocates around the country who are former recipients of the services they now work to improve.

Help for Women Drug Addicts

Kattie [pronounced 'Katy'] Portis also went through a dramatic personal transformation as a prelude to becoming an advocate. In dealing with her own addiction to heroin, she discovered flaws in the public policies that address drug addiction and rehabilitation, especially as they pertain to women.

"I was in Project Turnabout, the drug rehabilitation program," Portis said of her situation in 1976. "It's in Hingham, Massachusetts, an all-white community. A friend of mine had gone to an outreach of theirs here in Boston. I knew he was real dope fiend, and when I saw him he was looking OK. He told me where he had been, so I got out and researched it myself. I called them up, and they told me to come.

"I had three little kids at the time. So I went there. They had about fourteen women. The rest were men, out of a total of about thirty or forty people in the house. I was the only black woman in the dorm. What a culture shock! But it turned out great. I was very serious about my recovery at the time. I was the first black woman to make it through that program.

"My kids couldn't be with me at Turnabout. They gained some things from it. They wanted me to be good. Leslie, a staff member who became my friend, would say to the other staff members, 'She needs to see these kids. She's not going to do this until she sees her kids.' So all the clients in the program were very supportive.

"Even though it was an all-white group that I had never experienced before, what we learned about one another was that the things we were taught growing up didn't fit who we were and who we are now. In the end, we found that we fell in love with one another. That's where I got my training, that's where I was pushed and told that I could do things. It was good.

"Well, I went from there and moved to Connecticut. One of the staff at Turnabout had moved to Connecticut to start a program, and she decided she wanted me to help with this program. So I left Turnabout and went to live in Connecticut for two years, and my kids were still here [in Boston]. I helped start two programs. That was fun.

"I also hung around the Yale Women's Center. You see, in treatment they helped me a hell of a lot with my addiction and somewhat with other kinds of things. The one thing that nobody told us about was how to help me think about myself as a woman. The Women's Center did that. I hung around there a lot after I finished work and I was getting my head together, and finding out that I didn't have to take a lot of these things that I was taking. I didn't have to be what other people wanted me to be. I could be my own woman. That was the most important thing coming out of there."

After going through the system herself, Portis realized that existing policies and programs did not pay enough attention to the special needs of female and minority addicts, many of whom, like her, have children. Portis decided to get the system improved, and she persuaded the federal government to cooperate. Women, Inc., located in Boston, is the very successful, innovative drug rehabilitation program founded by Portis and run for women by women.

Older Women Share Problems

When Tish Sommers discovered that she shared her problems with thousands of other women, she, too, founded an organization—the Older Women's League (OWL). In order to solve the myriad difficulties that besiege older women, Sommers decided to "organize, not agonize" to change attitudes, laws and programs. She told Carol Krucoff of her beginnings in a *Washington Post* article dated April 19, 1983.

Prior to World War II, at age 18, she lived in the home of a Jewish family in Dresden while she was studying dance. "It changed my life," Sommers says of her first experience with prejudice there. "I thought art and politics were totally separate, but I learned everything was linked. I came out of that experience with a strong social conscience. When there is an injustice, the bell tolls for us all."

After Sommers returned to the U.S., she assumed a more traditional life in California as a wife, mother and homemaker, doing some volunteer work on school and civil rights issues. But, at age 57, her divorce plunged her into work for older women's issues. The reality of her situation was initially shocking.

"I had had a mastectomy, and I'd been on my husband's health insurance policy. After the divorce they wouldn't insure me, because I was at high risk. I also learned that I wouldn't be eligible for Social Security at age 65 because I happened to be older than my ex-husband. [The law has changed since, thanks to OWL's efforts.] I considered entering the job market, but my degrees weren't much good.

"I figured that if I were having these problems, other women probably were, too. I knew from volunteer work that when people organize they can make a difference. I decided that older women needed an advocacy group, because we had specific problems that neither the aging nor the women's groups were addressing."

Connecting her own liberation with the issues she shared with other older women, Sommers took a whimsical first step. "I threw myself a 59th birthday party," she chuckled. "I had it announced on the local radio station. I invited interested women to come and celebrate. The idea was to bring women together to help each other break into the job market. About 65 people came."

From that group Sommers created the Jobs for Older Women Project in Oakland, California, in 1973. Out of that grew the 10,000-member national organization, OWL. Tish Sommers was president of OWL, and continued to use attention-getting methods to bring people together to work on complex issues, until her death in 1985.

Abolitionists Become Feminists

Policy changes advocates work for are very complex. It is not surprising then that occasionally a person starts out championing one cause only to find out another issue claims more attention. That is what happened to Elizabeth Cady Stanton and other female abolitionists in the mid–1800s.

Elizabeth Cady and her new husband, Herbert Stanton, were both ardent anti-slavery advocates and Quakers when they met and married. In her book of reminiscences, *Eight Years and More*, Stanton described her startling introduction to the issue of women's rights. She and her husband were on their "wedding journey" at the time.

"Our chief object in visiting England," she wrote later, "was to attend the World's Anti-slavery Convention, to meet June 12, 1840, in Freemason's Hall, London. Delegates from all the anti-slavery societies of the civilized nations were invited, yet when they arrived, those representing associations of women were rejected."

The women, and some of the men, were shocked that such a decision had been made. A heated debate about whether to seat the women delegates began the convention. The women were not allowed to participate in it.

"Many remarkable women," according to Stanton, "were all compelled to listen in silence to the masculine platitudes on women's sphere" as the women "were waiting and watching on one side in painful suspense to hear how their delegates were received. . . ."

Although Herbert Stanton and other men protested, the women were kept segregated from the men and were not permitted to speak throughout the convention.

"The women," Stanton wrote, "sat in a low curtained seat like a church choir and modestly listened . . . for twelve of the longest days in June." They had time to think. "It struck me as very remarkable," Stanton wrote, "that abolitionists who felt so keenly the wrongs of the slave, should be so oblivious to the equal wrongs of their own mothers, wives and sisters."

Stanton and the other ostracized, silenced delegates formed close ties. "These were the first women I ever met who believed in the equality of the sexes and who did not believe in the popular orthodox religion," Stanton later wrote. "The acquaintance of Lucretia Mott, who was a broad, liberal thinker on politics, religion and all questions of reform, opened to me a new world of thought."

A movement was certainly born there. "As the convention adjourned, the remark was heard on all sides, 'It is about time some demand was made for new liberties for women.'

"As Mrs. Mott and I walked home, arm in arm, commenting on the incidents of the day, we resolved to hold a convention as soon as we returned home, and to form a society which would advocate the rights of women."

The movement they began succeeded in gaining some "new liberties for women." Most advocacy groups would not dream of excluding women from their activities today. Slavery was abolished more than a century ago. Women got the right to vote in this country in 1920.

Yet the work to change public policy continues. As struggles for "old" issues continue, new difficulties surface every year. And every year people, assuming a variety of roles, come forward to deal with them.

Chapter Two

The Spice of Life:
Advocates' Various Roles

Above all, do something.
—Eleanor Josaitis

The words women who work to change public policy use to describe themselves are as varied as their activities, ranging from "concerned individual" to "catalyst" to "foot soldier with a legal pad." The terminology covers a spectrum of attitudes—poetic, humanitarian, business-like, playful, political, and philosophical. Even though thousands of people across the country share similar roles, they do not share similar terms for those roles. The labels "activist," "spokesperson," and "advocate" were used most often by those who filled out questionnaires about their work.

"Advocate" seems to be emerging everywhere as the favorite title for people who try to change public policy. It applies to people who are paid as well as to volunteers. The name of the role, "advocate," and the action, "to advocate," make the nomenclature simple and easy to remember.

The verb "advocate" comes from Latin and means "to voice for." The term can be confusing; attorneys are sometimes called advocates. Attorneys and others sometimes advocate for people on a case-by-case basis. Public policy advocates focus on general policy.

Just as advocates have many names for their roles, they also have many roles that take limitless forms. Many advocates wear other hats in addition to being leaders in the public policy arena. Some have other jobs. Many have families and homes that are very important to them. Variety, for advocates, is the spice of life. Despite fuzzy definitions and multiple roles, advocates' commitment to issues emerges clearly when they talk about themselves. Time and again advocates say they *are* what they *do*.

In general, there are four types of public policy advocates: volunteer leaders, paid organization staff, government-employed advocates and freelance advocacy consultants.

Volunteer Leaders

Many advocates serve without pay. They are officers or members of organizations or just members of the public who are interested in issues. Some volunteer full-time. Most volunteers work when the issues require their time and they can spare it.

Although they are not advocates by profession, some volunteers do advocacy as part of other jobs. Others hold paying jobs in addition to their careers in volunteer advocacy. No matter how much time the person spends and no matter what the activity, everyone who works for policy improvements can be considered an advocate.

Journalist Turned President

Dorothy Ridings, former president of the League of Women Voters of the United States (LWV-USA), was required to spend a great deal of time in meetings in Washington, D.C. and speaking around the country.

Like many other volunteer advocates, Ridings also had a paying job as editor of the monthly *Kentucky Business Journal*, headquartered in Louisville, Kentucky. How did she manage the League from Washington and edit a journal in Louisville? "I travel back and forth every week." As the third major role in her life, Ridings is a wife, mother of two sons and a homemaker, too.

"I grew up in Charleston, West Virginia. My family was very socially conscious. We grew up in a home where people read and talked. We argued at the dinner table over issues. My parents were very religious and felt the imperatives of social consciousness.

"I became very interested early in becoming a newspaper reporter, and did all that in school and after school in the local paper. I went to journalism school and then took a job in Charlotte, North Carolina, as a reporter."

Ridings met her husband, also a journalist, when he came to Charlotte. "I was interested in social activism, but at that point more from an observer's perspective. I liked being around it, and I liked reporting on it, trying to be objective about what was going on.

"When we moved to Louisville I was pregnant with our first child, and I decided to take some time off. So I called the League and asked for a dues notice and the time of the next meeting.

"The first announcement I got said they were looking for someone to edit the local League bulletin. I thought, gee, I can do that with a small baby. I'm journalism trained, and I'd enjoy that. When I called up I found out that doing the bulletin meant you were on the board. So I was in the

League for about two months before I was on the local League board, and I took the baby with me to the meetings.

"Some interesting things were happening in Louisville. We were going through our early phases of the school desegregation program. I was interested in civil rights issues. Every state has an advisory committee for the U.S. Commission on Civil Rights. It was through the League I got on that committee. They were reconstituting it because it had been dormant for some years. They looked around, and the League seemed a logical place to go for people. I was on the committee for three years, the early to mid-seventies."

Ridings summed up her roles this way: "Traditionally women have been the nurturers, more oriented to human relationships. The women's movement has taken women more out of the traditional roles as homemaker and family nurturer from the way they once were, but still, nurturing is a very strong trait. I know I have it. I think I typify that because I'm in the workforce. I am part of the women's movement. I still have children at home. I have a husband. I have a family. I run a house. I do volunteer work."

Catalyst for Vitality

Gini Laurie gave herself a special role as an advocate in 1958 when she founded the *Rehabilitation Gazette*. She was editor and publisher of the international journal with her husband Joe Laurie in their St. Louis home until her death in 1989. "I am a catalyst. I gather and disseminate information, nationally and internationally," she said in an interview in 1983.

Laurie's advocacy focused mostly on written communication about issues. Through the *Gazette*, people with disabilities have communicated with each other over the years, sharing information about everything — including public policy.

Laurie tied her publication to other groups who work for policies for people with disabilities. "I very much encourage things like the American Coalition of Citizens with Disabilities," she said. "I was one of the first members on the first board. It's a coalition of all kinds of disabilities; people who are blind, deaf, in wheelchairs, and all the different organizations got together. This is vital so they can do the politicking. I tell the disabled about this coalition and urge them to join in and tell them what the organization does."

In May 1983, the *Gazette* held the first international conference on rehabilitation. Laurie, a 1979 Globe Democrat Woman of Achievement, and her husband, Joe, a retired business executive, received the President's Distinguished Service Award.

In the '80s Laurie planned for the future of the *Rehabilitation Gazette* to be sure that the work she and her husband, who were in their seventies, continued. "There's too much here that should be kept up on, but only if we get a younger executive director and get a part-time secretary. I've done all the typing for the *Gazette*. I'm getting really organized now. We're going to see if we can raise some money from corporations and foundations to employ an executive director."

Gini Laurie founded the *Gazette* because of her experience working as a volunteer in hospitals and respiratory centers beginning in 1949. "That's how I knew people and how they became my friends and how I knew they needed something like the *Gazette*, something written they could share and tell how they were getting along at home. That need to share and to communicate was universal. That's why the *Gazette* grew so."

Laurie's work came from personal loss. The year before she was born four of her brothers and sisters had polio, and two of them died, so she was the first in another half of the family. "My brother was extremely disabled. I was his mascot, his pet, his auxiliary arms and legs. He died when I was 16 and he was 21.

"We moved to Cleveland, and the big epidemics were starting, and they were short of nurses. They needed somebody to do hotpacks, and I did this because I was a natural at it. I had this attitude from being with my brother of expecting a lot from a person who was disabled: it didn't make any difference about the body, it was the head that counted.

"Later I started this group therapy of keeping up with each other, which is extremely important when you've gone through someting like one or two years together in a polio ward in an iron lung and watched all the progress. This kind of working-together spirit is vital to everybody."

Woman in Construction Builds Group

Connie Spruill is another advocate who appreciates the "working-together spirit." She has triple roles as a homemaker with five children, as a business owner and as the founder of a growing national organization.

Spruill is president of Central Ohio Forest Products, Inc., the subcontractor/supplier business she began in Brice, Ohio, in 1980.

The problems she and other women encountered drove Spruill to begin organizing the Association of Business and Professional Women in Construction, first in Ohio, then in the Midwest, and now on a national level.

Spruill says she began her business "without any bank assistance. I had no money to work with. I collected all my accounts, and that has got to be a damn good track record!"

Several years after her business was going, she reported, she went to a bank for a loan. "They didn't look at us with a lot of respect. They wouldn't even look at my financial statement, and within an hour they called and said, 'There's nothing we can do.'

"But one of the women bankers must have done some soul searching, because two days later she called me back and said, 'We can do something for you,' and she gave me a loan on my signature. She said, 'I know you want your company to succeed, and I want my money back.' I'll never forget that."

The organization of Women in Construction is the product of Connie's awareness of the problems all women in her business have. As president, she sees herself as the members' "representative, keeping constant contact with the women about issues which concern us." As their spokesperson, she airs grievances and works for legislation and enforcement of laws to protect women in construction from discrimination. "I was a victim, and I decided to do something about it."

Spruill works for the organization without pay. In 1982, Spruill received the Women in Business Award from the Small Business Administration. She also won the Emily W. Roebling Award, named for the woman who oversaw building the Brooklyn Bridge after her husband died, "for efforts enhancing women's roles in construction."

Helping Other Asian Immigrants

"I was very active in the Organization of Chinese American Women (CAW), and now I'm very active in the North Virginia Chapter of Chinese American Women," said Lotta Chi, another renaissance woman for whom personal, professional and advocacy lives are completely intertwined. Chi lives in northern Virginia where she works for rights for all Asian refugees.

"They have twenty chapters all through the United States," she said of the organization she helped found. "Then I have my own business. It was taking too much time to volunteer, so I'm not that active now.

"The main focus of CAW is to help Chinese women to survive well in the United States—how to cope with the two cultures, the everyday living, how to deal with family problems. We try to stay away from international political issues. So we say, 'People, we are here, so we must deal with the problems we are facing here.'"

An article in the March 29, 1983, *Arlington Journal* focused on Chi and her work with refugees: "Lotta Li Chi is an Asian immigrant to Arlington, but she hardly fits the stereotype of a travel-worn ragmuffin hustling to earn her next meal," the article says. "Her friends include former Democratic Congressman Joseph L. Fisher and Chinese Embassy officials in Washington, D.C. Chi and her husband run a lucrative engineering consulting firm here. Although the Chis are Chinese, the Chis try to help Vietnamese and Cambodian refugees find jobs. . . ."

Chi has a master's degree in microbiology from Rutgers University and is the daughter of two physicians. She and her parents came to the United States in 1947 to escape the Communist takeover in China.

"Asians in general are being ignored by much legislation for minorities, and many refugees need help," Chi observed in another interview. So Chi, mother of a daughter in law school and a son in college, decided to put her resources, personal and professional, to use.

"Before we got our first grant," she remembered, "the CAW didn't have very much money. We had a small grant from ACTION and that just produced one small conference for each center. Everyone volunteered. I volunteered my time, and I paid for my staff time to write the proposal.

"You know about proposals. It takes a long time to do one—a couple of months. We finally got it, and then I helped to set up. We had to get an office and do many things. I do have a full-time job. Then I turned the position over to someone who really needed a full-time job and who can devote a lot of time to the organization. She works very hard."

"Now I just do a lot of the legwork," Chi said. "I give them mailing lists, for example. They say, 'Who shall we mail this reception invitation to?' I went to a planning meeting and we discussed who was going to mind the registration tables from what hour to what hour—the little details."

Teaching and Living Political Themes

Norma Wilson is a poet and teacher. She combines these professions with advocacy while bringing up a family in her home of Vermillion, South Dakota. Born "a poor farm girl from Tennessee," Wilson is now a full-time associate professor of English at the University of South Dakota. As a teacher of literature and composition for more than ten years, Wilson purposely draws out the social and political themes inherent in the courses she teaches for the benefit of the students and the issues.

In addition to teaching, Wilson is very active in two organizations. In 1979 she helped put together the Vermillion Chapter of the Black Hills Alliance to fight uranium mining and to work for Native American rights. The other group, the South Dakota Resources Coalition, advocates for environmental, economic, nuclear waste and farming policies.

"I have taken mostly a supporter's role in these two groups," she said.

"My leadership is mostly in my local area. In the Vermillion area I would say I have had a leadership role, but in terms of the organizations, since they are not headquartered in this area, I am a supporter. I have tended to be one of the leaders of both groups here. One of the things I like about this state is that whenever we form a group, it doesn't tend to have just one leader."

Wilson—who has a home, a husband and two young children to take care of—laughs when asked how she manages. "I can do all these things maybe because I'm not doing a good job at anything. On the other hand, I think I'm more understanding and more patient because I have children. It makes me more attentive to individual people and more concerned than I used to be about the future.

"I think it's real important to have children. I hope I can educate them about the importance of social issues. We can't just hope for things to miraculously change for the better. It takes a lot of work."

Clout for Mexican American Women

Martha Cotera has worked at one job or another since she was 12 years old. And for the past 25 years she has been a librarian and information specialist.

"I have a business called 'Information Systems Development,'" she said, "and I work on that. Thank goodness," she laughed, "because I'd be fired if I worked anywhere else."

The lines between Cotera's business and volunteer work as a promoter of policy to benefit women and Mexican Americans in Austin, Texas, are blurred. "I have the resources right here in my office," she pointed out. "A lot of my work is community research.

"I spent an hour today with a school principal strategizing and figuring out what we are going to do on Friday and on lining up the right people. I'm going to spend a lot of time this week getting the people to be there and writing a letter. I take a lot of time for my advocacy work. Lots of meeting time. It's voluntary. It's not part of my job."

For more than 15 years, Cotera, president of the Mexican American Women's Business and Professional Association of Austin, has led local movements for such issues as forming a state commission on the status of women, keeping the women's educational equity program, preventing police brutality and establishing and maintaining bilingual education in the schools.

"I and others work on three to five political campaigns every year and thus enhance Mexican American women's clout," she said. "I find this pretty

effective. Once our candidate wins, we can lobby for appointments, contracts for minority businesses, and affirmative action policies."

Organization Staff

Being paid for advocacy is becoming more and more common. Staff
members of non-profit organizations are employed to do policy advocacy
as part or all of their jobs. Non-profit organizations whose primary goals are
education and policy change have become aware that to really affect policy,
professionals with specific skills and experience doing advocacy are needed
on the staff.

Even agencies that deliver services are realizing that advocacy for
policies affecting their clients is required in order to serve them. In some
cases, organizations may not formally or officially recognize the necessity
of staff working on policy issues, but the staff finds itself doing advocacy
anyway. Advocates who are paid staff of advocacy organizations often have
loose, self-defined advocacy roles. Some advocates combine paid and volunteer advocacy.

Caring for Children's Policy

Barbara Reed's jobs with a variety of organizations give an overview,
in one person's history, of the range of employment possibilities that exists
in the advocacy field. Although her home state of Georgia has been her
base, the geography of Reed's responsibilities has been far-reaching. She
has been president of a local teachers union, an anti-poverty advocate, director of an advocacy project, and is now a day care center director. In addition
to her paid advocacy jobs, she has voluntarily chaired the board of a non-
profit housing corporation.

Reed's first advocacy experience in 1960 as a high school teacher and
president of the local education association was not a pleasant one. "It was
an extremely political kind of situation. My first lobbying involved the
school board, talking in terms of teachers' rights and establishing those
rights.

"Ultimately the county where I was working forced the local teachers
to drop out of the state organization. The only thing I could do to make
any kind of an impact was to resign as president of the organization publicly." Because of that "bitter experience" she quit teaching too, soon there-
after.

"I went to work for the Poverty Rights Office (PRO) in Atlanta. We did two kinds of advocacy, I guess. We did advocacy on an individual basis, where clients would tell us about their problems dealing with various aspects of the bureaucracy.

"As part of that work, the center and I got involved in more general kinds of advocacy. We looked at things that were wrong with the system, both locally and at the state level. We worked closely with welfare rights groups and organized protests when they were cutting back benefits. It was our job to get people to the demonstrations. So, although the work at the PRO was an individual rights thing, if you were interested in going beyond that [to policy advocacy] you had the freedom to do it."

From the mid–1970s until 1982 Reed was employed by the Children's Foundation, headquartered in Washington, D.C., as the Southern Regional Director of the Women, Infants and Children (WIC) Advocacy Project. Her job was to communicate constantly with all parties involved — from government officials in the nation's capital to local officials, advocates and program participants in southern states.

Now, as director of the Fulton County Day Care Center in Georgia, Reed said, "We do a lot of advocacy with the public school system. If we did not go over and make the school system test children before they got in school, they would never be placed in the educational programs they need." She also finds herself persuading parents and others to work with the health care system and to get adequate funding for day care programs.

"Now that I am a service agency administrator," Reed observed, "I still consider myself to be an advocate. Immediately, although this is a new field to me, I was plunged into the advocacy part."

Mental Health Services People Want

Sally Mead started doing advocacy as part of a job with the North Pacific Rim Native Corporation. Originally from California, she explained, "I started going up to Alaska in 1969. It was kind of a lark thing to do, but once I made it to Alaska the first time, it seemed like it was home. I moved here permanently in 1971. The mailing address for Birdcreek and Indian, Alaska [is] the same; there are about 400 people in the two communities here."

Mead worked for a native corporation, set up with federal money paid to the natives of Alaska for land taken from them. A psychologist, Mead was a "family services trainer," who helped villagers learn how to work out their own problems about 80 percent of the time and did more traditional counseling and consultation the other 20 percent.

"Initially," she said, "my job was to set up the program. There was no job to begin with. So I started out by doing basic needs assessment, spending a lot of time in the communities, letting them get to know me and my getting to know them and their ways of doing things. I did a lot of observing and keeping my mouth shut.

"Then it became time to start developing the program, writing the grants. I was doing a lot of work with the government bodies, the village councils and the community, so they had a say·in what the program was going to look like. Finding out what they wanted was a process in itself.

Mead involved the village councils in hiring staff. "I took the resumes to them and said, 'Here are the four people we're looking at.' We talked it over, and they said, 'We think it should be this person.'"

In addition to her paid advocacy job, Mead was the volunteer coordinator of the Carolyn Brown Legal Fund. "She's an obstetrician-gynecologist," Mead explained. "A right-to-life group has defamed her, and she has pressed a libel suit against them. She's the doctor who delivered my son. I volunteered to coordinate her legal fund. I'm also putting together an advisory committee for her."

Serving Senior Citizens

Charlotte Tropp was the director of RSVP of Humboldt County, California, a senior volunteer organization, from 1975 until her death in 1987.

"This has been a great job for me, and I think I've brought lots to it," Tropp said in an interview in 1982. I think that I'm really charged by administration and the kinds of P.R. work I do. I really like being able to effect change.

"Administration is something that I'm very comfortable with," Tropp added. She supervised 17 paid staff members and 500 regular volunteers over age 60 who serve 10,000 people of all ages.

As if she did not have enough people to supervise, she also had "twenty-three funders—federal, state, city, county and foundations. I am responsible to every one of those funders. Since we depend on funds and laws and regulations at all of those levels I found long ago that I could not do my job without doing advocacy work. About fifty percent of my job is advocacy.

"I really got this job because of serendipity. I had been in the east and came back here with my husband who teaches at Humboldt State. I needed a job. I had taught theater, but teaching jobs were hard to get. RSVP was just starting out in its first year, and the advisory council was not looking for someone with gerontological experience. They wanted someone who knew about public relations, and they needed someone who could give it visibility in the community. I got the job on that basis really. It was pure luck. If I applied for this job today, I wouldn't even get an interview."

To those who watched children's television in the 1950s, Charlotte Tropp will always be remembered for another role; she was Miss Charlotte on the nationally televised "Romper Room" program.

"I've also had some bona fide jobs in between raising my four kids and being a faculty wife and playing duplicate bridge. I've had a checkered career," she chuckled.

"I was born in 1934, and I'm white. And Jewish," she described herself. "I grew up in a very, very Jewish atmosphere, so that I'm culturally Jewish, not religiously Jewish. I'm mostly a Democrat, but certainly never a Republican. I think my background really enabled me to be tough and secure and to be aware."

Tropp helped draft resisters during the Vietnam War. "During the Nixon period, when things were getting awful, my husband went to finish his Ph.D. at the University of Toronto. I worked there as a runner for draft resisters, as a volunteer for the Women's Strike for Peace. We had a wonderful, wonderful thing going for the draft resisters who were escaping the Vietnam War.

"We had about six businesses in the Toronto area that made bona fide job offers to any draft resister that came in. We would give each resister a suit of clothing. We would give them five hundred dollars so they could go back down to the border. They would cross the border at Buffalo or Detroit and wear the suit of clothes and have five hundred dollars and a bona fide job offer, which was what a person needed to become landed Canadian immigrants at that time.

"They got landed immigrant status, came directly to our office in Canada, returned the suit of clothes and the five hundred dollars. We processed five thousand draft resisters with the same suit of clothes and the same five hundred dollars in that two-year period."

Civil Rights in Arkansas

Sandra Kurjiaka was the director of two organizations, the Civil Liberties Union of Arkansas (the state chapter of the American Civil Liberties Union) and a related organization, the Women's Rights Project. She described her work one day in 1982. "I'm sitting here going over five years of work for a proposal I am doing. It's to a foundation to get money for the Women's Rights Project. I have to do charts, and I really hate to do them." She read from the form: "How many people attended the conference? What were the results?"

Kurjiaka did community organizing before she joined the CLU of Arkansas staff in 1977. Divorced with a daughter and son in their 20s, "I was a homemaker for thirteen years before I entered the workplace," she said.

"As director I have to deal with all the clients, do all the screening, raise the money, recruit the members, do all the necessary board work, plus tons and tons of paperwork and financial reports. Those are the kinds of things a director does."

Kurjiaka is well-known in Arkansas and is often quoted in the press. In addition to her office work, she travels around the state to inform people about their rights and to help them take action.

The June 2, 1982, *Arkansas Gazette* reported on a Gay Pride Week Rally at which she spoke. "Only a few participants wore paper bags on their heads," according to the article. "Sandra Kurjiaka, the state ACLU director, asked news photographers not to take close-up pictures of the audience. . . . The crowd cheered as Kurjiaka and other speakers praised them for 'coming out of the closet' and urged them to become politically active.

"'We're talking about gay pride, not gay hide and gay shame, and proud you ought to be,'" the article quoted her as saying. It also reported that she "chastised homosexuals for remaining silent when the state's sodomy law was enacted in 1977. 'Your silence speaks loudly,' she told them."

Government-employed Advocates

Most paid advocates are staff members of non-profit organizations, but some are employed by an important, controversial boss—the government itself. Contrary to popular belief, government employees and agencies are very much allowed to advocate for public policy issues. Advocates are often hired at local, state and federal levels because they are experts on the issues and experienced in communicating information to a variety of people and groups.

Welfare Mom to Welfare Department

The story of Janet Diamond's movement through two distinct roles to becoming an employee of the Massachusetts Department of Public Welfare is a modern classic.

As a divorced mother forced to go on welfare in the mid–1970s, Diamond rapidly became aware of many hard facts. "When I look at poverty," she said, "I track it through an entirely different indicator than most people. I track it through the divorce rate. The relationship between divorce and poverty—what happens to families economically when families split—is not taken into account by most people. As far as I can see, AFDC [Aid to Families with Dependent Children] is an invention of divorce."

When she was a divorced welfare recipient, Janet "began to lobby because of my commitment to an issue which affected me personally. I was one of the token poor people on a welfare advisory board," she said. "I didn't know very much about the programs. I just knew I wanted to get involved."

Diamond later became the media coordinator for the Coalition for Basic Human Needs (CBHN). "It's not like I invented the recipients' point of view," she said. "That was my job, not to invent things and situations, but to filter the grassroots through me in our statements."

Not long after Michael Dukakis was elected governor the second time, one of his first actions was to appoint Diamond to a policy-making position in the Department of Public Welfare.

"I have a different job. I do different things. I manage day care for the employment and training program," Diamond said. "The question is, who's going to take care of the kids?"

Diamond's point of view is "not that much different, though," in her new job. "Those women are out there trying to get training, trying to get ahead. I understand that it is just as important for women to have the opportunity to transfer from AFDC, which will never be anything but second best. Even if benefits were wonderful, which they will never be, there's something about depending on government for your support that goes against the American way."

Freelance Consultants

A growing advocacy field involves providing advocacy services — especially for work on legislation — for a fee. At city, state and federal levels, freelance public policy consultants — sometimes called "lobbyists" — are being paid by non-profit organizations to work for policy change. Other consultants like Lois Gibbs and Citizens Clearinghouse for Hazardous Wastes help with the entire scope of advocacy — not just legislation.

A Skilled, Experienced Strategist

Carol Tucker Foreman's work experience in the nation's capital is a compendium of top-level positions as a lobbyist and government employee. She began her advocacy as a staff member of Planned Parenthood and the Consumer Federation of America.

She has also been employed by government as assistant secretary of agriculture for Food and Consumer Services during the Carter Administration. Before that she was employed by the federal government as a legislative liaison between the Department of Housing and Urban Development (HUD) and Congress. Currently, Foreman is a freelance policy consultant with a private firm in Washington, D.C.

The first paragraph of Foreman's résumé describes her advocacy skills: "Experienced executive of proven leadership and managerial ability. Effective administrator of programs with annual budget of $15 billion and staff of 15,000. Skilled strategist, advocate, analyst, writer, organizer and fundraiser."

Foreman offered this review of her career so far: "I have been lobbying in Washington on various issues since late nineteen sixty-one when I went to work for a small lobbying firm called 'Federal Council Associates.' I was lobbying to repeal the Silver Purchase Act of nineteen thirty-six.

Later I was a legislative rep for HUD, and then I did some lobbying work for Planned Parenthood in the late sixties and early seventies. I then held positions with the Consumer Federation of America and with the Department of Agriculture. Now I work for a number of clients. All my work has involved lobbying."

When she was executive director of the Consumer Federation, Foreman said, "I probably spent seventy percent of my time managing the organization and raising money and thirty percent of my time lobbying. There were also people on the staff who lobbied.

"Now," she added, "I am essentially back to where I started in 1961, working for private clients as a lobbyist. In the past I lobbied on such issues as removing the purchase requirement for food stamps and creating a consumer protection agency. Now I'm working to amend the bankruptcy law for the benefit of asbestos victims."

Trial and Error Training

Advocates' formal education is as varied as their personal histories. The amount of school learning they have ranges from not finishing high school to Ph.D. level. Most fall somewhere in the middle, with high school diplomas and college degrees. Typically, some have gone to school part-time as adults. Brenda LaBlanc got her B.A. in English in night school. Formal education does not seem to be a prerequisite for being a good advocate. And subjects advocates who speak in this book have studied are equally diverse, encompassing journalism, bacteriology, education, English, law, history, theater arts, American studies, interior design and business adminstration.

What advocates have in common is the extremely informal way they learned advocacy skills. Betsy Reifsnider's experience was typical. "The person who had my job—conservation coordinator for the Angeles Chapter of the Sierra Club—quit. I was already a Sierra Club volunteer. I used to take minutes at executive committee meetings. I was interested in politics, and when something like that came up, I would volunteer to do it. When the person I replaced quit, I was in the right place at the right time. They asked me if I would like the job and I said, 'Sure.'

"Slowly they gave me more responsibilities. I started out not knowing what to do at all. Slowly I gained more experience. It was like taking a kid and throwing her in the swimming pool and saying, 'Swim!'"

Most advocates have learned what they know from experience. They have also learned much by observing other advocates and less by reading books and attending workshops. Few received any formal training.

"On-the-job" and "trial-and-error" training can be difficult for the advocates and the issues. Charlotte Tropp wrote an entire funding proposal she didn't need to write when she first took her job as the head of RSVP/Share in Humbolt County.

Lack of confidence is also a problem. Betsy Reifsnider remembered, "When I first had to go to legislators' offices I would be so frightened. I thought they were gods. I thought this person is so far above me, the honorable so-and-so! I felt like I was some little insect. Slowly," Reifsnider reported, "I realized that they are public servants who are supposed to listen to what the people say. Usually I had a lot more background on the issues than they, and I could answer their questions very well. Now I can go in and speak on a much friendlier basis, and there's more give and take," she said. "I'm not frightened at all any more."

Part Two
THE PUBLIC IN THE POLICY

Chapter Three

Being a Bridge:
Advocates Work with Groups

I think of us as a bridge.
— Carol Garvin

Bridge, link, connection. . . . No matter what comparison advocates use, about half of their activities are geared to putting together and maintaining diverse groups of people involved in issues. The "public" in public policy is the large pool advocates draw from to find people to take responsibility for change. Advocates are perpetually creating and guiding groups of people who will deal with the issues.

Advocates define "community" in the fullest sense of the word. They not only bring average citizens together, but they also work with all sorts of other groups. When asked, "Who benefits from your work?" one advocate answered, "Everybody." And "everybody" is who advocates keep in mind when they set to work on issues.

To carry out actual policy change, advocates work with the public as separate types of groups. Then they try to keep the groups together to settle the issues. In this modern, mobile society, advocates have to find interested people, bring them together, then keep them informed and involved.

Advocates bring together and work with three major types of groups: advocacy organizations, constituents for the issues and government. They also work with special groups like institutions, businesses and experts. Each group benefits from the give and take of advocacy for issues; each contributes to and gains from one another's efforts. (See chapters Four, Five and Six for specific methods advocates use to mold and maintain these groups.)

Advocacy Groups: Hubs of Activity

One lone person can do little for a cause, no matter how skilled or "important" that person is. Most advocates are affiliated with a non-profit group that focuses on issues. An organization provides a center from which people and issues flow in and out. The group offers credibility, permanence, structure and identity to issues and to the citizens concerned with them.

Advocacy groups come in every size, shape and structure imaginable. And — like individuals — they vary greatly in the amount of policy advocacy they do in any one year. The Sierra Club is a national advocacy organization, with 365,000 members affiliated with local chapters. The Black Hills Alliance of South Dakota may deal with similar issues, but it is located within one state and has hundreds of members.

Some organizations, like Common Cause and the League of Women Voters, deal with a broad range of issues. The Arkansas Civil Liberties Union operates under a very tight structure with established rules and hierarchies.

The neighborhood groups Lois Gibbs helps fight hazardous wastes are much less formal and are often not officially incorporated.

The primary goal of some groups that do policy advocacy is the delivery of services — day care, education, health care, elderly services, etc. — but they find themselves doing policy advocacy as a necessary ingredient to maintain services and fully serve clients' needs.

The Minneapolis/St. Paul American Indian Center and RSVP/Share in California deliver direct services first and work for government policies that support those services when necessary.

Coalitions are large, temporary groups made up of several separate advocacy organizations that work on specific policy goals.

Despite differences in size and structure, advocacy organizations have much in common. They all work to make public policy. Almost all are non-profit, either officially incorporated or unofficially.

The three most common types of non-profit advocacy groups are service providers, membership and professional organizations. Officially these groups are called 501 (c) 3s, 501 (c) 4s and 501 (c) 5s, respectively, after their sections in the tax code. Some organizations function as combinations of types. (See Chapter Four for more information about non-profit advocacy groups and the tax code and Chapter Thirteen for how their advocacy activities are regulated.)

An Informal Group

Martha Cotera described a neighborhood advocacy group in which she was active. "Membership fluctuated between eight and ten of us, and we each had a constituency. There were three or four members from different neighborhood associations [in Austin]. I'm with several Mexican-American groups. We had the potential for working in the neighborhoods and citywide" on a variety of issues that concerned them. One thing the group did was support local candidates who agreed with their policy stands. (See Chapter Six.)

A Service Organization

The Mental Health Association in South Carolina (MHASC) is a division of the National Mental Health Association (MHA), which is organized—like many national groups—with various geographic levels of operation.

On the back of a brochure called, "How to Deal with Your Tensions," appears this description: "The National Mental Health Association is a nationwide, voluntary, non-governmental organization dedicated to the promotion of mental health, the prevention of mental illness and the improved care and treatment of the mentally ill. Its 850 chapters and divisions and more than one million citizen volunteers, work toward these goals through a wide range of activities in social action, education, advocacy and information. If you need help," it goes on, "or can help others, get in touch with us."

Carol Garvin, former president of the South Carolina MHA, now president of the national organization, described the MHA as a "citizens volunteer group, not a professional group" founded by Clifford Beers. "He was a young man in the early nineteen hundreds who was mentally ill and had to be hospitalized several times. He became convinced that some sort of group was needed that was not composed of professionals but of people who would be advocates."

The brochure, "Who We Are, What We Do," describes the MHASC set-up: "Our Division [South Carolina] has thirty-three affiliates covering thirty-seven counties and operated last year on a budget of one hundred seven thousand one hundred fifty-nine dollars. The Board of Directors is composed of ten directors at large, fourteen regional directors, thirty-three chapter presidents and thirty-three delegate directors. The MHASC has three paid staff. Six of the chapters have either full or part-time staff."

"In a sense," Garvin says, "we feel we serve citizens of the whole state, but of course our emphasis is on people who are mentally ill, and that's usually estimated to be fifteen percent of the population that need some kind of service. About one and one half to two percent of the population is considered to be severely affected."

The Association has three purposes: promoting mental health, preventing mental illness and improving the care and treatment of the mentally ill.

Garvin outlined the group's activities. "We do a lot of public education and . . . we do a lot of legislative work, essentially lobbying," Garvin said. "We do a lot of work for funding because mental health has never been funded to near the extent that physical health has.

"We do a lot of direct volunteer service for people in mental health centers and in hospitals. We go to the six state hospitals in South Carolina regularly. Volunteers make sure the clients and patients are in good condition by the simple act of going in to be a friend. There's an evaluation of each situation that goes on informally."

A Membership Organization

The League of Women Voters, also organized at the national, state and local levels, has thousands of dues-paying members. The League's program handbook describes the group's role in policy-making: "We are in the forefront of the citizen advocacy movement, but we are not at all new to this method of political participation. We've been at it since nineteen twenty . . . we can speak from every corner of the nation, every state and, indeed, all but a few congressional districts. . . . The League itself was founded out of one of the largest and longest action campaigns this country ever witnessed — the fight for women's suffrage."

Then president of the League, Dorothy Ridings, added, "We've been around for more than sixty years, and we're a very healthy, viable organization. We are aided by the fact that we are a non-partisan organization that does not support or oppose candidates. That gives us a lot of credibility.

"In addition, there is the fact that we are a multi-issue organization. If a member of Congress from Oshkosh can't be with us on acid rain, we say, 'We'll be back to you next week on domestic content or on the ERA or on something on which we can agree.' That gives us strength, too."

A Professional Organization

In June 1983, the Association for Business and Professional Women in Construction (BPWC) in Ohio held a successful first conference, "Women Building Bridges for the Future."

"We're timing it with the centennial of the Brooklyn Bridge," Connie Spruill, one of the founding members of the fledgling organization, explained before the conference. Spruill won an award that year named for Emily Roebling, who oversaw the completion of the bridge after her husband died.

The first day of the conference women from Michigan, Ohio, Illinois, Indiana, Kentucky, Pennsylvania, New York, New Mexico, Washington and

Colorado talked about the growth and development of an association. "All the new women coming in from the various states will be able to go back and start their own chapters of the Association for Business and Professional Women in Construction," Spruill said.

"Now I just have myself as executive director. We're not going to elect national officers until we get the other chapters completely set up and then we will have a representative from each area in the various states."

Spruill explained how she became involved in the organization founded by Lenore Janus in March, 1980. "I read an article in the 'Engineering News Record' that they were trying to begin new chapters outside of New York. I called her, and I met with her in October, nineteen eighty for their first annual conference, which turned out to be one heck of a conference.

"They had a hundred people, and they'd only been in existence for six months. After meeting with her I found out that this is what I need. It's a group that can identify with my problems as a female in the construction industry.

"So I came back to Ohio and set up a newsletter and started addressing it to a list of women business owners that I got from the Ohio Department of Transportation. Every month that newsletter went out. For six months the association in Ohio was nothing but a newsletter.

"However, in the newsletter the image was given in a different way, you know: 'We're a growing association, come join with the rest of us.' And within six months we had about twelve members. We had our first meeting in January of nineteen eighty-one, and the Association has grown from twelve members in Ohio to hundreds from all over the midwest. I have recruited women from all over the midwestern states."

Cooperation Among Advocacy Groups

Most advocacy groups "network," that is, they make connections and share information informally with other groups that are or may be interested in the same issues. The benefits are huge. Treating other groups coolly or, worse, competitively, always causes harm in the end. (See Chapter Twelve.)

Betsy Reifsnider of the Sierra Club reported, "We coordinate a lot of things with the Wilderness Society. Sometimes we call on the Audubon Society for support. We lend a hand to Friends of Wetlands and Friends of the Marsh on their efforts at a particular local issue that we agree with."

Sometimes advocacy groups join more formal, though temporary, alliances, called "coalitions," which are among the most misunderstood groups around. Coalitions are large advocacy groups made up of several separate advocacy organizations that work in concert for a limited time for a specific goal or goals. A "permanent coalition" is really an amalgamated advocacy group. An association where one group does all the activities and others simply endorse the stand is not a coalition. A group should never call itself a coalition unless it can name separate member organizations.

Forming a coalition can make sense for many reasons. Tish Sommers of the Older Women's League (OWL) wrote in the group's Organizing Manual that coalitions are "important and will proliferate" as more and more groups find themselves affected by budget cuts.

"Coalitions are formed for greater clout," she wrote, "and also to show how broad the support or opposition is to a particular question or to overcome splintering. Most of all, coalitions are formed to put up a united front vis-à-vis the opposition."

One of the best reasons for forming a coalition is that the number of constituents and amount of resources gets multiplied by the number of organizations. For example, Boston NOW has worked with several coalitions. The Coalition for Reproductive Freedom has more than 100 member organizations, from the Civil Liberties Union of Massachusetts to the Simmons College Women's Center.

Constituents Care and Count

The largest, least formal, yet most important group advocates strive to put together and keep together is constituents for the issues. These are the members of the public who care about particular policies.

Because we elect representatives to create policy on the public's behalf, those in power tend to count; they count money and votes. And the less financial power an issue or group has, the more countable constituents it needs.

A NETWORK newsletter quoted a summer intern of the Washington-based organization after she visited a congressional office. "All the legislative aide wanted to know," she said, "was how many members we have in his district!"

Constituents are needed to support the work of advocacy organizations by lending their names, their experiences, their voices and, often, their time, energy and money, to the causes they care about. Of all the groups involved in advocacy, constituents for issues have the most to give and the most to gain from successful advocacy efforts. They can vary their participation in amount and kind, depending on their interests and schedules.

Constituent groups are made up of people who have characteristics and concerns in common. Constituents generally fall into one of four categories according to the difficulties that bind them: local problems (later we will distinguish between people who live near each other and those who have particular local issues), ethnic or gender identity, life experience or general concerns.

Local Problems

Location is significant to advocates looking for supporters for a specific issue when all the inhabitants are directly affected by that issue. A hazardous waste site, a plant closing, a crime wave, a dangerous intersection, a school closing and bank red-lining practices are examples of problems people in a particular location might share. Constituents for local issues share a common geography *and* a common problem peculiar to their location.

"There's a really good group in Lake Charles, Louisiana," Lois Gibbs said. She worked with them since they asked the help of her national organization, Citizens Clearinghouse for Hazardous Wastes (CCHW).

"It's really two groups," she pointed out. It became one because they have the same problem. "On one side of the highway is a very poor black community," she said. "And on the other side of the highway is a very wealthy more educated professional community. And in between these two communities is the Bolling Fass Industrial [BFI] site. It was going to grow. It's a landfill — a major landfill. And the citizens were complaining. The poor black community was complaining that the landfill was already leaking in their environment.

"What we had to do from there," Gibbs said of CCHW's task, "was begin by getting these two groups of people who are usually considered socially incompatible in our world today to talk to one another and to utilize one another's resources.

"That was done," she said, "by explaining to them that they're all in this together. We said, 'These people have this to offer. You have that to offer.' For example, the more professional people have contacts in the university and the medical community. The black people have a lot of people power — to help distribute newsletters, do fund raising, things like that," Gibbs pointed out. The two groups got together and formed one organization called Citizens Against Landfill.

"This group successfully beat BFI because of the amount of people they were able to turn out, and because two very different societies joined forces...."

CCHW works with groups all over the country dealing with specific local hazardous waste problems every year. In 1984 the national clearinghouse for information and help listed Martin County, Kentucky; Featherstone, Virginia; Waterloo, Ontario; Merritt Island, New York; and Eureka, Nevada, along with 111 other locations they had worked with that year.

When it comes to bringing constituents together, people with local problems are sometimes treated as the only type of constituent group. But most advocates realize there are other complex problems besides local ones that mold people into groups.

Ethnic and Gender Identity

Who they are at birth gives some citizens special concerns about public policy all their lives. Gender, race and ethnic background are automatically common, sometimes troublesome, characteristics people have in common.

Native Americans, because of their heritage and history, share many problems. Sally Mead worked for the Native American Corporation on the North Pacific Rim in Alaska.

"In Alaska," she said, "the native culture is on the edge of being destroyed. But it's on the edge of surviving, too."

Mead maintained that the federal legislation in the 1970s contributed to "taking the power back into the native communities around the country and have the community be able to resolve some of its own problems.

"It's a real exciting and fascinating time to watch the culture trying to evolve itself. It's like they've jumped from the nineteenth to the twenty-first century in about twenty or thirty years. It's causing conflict and how it's being manifested is an alcohol problem," she said. Mead blamed past treatment of Native Americans. "There's been a long process of breaking down a beautiful system," she explained.

"The intent of the acts we work under is to return the power back to the villages—so that people find their own strengths again. You can't provide services in the arenas of the mental health and alcoholism from the outside. They have to come from a natural helping system inside the community itself."

When she got to know the villages, Mead learned that "a natural helping system existed already. It's just a matter of revitalizing it. So it's a matter of trying to help pull out some of those folks who are the natural helpers and helping them see what's going on."

Life Experiences

Age, illness, disability, chemical dependence and other problems bind people together to form constituent groups for certain issues. Victims of poverty, crime and abuse also fall into the life-experience category.

But life experiences that connect people are not necessarily negative ones. People who work together or have the same professions are constituents for common issues. Recipients of similar services or services delivered by the same organization are often bound together in support of programs and other services.

"Older women are an oppressed group in our society," said Tish Sommers, the often-interviewed president of the Older Women's League (OWL). Women are a group with special issues because they were born female. Getting older is a life experience which may bring other forms of "oppression."

"To overcome the oppression," Sommers said, "requires a maximum amount of energy and effort. One of our slogans is, 'Don't Agonize— Organize.' And another is, 'We're growing in numbers, and we're growing in power.' We're rolling forward.

"The demographics are with us. There's no question we can be significant and have a significant impact on society. It requires this huge percentage of older women to do it. But, if an organization is seen as an opinion-maker, older women will not feel so helpless—that nothing can be done."

The first question posed in the OWL Organizing Manual is "What is an older woman?"

This answer is offered: "She's anyone who is willing to admit to it in this society which battles wrinkles and thinks of aging females as pitiful or comic. She is anyone who has experienced the combined impact of age and sex discrimination in the job market. . . . She is anyone who has been turned aside for a youthful counterpart and learns how vulnerable older women alone are. . . . She's one of millions of middle-aged and elder women, the fastest growing segment of the population in this country, and the least organized."

General Concerns

Some constituents share only concern for an issue as their most common denominator. They may live thousands of miles from each other and possess little or no ethnic and gender identity or life experiences. What they do share is caring; they want to improve the environment, end the military weapons buildup, or safeguard human rights, for example. It is their concern that brings them together.

Sandra Kurjiaka was the director of the state branch of an organization which appeals to people who share a concern, but not necessarily any other characteristics.

She described the membership of the Arkansas Civil Liberties Union. "There's not a particular type of member. I keep trying to find out if we have a type, because that would help in membership recruitment. If it was like mostly legal people or mostly college professors or mostly professional people. . . . If there was some way I could get sort of a reading on who is attracted to us. It's just that there is no way to label members of this organization in this state. It's good, I think.

"We get a much more balanced board," she said, "just in terms of making decisions. The board is elected from each of the four corners of the state. The board sets policy mostly, and they charge me with carrying it out. I mean in Arkansas people don't just run for the CLU board unless they have strong feelings. So we end up with some really good people."

A Happy Mix

Because each issue has multiple implications, most constituency groups are not *purely* one of the four types, as the above examples vividly illustrate. A person might be a constituent for mental health issues, for example, because of general concern or because of a personal experience with mental illness.

Issues blend sometimes. Two people who have in common that they are women (gender identity), and grow older (a life experience) support certain changes in Social Security for both reasons.

Being aware of the four fundamental groupings of constituents provides a foundation that enables advocates to find and appeal to members of the public interested in common issues.

The OWL Organizing Manual poses a question about the constituents of the organization. "Who is elibigle to join OWL?" The answer includes women of all ages, people of both sexes who share concern with older women's issues and, of course, older women.

"All politics is local," former House speaker Thomas P. (Tip) O'Neil has been quoted as saying. Advocates often structure their organizations to respect that notion. Many national advocacy groups subdivide into geographic levels, but mechanical divisions by location are not to be confused with issues that will attract everyone in a particular location to a particular cause. National groups often try to "localize" state and national issues for grassroots efforts to make recruiting easier.

Government: In Constant Flux

Of the three major groups advocates work with—advocacy organizations, constituents for the issues and government—government has the most power over policies. All three branches of government—courts, legislative bodies and administrative offices and boards—make decisions and take actions which directly affect issues every day. Government tends to receive much more public attention than the other two major groups.

Nevertheless, to many advocates, government is not really "over" the rest of the public. Government is just the third major group, on a par with the others. Many advocates work to mold and maintain responsive government groups and officials just as they do non-profit organizations, so they will do the right thing for policy.

Some advocates spend a lot of their "people time" on straight politics, making sure officials that agree with them get inside government and stay there. That means they deal with elected, appointed and employed people in the three branches of government.

The list of groups just one advocate deals with in a year is long. Barbara Reed, for example, regularly deals with the United States Department of Agriculture, the Atlanta Housing Authority, the Atlanta Health Department, U.S. Senators and representatives, Georgia state senators and representatives and the Georgia Department of Human Resources.

The great variety of government groups is typical. Advocates keep track of which government groups are dealing with their issues. Advocates research, stay familiar with and continually update information about people involved and the agendas of each group. (See Chapter Eight.)

The Mental Health Association of South Carolina distributes a chart to its members which shows the hierarchy of the state's dealings with mental health issues. Under the governor is the state mental health commission, then all the various "offices," divisions, then the hospitals and clinics and centers where services are given. The chart also provides the name of the person in charge of each and names all the mental health commissioners.

Advocates in Government

Some advocates are part of government because they hold official government positions. Eleanor Josaitis and Carol Garvin were both appointed to government groups because of their advocacy and expertise. Josaitis, associate director of Focus:HOPE in Detroit, is a member of the U.S. Department of Agriculture's national advisory council on maternal infant and fetal nutrition. Garvin serves on South Carolina's Mental Health Commission. Martha Cotera has been appointed to numerous boards in Austin, Texas. None of these women, it should be noted, are college-trained professionals in their fields; they learned what they know through advocacy experience.

Carol Tucker Foreman, Janet Diamond and Marlene Sciascia are all advocates who were hired by government agencies at national, state and local levels, respectively, because of their skills.

Although not directly employed by government itself, advocates who work for agencies that deliver services receive government grants as major sources of funds for their programs. Diane Roach of the St. Paul American Indian Center and Kattie Portis of Boston's Women, Inc. all work closely with government as they manage programs government agencies fund.

Advocates also find themselves working to see that other advocates gain government positions, especially elected ones. Lotta Chi, Martha Cotera, Juanita Kennedy Morgan and Brenda LaBlanc have all worked in the campaigns of candidates sympathetic to their causes. They also support appointments of other citizens who share their concerns.

Although government officials may seem to be the most powerful, they are not necessarily the longest lasting or most reliable group advocates deal with. Changing attitudes, administrations, relationships and times affect government officials' and groups' advocacy very strongly. When advocates try to persuade government officials to take stands on a policy, officials' responses vary.

A Range of Attitudes

"Last week I went to a meeting at the state Department of Transportation," Connie Spruill of Ohio's Business and Professional Women in Construction related in a 1982 interview. "There was a panel of state people to address the Women Business Enterprise people certified with the state. There were eight people on the panel, and two of them were women.

"We had forty-five women in the room," she said, "and they didn't even know how to address us—'young ladies' or 'girls,' they called us. And I thought: I don't believe this! They were completely oblivious as to what our grievances and problems are. . . . We would ask questions that pertained to our exclusion, and they beat around the bush and never did answer us.

"The two women on the panel have probably been with the state for twenty years—that kind of person. They had no idea what was going on. They only see what goes across their desks on bid forms. And, of course, they don't see many women's bid forms because there are no opportunities out there for them to bid.

"In fact," Spruill contended, "they feel that there aren't enough women contractors—even though there are three hundred registered with the state—who are actually qualified to do anything."

With some officials and groups, the relationship is more positive. Janet Diamond spoke very highly of one powerful Massachusetts legislator, a former champion boxer. "Joe DeNucci is a wonderful man. He's a very compassionate man. There's really no other reason [for his constant help for welfare issues]. It's not that his district is so full of poor people. It's just that he's very compassionate. The stories move him. The testimony from poor people moves him. He's always been an advocate for poor people. It's not that he doesn't understand the issues; it's that he is also a man who will literally weep over a hurt child. It distresses him to think there are children without shoes in Massachusetts. I mean he can do something about it. He becomes a person carrying a banner for those children. And if you can get a handful of people in the state house like that. . . ."

Stefan Harvey named certain congressional committees she and other WIC advocates "counted on. One of these was the Senate Select Committee on Human Needs. . . . We are much more involved with the appropriations committees than we were ten years ago. If you look at the congressional work we did, as we developed relationships with key staff people and committees, it was easier to go back the next time because we had already established relationships."

Eleanor Josaitis has had many dealings with Washington political bigwigs in her role as advocate for the poor in Detroit. When she and another Focus:HOPE staffer were having trouble getting an appointment with Earl Butz, Secretary of Agriculture under Richard Nixon, Josaitis finally just went to the office and persuaded a secretary to let her in to talk to the cabinet member.

When George Bush was running for president in 1980, Josaitis arranged to have him and Michigan's governor tour the Focus:HOPE food operation. When some questioned why she would invite a Republican candidate to tour a heavily Democratic operation, Josaitis countered, "I don't care if they were using us politically. It gave me a chance to invite them into the solution."

Betsy Reifsnider contrasted how different officials treat environmental issues in the Los Angeles area. "The L.A. County Board of Supervisors has a conservative majority and all the control. We can't get anything done there. They passed a local coastal plan that is terrible."

On the other hand, she pointed out, there is hope. "The plan has to be approved by the Coastal Commission. At this point the commission is still pretty good. There are some good people on it, so we can approach them."

Different Administrations

Sometimes government is a help, and sometimes it's a hindrance, Reifsnider observed. "It all depends. Is it the Reagan administration or the

Dukmejian administration. The staff at the state parks you can always depend on. They are excellent people. They will tell us the truth.

"Now with the Dukmejian administration coming in, and the crap coming from them, I can't believe a word they say. The long-term people, like the ones who have been in the EPA [Environmental Protection Agency] since it was started and really believe in environment protection, we can talk to them. But the people like Rita Lavelle or Ann Gorsuch we can't, because there is so much doubletalk going on."

Stefan Harvey, Washington nutrition advocate, has seen contrasts within the Department of Agriculture (USDA) and between presidential administrations' attitudes. "In my early years of doing advocacy, it was impossible to get information from the Department of Agriculture," Harvey remembered. "From nineteen seventy-two to nineteen seventy-four, they refused to provide what was public information.

"If you look at the years of a Republican administration as compared to the Carter administration, the biggest difference is that during the Carter years the USDA policy-making people worked very closely with the advocacy community. They asked for our opinions. They asked for our assistance.

"During Republican administrations, we had to watch much more closely what their departments were doing. We were much more on the defensive," Harvey reported. "We had to spend a good deal of our time prodding the agency to do what the Congress already said the agency had to do. We had to do more work at the state and community levels when the Republicans were in power than when the Democrats were."

Special Groups: Special Functions

Advocates must work with specialists from time to time. Lawyers, scientists, academics and others contribute their skills to the progress of policy change in specialized ways. Some special groups advocates work with include: content and process experts, institutions, businesses and the media.

For example, Carol Tucker Foreman said that in dealing with bankruptcy laws and corporations escaping compensation for asbestos disease victims, she will work "with lawyers and economists and law professors and maybe some health people and maybe some scientists about this issue."

Process Experts

Lawyers and freelance consultants often help advocacy groups. Legal experts advise advocacy groups about their organizational set-ups and ongoing operations. In addition, specific legal services are required if advocates must use litigation to bring about policy change.

Many organizations consult lawyers and try to have a lawyer on their board of directors or in other permanent volunteer positions. For example, the board of the St. Paul American Indian Center has eight members. "The one non–Indian is an attorney who has three kids," Diane Roach said.

Lawyers help advocates analyze laws that might need changing. Carol Garvin said she was "hoping to pull together some sort of committee which would include some lawyers from around the state to look at commitment laws. We really need to engage a number of lawyers, because there are certainly a lot of legal overtones in the mental health area."

The MHASC ended up working in cooperation with the Mental Health Law Project in Washington, D.C. after the group collected case studies of mentally ill individuals in South Carolina who were thrown off the Social Security Disability rolls without review of their cases.

"They were reprinted by the Project," Carol Garvin recalled. "A staff person at the National Mental Health Association talked to someone at the Law Project and a number of other groups concerned about this. They did a lot of networking and disseminating information, and they sent us a packet where they pulled together six possible strategies, one of which was take-'em-to-court."

When a group chooses the take-'em-to-court strategy, and many have to, lawyers become front-line issues workers aiding advocacy campaigns. Focus:HOPE in Detroit used a lawyer to sue AAA. The Anti-Poverty Center in Atlanta sued the federal government. Carolyn Brown sued publishers in Alaska. Lawyers are important experts.

Most people who call themselves public policy consultants are lobbyists, that is, they specialize in working with legislatures to get laws passed. The professional organization of which Charlotte Tropp was a member had a Washington, D.C., lobbyist, for example.

Some policy consultants, like Lois Gibbs, offer a spectrum of advocacy services, including working with groups and conducting policy campaigns of all kinds. Those consultants also offer information on issues to their clients.

Content Experts

Experts in medicine, sociology, psychology, chemistry and other fields contribute a lot to advocacy when called on. They educate members, conduct studies, testify at hearings and write materials.

Stephan U. Lester, for example, is the Citizens Clearinghouse on Hazardous Wastes (CCHW) science director. One of his jobs is to write a regular column in "Everybody's Backyard" where he explains scientific facts and gives other information useful to the average person concerned about hazardous wastes. At the end of the column readers are told, "If you have any questions, or need help with a technical or scientific problem, give Steve a call or write to him."

Gini Laurie, chair of the board of the Gazette International Networking Institute, compiled a handbook co-edited by two physicians on the Late Effects of Poliomyelitis for Physicians and Survivors.

Sometimes experts conduct studies. Lois Gibbs said CCHW has "several scientists on the staff who will review any case studies that we've done. In case of a closed facility, they'll review the proposal. . . . In the case of an existing site, they will look at the level of exposure and try to estimate the risk to the community."

The National Institute on Drug Abuse did a study about pregnant drug addicts that Women, Inc. found useful. Statistics showing the seriousness of the problem were given to the press and provided in testimony at congressional hearings.

Speaking at hearings is another useful service experts perform. Two physicians testified alongside drug rehab advocate Kattie Portis at another committee hearing. Psychiatrists, lawyers, psychologists and other professionals speak on behalf of mental health issues for the Mental Health Association of South Carolina.

Even when the experts do not write or speak themselves, their names and statements lend credibility to statements of average citizens.

Kathleen Sheekey of Common Cause used experts to help with the complex MX missile issue in Congress. "I think the best thing to do for somebody like you or I who's not an arms control specialist, is to quote experts. There are military experts on our side of the issue," she pointed out.

"The former head of the CIA, William Colby, has testified against the MX missile. He doesn't think the Soviet Union is superior to the United States. Paul Warnke is another one. He was the SALT II negotiator during the Carter administration. Gerard Smith was the SALT II negotiator during the Nixon administration. All of them oppose the MX missile. All of them say that they would not trade the Soviet position with ours.

"So I think a good way to allay fears is to quote experts from the field so that it's not a lay person coming across as someone who might 'trust the Russians.' It really doesn't have anything to do with trust."

Institutions

Advocates and advocacy groups often have strong affiliations with major non-profit institutions such as churches, universities and foundations.

Churches provide facilities, funds and moral support for advocacy for policy change. Barbara Reed's Interfaith, Inc. is a church-created non-profit advocacy group which deals with housing problems in Atlanta, Georgia.

Local groups often find themselves meeting in church basements to talk about issues from hazardous wastes to bank red-lining. Eleanor Josaitis began Focus:HOPE with a priest partner, Father Frank Cunningham. Sermons were what first ignited people's awareness of racial and economic injustice in Detroit.

Universities make fertile ground for advocacy efforts. Humboldt State University in northern California was the umbrella institution for Humboldt County RSVP and channeled its funds for them. Norma Wilson and others use their classrooms to educate students about the socio-political ramifications of academic subjects. Universities also do research and furnish studies on subjects like child nutrition to the Center for Budget and Policy Priorities, which the Center can use to back up advocacy stands.

Foundations are a familiar group that provide funds for advocacy organizations as well as information. The United Way is one of the largest, providing money to organizations that deliver services. The St. Paul American Indian Center and Mental Health Association of South Carolina are two such recipients.

Business

Business may not come immediately to mind as an advocacy help group, but private enterprise sometimes contributes money and expertise to advocacy causes.

"Our special thanks and gratitude is also due to Simpsons Timber Company for a contribution of $1,000, to Humboldt Board of Realtors for $500 for our Homesharing Program, Eureka Rotary Club for $500 and to Coastal Care Centers for doubling the amount of their monthly contribution from $50 to $100 ," says the RSVP/Share newsletter.

Focus:HOPE News says, "Business and industry leaders joined Focus:HOPE in the special celebration held at the training center in Industry Mall. . . . Father Cunningham continually comments that success here at the Industry Mall is due to the teamwork of local industry, business, foundations, government and individuals working together to solve problems of unemployment."

News Media

Television, radio, and newspapers are useful in educating the public about issues. (See chapters Six and Nine for specifics.) Advocacy groups put out reams of instructions on how to work with "the fourth estate" because of its influence.

"Without media we could get nowhere," begins 20 pages devoted to using this special group in the OWL Organizing Manual.

Kattie Portis gave an example of how media attention can help get a problem solved: "I did some work around MCI [Massachusetts Correctional Institution] Walpole. When they had a lockup at Walpole a friend of mine organized a prayer vigil on the State House steps. The threat from the government was that the community should not demonstrate—that people would get killed if we did.

"There were one hundred fifty people on the steps. I took everybody I knew. We didn't want the inmates in Walpole killed. There was a lot of crazy stuff happening. And there wasn't anybody saying anything. We knew we couldn't make the institution do anything. But we thought, maybe if we got on NBC, maybe they wouldn't kill anybody else. The news was there. We got on NBC. And it worked."

All the special groups advocates work with are controversial. Often these groups turn up on the other side of important issues. Working with them can be tricky at times and requires skill and knowledge of how to best use the groups. (See Chapter Six.) Nevertheless, advocates recognize their usefulness.

Chapter Four

Centers of Activity: Creating and Maintaining Advocacy Groups

This kind of working together spirit is vital to everybody.
— Gini Laurie

When it's obvious that a public problem exists, it's time to look around. An advocacy group that deals with that issue may already exist. Or perhaps an organization that focuses on similar issues can be persuaded to look at a new one.

Janet Ferone joined NOW when she became concerned about women's rights. Kathy Kelley introduced new issues to the teachers union she belonged to. A new group does not need to spring into existence every time someone discovers a problem. When a suitable organization does not exist or existing groups cannot or will not take on an issue, then new advocacy groups come into being.

How Some Advocacy Groups Were Born

The stories of how a few advocacy groups were formed tells a lot about all of them. Some groups remain informal and some incorporate as nonprofit organizations.

Local Hazardous Waste Groups

Advocacy groups to deal with local problems come into being "when one or two people become convinced that something is wrong. Do you think you have a problem? Observe what's going on around you. Talking to your neighbors is the first research stop in forming an organization." This is what Citizen's Clearinghouse for Hazardous Wastes (CCHW) says about putting together an advocacy group to deal with a local problem in its "Leadership Handbook on Hazardous Wastes" (LHHW)—a book by Lois Gibbs and Will Collette.

Gibbs said in an interview, "Most communities have never organized before, don't have any idea how to organize and have no idea where to go with the problem. What we do," she said, "is help show them."

She described how local advocacy groups—most of them unincorporated—have been created with CCHW's help. "We show them the way to research the issue. . . . After that's done we explain to them how to organize the community. . . . Then we show them how to hold a local community-based meeting. After they've successfully done that, we help in other techniques such as fund raising and so forth." Gibbs and CCHW have worked out a clear way to put together local people who had no advocacy group to begin with.

Women, Inc.

Sometimes groups spring out of already existing groups or movements. And they can be organized at all levels, including nationally. "We started to raise hell in nineteen seventy-one," remembered Kattie Portis, "and Women, Inc. was first funded in nineteen seventy-three.

"There was a national drug conference in Chicago in nineteen seventy-one," Portis said. "The black folks, the women, the gay people, the American Indians, the Hispanic people, we would always go to this conference. It was required of us; we were supposed to learn something. We got there and here were all these doctors, and we were tired of them telling us about methadone. We didn't want to hear it."

"So a group of women, black folks and Hispanics broke off and started a caucus. We were the people nobody wanted to deal with. A lot of things happened at that conference. Blacks came out with an agenda. Women came out with an agenda.

"When we got back to Boston people were really starting to get stirred up. So the state decided to have a conference at Amherst [Massachusetts] to deal with some of the issues.

"Things got so crazy you wouldn't believe it. Somebody from the state brought a tape recorder into our session. They were taping the session to show how bad these people were. So we took the tape recorder and threw it out.

"At that time Dr. Duma was the commissioner of drug rehab. He was a terrific man. He knew. As a matter of fact, he was giving us feedback. And he made sure we knew what our rights were. He was our support. And then we went to Washington [to seek funding], and that's how Women, Inc. really got started."

Older Women's League

"OWL was an outgrowth of the displaced homemakers movement," Tish Sommers explained. "Laurie Shields and I had been working to get legislation passed to help women move from dependency to self-sufficiency and get centers set up to give them assistance during that process. It was quite clear to us that there needed to be a national membership organization which would address some of the problems that older women face but no one else was tackling.

"The women's organizations had not gotten to these questions, and the aging organizations seemed to be oblivious to the fact that women had some special problems that need their attention.

"In about nineteen seventy-eight we formed the Older Women's League Educational Fund, which we saw from the beginning as a midwife to get OWL off the ground. We had a 501(c)(3) status from the IRS, and we researched the issues. We got up 'gray papers' on older women's issues, social security, pensions, etc.

"At any rate, the opportunity arose in nineteen eighty when we were asked to co-sponsor—well, co-sponsor is perhaps too strong—we pushed for a White House mini-conference on older women. In October, as a preparatory conference for the White House Conference on Aging, we held a conference with the Western Gerontological Society. At that time part of the purpose was to launch the Older Women's League. They asked people to stay over one more day, and some three hundred delegates did, and we formed the Older Women's League then.

"As you can see," Sommers said of the origins of the membership organization in a nineteen eighty-three interview, "it was one stepping stone after another. We've just finished a new stage. We just got a national office in Washington, D.C., where we can network with other organizations and play a role as a bridge between, again, activism and women's organizations.

"When we first started we used the downstairs of a house that Laurie and I share. And it was on a very, very small scale with a very small budget. And right now we're moving to the big time."

Managing Advocacy Groups

From the first glimmer of existence, as the anecdotes about creating groups show, the groups grow, divide, develop and change. In order to survive, they need constant care and attention. They need goals, structure, funds, and good communication within the group and with the public to flourish.

A Sense of Purpose

"The Group Must Have Goals!" Lois Gibbs says in the CCHW Leadership Handbook. The goals and purposes of the advocacy group determine everything else. Advocates formulate, state and act on the group's agreed-upon purpose on all activities.

Many organizations spell out their purposes in their publications. The purpose of Focus:HOPE is written in the form of a pledge in the August 1982 newsletter. Titled "Recognizing the Dignity and Beauty of Every Person," it begins, "We pledge intelligent and practical action to overcome racism, poverty and injustice. And to build a metropolitan community where all people may live in freedom, harmony, trust and affection...."

The brochure describing Gini Laurie's *Rehabilitation Gazette* features the three purposes on the front: "Group therapy by mail; Guide to independent living; and Guide to coping with disability."

The League of Women Voters' "Guidelines for League Boards" states League purpose and policy have changed "little" since the founding days. "The purpose, as it appeared in the national bylaws in 1920, was 'to foster education in citizenship and to support improved legislation.'

"The bylaws also said, 'The National League of Women Voters urges every woman to become an enrolled voter, but as an organization it shall be allied with and support no party.' In nineteen twenty-three, the purpose was enlarged to include efficiency in government and international cooperation to prevent war."

Citizens for Community Improvement of Des Moines states its purpose in the first paragraph of a funding proposal. Brenda LaBlanc's group says it is "a people's organization [where] residents are assisted in organizing themselves to resolve community, neighborhood or block issues."

Just because goals are not written down does not mean groups do not formulate them. Martha Cotera and a small group of parents formed a short-term advocacy group that knew its purpose very well. "We've got a bilingual program," she explains, "but now they are restructuring it. They're doing some school policy and it seems very hush-hush and very rapid, and we've got to slow down the process."

The Mental Health Association of South Carolina and President Carol Garvin delineated five pages of specific goals for 1983 for distribution throughout the organization's chapters. The goals are introduced by saying, "The highest priority for 1983 will be chapter development and field services . . . ." After the organization's general purposes are stated, the next pages detail specific program, membership and administrative goals for the coming year.

Structure Is Security

"Structure," according to CCHW's Leadership Handbook, "means some established process for making decisions. You need to develop a structure that works and is based on your circumstances," it says to local groups fighting hazardous wastes. "While you don't have to use 'Roberts Rules of Order' or have a formal constitution . . . you must be able to function and, if yours is an organization fighting for justice, you must operate democratically."

The structure an organization chooses depends on the size and scope of the group's goals. Clearly, the League of Women Voters will be a long-term, tightly organized group. Cotera's bilingual parents group does not need to be formally organized to reach its short-term goal.

Martha Cotera said of another group, "Now that we have enough groupies and we have enough people who are actively involved . . . we can go ahead and formalize our group. I always do things backwards. You know, I don't like to formalize a group and then start with two people. I like to go ahead and do a lot of work, and then, when people are ripe and ready, to get some kind of formal structure."

Non-Profit Incorporation

Although it is not always necessary, some groups choose to incorporate as one of three common types of non-profit-organizations—known informally as service providers, membership or professional organizations. They incorporate, among other reasons, because they want special financial treatment offered by the tax code. (See Chapter Eleven for details about how the tax code regulates funding and policy advocacy efforts of various types of non-profits.)

Service delivery groups like Women, Inc. are 501(c)(3)s. This type of group can get tax deductible contributions and government funding, but advocacy activities are severely limited. Most churches, many hospitals and other service and educational agencies are 501(c)(3)s. Informal terms— many of them misnomers—exist for service delivery groups, such as "charity." Some people use the word "non-profit" synonymously with 501(c)(3)s, but that is inaccurate, because there are other types of non-profits.

Membership organization is a term often applied to groups incorporated as 501(c)(4)s. Other terms include "citizens' groups," or "people's organizations." Membership organizations may advocate policy change, but they cannot get government money, and donations made to them are not tax deductible. Funds come from dues and other fund-raising activities. Common Cause, the Sierra Club, the League of Women Voters and many others are 501(c)(4)s. Obviously, 501(c)(4)s exert a great deal of effort to appeal to a large number of people for support and membership.

Professional organizations and unions are 501(c)(5)s. They have the same fund-raising limitations as 501(c)(4)s. The Boston Teachers Union and the Association of Business and Professional Women in Construction are 501(c)(5)s.

Combinations. Some organizations have separate incorporated branches. Maintaining a membership and a service organization—as does the Civil Liberties Union of Arkansas—is fairly common. The Women's Rights Project, a 501(c)(3), works on behalf of women and their rights, mostly doing education. The 501(c)(4) membership organization handles court or legislative actions.

Another successful combination comes when staff of 501(c)(3)s form 501(c)(5) professional organizations. Barbara Reed, director of a 501(c)(3) day care center, belongs to the Georgia Title 20 Directors Association, a 501(c)(5).

In addition to their non-profit status, a membership or professional organization may choose—like NETWORK—to register officially as a "lobby." Groups may also have affiliated Political Action Committees (PACs).

Nomenclature can be confusing. Service delivery and informal groups often have "members" or "volunteers" who show their support for the group by paying nominal dues, just like official membership and professional organizations.

Who Decides?

Decision-making usually has a structure to it. A section of a 1982 NETWORK newsletter called "Setting the stage" described two diagrams. "Within the state, one structure which has proven very helpful is the formation of a steering committee to assist the state or regional coordinator in carrying out NETWORK activities...

"Regular meetings of this committee allow close coordination of activities without the necessity of frequent meetings of the general membership. The existence of a steering committee also promotes a participatory model of NETWORK organization, with a strong level of secondary leadership to share in decision making and help carry out necessary tasks."

The Mental Health Association of South Carolina also puts out diagrams showing its decision-making structure. Typical of the democratic orientation of most advocacy groups, at the top of the pyramid is "membership." Included are an 11-person executive committee and board, and three staff members. The statewide organization has seven standing committees: nominations, legislative, financial development, professional advisory, annual meeting, organization development and personnel.

Most advocacy groups operate with a mixture of a few staffers and many volunteers working together. "Our group is very much directed by volunteers," Carol Garvin said of the MHASC, which has 30 chapters in the state. "The executive committee pretty much runs the day-to-day business of the association. . . . It's hard to run a large state organization," she pointed out. "It would be helpful if we had a little more sense of paid hands so we could get our volunteers to a place where they could do more. I think we need more staff." The MHASC had an executive director, an administrative assistant and a field services coordinator.

Sandra Kurjiaka described things from the staff view at another state branch of a national organization. "The board," she said of the Arkansas Civil Liberties Union, "sets policy and charges me with carrying that out."

At OWL Tish Sommers said both volunteers and staff members "have come forward and said, 'I'm involved, or I want to be,' and we've gotten very terrific talent that way. Then we work as much as possible in a team way."

The OWL Organizing Manual says, "For most OWL chapters the possibility of staff is not yet feasible, but should be considered for the future. In some cases it may be possible to secure a volunteer staff person. . . . Sometimes staff may be 'loaned' from an agency. . . . Whether paid or unpaid, the role of staff," the manual points out, "should be clearly distinguished from chapter leadership. The employer is the chapter and the staff person helps carry out the mandate of that body."

Brenda LaBlanc considers having staff highly beneficial. "Our staff people have done an awfully good job of investigating," she said. "Now we've got staff. When it was just the neighborhood group, we had to spend an awful lot of time and go down to City Hall and look into things and find out information. That's why National People's Association is such a great organization. Their staff people know where to go, who the people are and how to get information."

Committees are common in advocacy groups. "If you break your work down into small tasks," suggests the Leadership Handbook on Hazardous Wastes, "it's easier to get volunteers to do them. . . . Committees are usually the best way to share the work load."

Spending Money

As the OWL manual says, "Organizations cannot run on love alone. . . ."
Fund raising is a basic necessity for all advocacy groups. Typical sources of
funds are membership fees, especially for membership and professional
organizations. Service delivery groups receive grants from foundations and
government. And all groups take donations and organize fund-raising activities of various kinds.

Tish Sommers said, "If you can't raise the money, you're not going to
grow and you're not going to be able to develop the staff needed to do what
you want to do. So, I'd put fund raising right at the center of organizational
tasks.

"My major job is fund raising and financial planning. I also teach older
women who've never done fund raising some of the skills because on the
chapter level they have to learn."

Where the money comes from depends not only on the group's tax
status but also on the principles of the organization. Citizens Clearinghouse
on Hazardous Wastes refuses to take grants from businesses or government
to be sure it is not compromised in its efforts. CCHW gets its funds from
dues, donations and fees it charges grassroots groups for advice.

Citizens for Community Improvement of Des Moines, on the other
hand, does not want to exclude anyone because they lack money, so the
group relies on grants to fund its operations.

The RSVP program at Humboldt State in California, a 501(c)(3), got a
lot of its money from government, by way of the university, through 23
separate funders—federal, state, city, county and private foundations.
Charlotte Tropp said, "The institutional routing has to happen. Everyone
not only reads and approves the commitments made on behalf of the university for the money, but also specifies what is appropriate and consistent with
the goals and mission of the university. So there's that kind of a check-off
that happens automatically."

"We are funded through the local chapters . . . through membership
dues," said Carol Garvin of the Mental Health Association of South
Carolina. "Each chapter provides what we call a 'fair share.' But we're largely
funded by the United Way. I'm quite happy to let them do the fund raising,
which they're good at, and let us do the work."

Advocates and advocacy groups are continuously dreaming up creative
ways to raise money to supplement often meager incomes from traditional
sources such as dues. But good planning is "the first requirement of all successful fund raising," according to OWL. "First you determine what you
need to raise and then you consider varied means of raising it."

There are several methods for appealing for donations from the public.
The two types of donations are monetary and in-kind—a donation of goods

or services which the organization can use or sell. CCHW says: "Donations should be encouraged at each public meeting, at membership meetings, at social events and in publications." OWL mentions canvassing for donations, going door to door.

Sometimes an organization can be persuaded to make a donation. "Links benefit raises $$ for drug program," the headline reads. The third annual Harvest Ball of the local chapter of the national organization LINKS raised $3,000 for Women, Inc. in 1980.

Direct mail is another way to solicit donations. Almost all national organizations have found it cost-effective to pay for mailing lists of strangers or mail to sympathizers to ask for contributions. In most cases the appeal includes a statement about a particular problem the organization is addressing or a service it provides. Often a newspaper article is also included, because it tends to convey legitimacy quickly.

CCHW sent a letter describing a new project saying, "The purpose of Project Independence is to raise enough money from *you*—from concerned people and groups that share our philosophy—to ensure that CCHW is insulated from changing trends and able to continue to serve your needs, come what may."

Telephone solicitation is the local version of the direct mail method. According to CCHW, "It is a very inexpensive way to make direct appeals and can be done with a pool of volunteers."

Citizens Against Landfill in Lake Charles, Louisiana, "went to local merchants asking for a direct donation or things they could raffle off," according to Louis Gibbs. "A lot of the professional community went to their colleagues and asked for direct cash donations of a couple of hundred dollars. They raised funds and were able to further establish their group by getting letterhead paper and renting halls and starting a newsletter—things like that. Also, they were able to hire a scientist to come in and look at the situation."

From books to bumper stickers, advocates sell materials that educate the public more about the organization and its issues. Often they sell them above cost in order to raise funds. They advertise the materials in other publications they send out and display them at meetings and conferences.

With almost every other mailing it sends, CCHW includes a list of items available for purchase. "New Items from CCHW," is the title of one insert, complete with order form. Items include a "no spilled barrels" button for $.75, testimony by Lois Gibbs on victims compensation ($1.50), a CCHW baseball-style cap, two more publications and a T-shirt that says "Hysterical Housewife! You Wish." Customers can pay cash or use a charge card.

Except for occasional donations, most of the operations money for the

Rehabilitation Gazette comes from purchase of the *Gazette* and other books. Back copies are always available.

Grants are another source of funding. Many foundations and government award grants only to 501(c)(3) non-profit organizations. "We get funds mostly from churches," said Citizens for Community Improvement's Brenda LaBlanc. "The staff is forever sending in proposals. One group pays for the tenant-landlord thing and another pays for the anti-crime.

"I spend a great deal of my time writing proposals," said Tish Sommers. Her statement holds true for most directors of advocacy groups.

Special events can also bring in money. "Once in a while we put on a fund-raiser," said Juanita Kennedy Morgan of the Black Women's Political Caucus. "We had Maya Angelou read once, and half the time we put on that kind of program. Last year we had money donated from a performance of the 'Black Nativity.' Otherwise," she said, "we only get money from membership. We've tried on several occasions to get government money, but we got turned down because we've got the word 'political' in our name. It's hard for us to raise any money except through events."

Events "should be things people like to do and that you have the capability to pull off," says CCHW. OWL adds that a fund-raiser can also be a "consciousness raiser and a membership builder."

Communication Begins at Home

The necessity for excellent communication permeates all advocacy work, starting with communication within the advocacy groups themselves. It involves a lot of telephone calls and meetings. Conferences are also used to assemble and maintain advocacy groups. And many advocacy groups end up being small publishers because of all the written communications they send their members.

Advocates use the telephone daily. Some groups set up telephone trees to facilitate communication. "Basically," says the OWL manual, "a chapter phone tree is a means to communicate rapidly and regularly with chapter members. . . . The set-up varies, depending on the purpose of the calls and on the number of people." Sommers wrote, "Callers can build up personal contact with others that will further promote a 'team' feeling. . . . The larger the chapter, the greater the need."

The fax works the same speedy way as the phone, especially when members of the group are all professionals with offices.

Meetings are another key element in maintaining groups. OWL, CCHW and the League of Women Voters (LWV) have written useful descriptions of good meetings.

The League says that "successful discussion units have certain key ingredients: the atmosphere is friendly . . . objectives of the meeting are stated briefly and succinctly . . . information on the topic is available . . . sufficient time is allotted for discussion . . . free interplay and exchange of ideas and viewpoints is encouraged . . . periodic review and wrap up . . . include a total review of any member agreement/consensus . . . the topic of the next meeting is announced . . . appreciation is expressed to those present. . . ."

Conferences are often used to create an advocacy organization, or, more truthfully, announce the creation of one to the world.

Elizabeth Cady Stanton called conferences "conventions" in *Eighty Years and More*, the autobiography of an advocate in mid–19th century U.S. She referred to the fact that women were not seated and could not speak at one conference when she describes another.

> My experience at the World's Anti-slavery Convention, all I had read of the legal status of women, and the oppression I saw everywhere, together swept across my soul, intensified now by many personal experiences. It seemed as if all the elements had conspired to impel me to some onward step. I could not see what to do or where to begin — my only thought was a public meeting for protest and discussion.
>
> My discontent, according to Emerson, must have been healthy, for it moved us all to prompt action, and we decided . . . to call a "Woman's Rights Convention." We wrote the call . . . and published it in the *Seneca County Courier* the next day, the 14th of July, 1848, giving only five days' notice, as the convention was to be held on the 19th and 20th.
>
> The convention, which was held two days in the Methodist Church, was in every way a grand success. The house was crowded at every session, the speaking good, and a religious earnestness dignified all the proceedings.
>
> These were the hasty initiative steps of "the most momentous reform that had yet been launched on the world — the first organized protest against the injustice which had brooded for ages over the character and destiny of one-half the race."
>
> But we had set the ball in motion, and now, in quick succession, conventions were held in Ohio, Indiana, Massachusetts, Pennsylvania, and in the City of New York, and have been kept up nearly every year since.

"Somewhere down the line," OWL begins its chapter on conferences, "the chapter will probably decide to hold a conference. . . . For the organization they provide the opportunity to raise consciousness on issues, build membership, perhaps raise funds, develop leadership skills and gain identity and a sense of accomplishment."

The *Rehabilitation Gazette* published since 1958, held a post-polio conference in May 1983 in St. Louis which did just that. That organization was in a transition phase. Publisher Gini Laurie, 70 at the time, was looking for funds to continue her work. "It's only going to done if we get a younger executive director and get a part-time secretary."

The 429 people who attended the conference on independent living came from all over the world. "All these people came because of the *Gazette*," said Laurie. "All these people paid their ways from South Africa, from Japan, from every place—all their own expenses and they came because of the *Gazette*.

"This conference should make raising the money for salaries a lot easier because we got awfully good publicity here and then on the Charles Kuralt show nationally. I have a lot of darling young friends who are in P.R. and have been helping us out on the conference. I'm going to get a bunch of these young people on the board and help us get this done."

Workshops are also common advocacy group get-togethers. Usually these are shorter and designed to educate members. NETWORK offers workshops, seminars and practicums on management, skills training and a week-long lobbying practice course.

"One unique idea for gathering NETWORK members," says its organizing brochure, "is being tried this fall. Members will be invited to a weekend NETWORK retreat. . . . Planning a NETWORK potluck or picnic is another effective way to gather members to share ideas for action while enjoying each other's company.

"Whatever the format of NETWORK gatherings, they should always attempt to include the goals of sharing faith, sharing strategy, sharing action and sharing fun."

The newsletter—the most common written tool advocates use for inner-group communication—is a strong block in the organization's foundation. With the exception of a membership card, the newsletter that arrives periodically at members' and others' doors may be the only tangible evidence of the organization's existence to some members.

Practically, newsletters keep members informed of basic organizational information. Charlotte Tropp's RSVP/Share Project features a "Circle the Date" in the newsletter listing craft groups, meetings, and special events with dates, times, places and phone numbers.

Bell Ringer, the newsletter of MHASC, gives lots of news about what is going on in the organization and its committees. "Plan to attend, Toward a Caring Community, MHASC Annual Meeting," says a front-page headline of the tabloid. Later in *Bell Ringer* "Meet Your Executive Committee" gives information on four of the group's leaders.

Bell Ringer reminds people of why they are involved in a mental health organization by placing short messages throughout saying things like, "Mental health is everyone's business" and "If I am not for myself, who will be for me? If I am not for others, who am I for? And if not now, when?—from the Talmud."

Newsletters promote all elements of the organization, including fund raising. Most of Focus:HOPE's August 1982 issue is devoted to promotion of its annual "Walk for Justice" in which thousands of Detroit people get sponsors to pledge contributions for the organization. "Why: To celebrate a belief in justice and to express commitment to working for justice throughout Focus:HOPE and its projects. To raise funds for Focus:HOPE."

Most imporant, newsletters grab attention. A photograph of a dump in Pennsylvania in CCHW's newsletter, "Everybody's Backyard," makes a distant problem vivid and immediate.

In addition to regular newsletters, organizations sometimes send special letters to people associated with the organization. CCHW, for example, publishes an "Action Bulletin" and periodically sends letters requesting funds and other help.

Some organizations publish books about themselves, how they operate and related subjects. Be they bound copies of typed information, such as the "OWL Organizing Manual," or the glossy typeset manual from the League of Women Voters, the books explain to anyone who wants to know, how the organization operates.

Telling the Public About the Group

In all the public relations work advocates do, one of the most important objectives is to get attention for the organization itself. If the group has name recognition and positive public regard, the group has a strong basis for conducting public policy campaigns. Constituents for the issues, government and other groups come to respect the organization and pay attention to it.

Organizations get media attention in two ways: by directly publicizing the organization and its activities and by including brief information about the organization in all other publicity, including announcements and issues information.

Tish Sommers issued a press release on OWL stationery about ex-spouses being denied army pensions. The release contained descriptive information about OWL as well as information about the problem. "Speaking for the Board of Directors and members of the only grass roots advocacy organization for older women, the Older Women's League," was the introduction of Sommers's remarks.

Most information about the organization usually appears at the end of the release. "The Older Women's League, a rapidly growing organization, currently has 42 chapters nationwide and a national action agenda focused upon the impact on older women of pension inequities, the need to defend and reform Social Security and work for easier access to health care insurance."

In 1981 WXYZ-TV in Detroit broadcast an editorial three times praising Focus:HOPE. It began, "We've often had kind things to say about Detroit's premiere human rights organization Focus:HOPE. There's a reason for it. Focus:HOPE has a reputation for zeroing in on basic human problems and resolving those problems with constructive action."

Eleanor Josaitis of that group has an eye for publicity opportunities. "On opening day of the baseball season at Tiger Stadium there was a picture that appeared on the front page of the Detroit Free Press," she said. "It showed the stadium, and underneath it said, '102,000 people crowd into Tiger Stadium for opening day.'

"Well, we fed fifty-three thousand people last month, so I went out and bought twenty copies of this newspaper, colored in half of the people, with a note on it that said, 'This is what 51,000 people look like. Focus:HOPE fed 53,000 people last month.'"

Letters to newspaper editors about issues are another way to get advocacy groups favorable attention.

Sometimes other newsletters give organizations publicity. The Michigan Catholic magazine featured pictures of "more than 8,000 persons from the metropolitan Detroit area . . . together to demonstrate their commitment to racial justice as they marched in the annual Focus:HOPE Walkathon."

In the OWL Organizing Manual, Tish Sommers listed "media positives" about the organization, including that older women speaking out is new, and chapters are sometimes new. "We have potential for good human interest stories," and "Demographics are on our side," she said.

Although media coverage does not directly help the organization, what media say can be used later. Common Cause put out a brochure, "What the press has to say about Common Cause." The group collected positive quotes about itself and put them together to serve as a group promotional tool.

The American Civil Liberties Union has a brochure called "Guardian of Freedom" that describes the entire organization. It includes "how the ACLU works, an army of volunteers, how the ACLU is governed, how your money is used, and tax deductible gifts." Almost all advocacy organizations have brochures or other materials that describe the group.

Some organizations have speakers bureaus. Although the choice of speakers and programs usually covers a range, some are specifically for educating people about the organization. On a list of possible speakers from the MHASC appears "James Allen, Jr. . . . from Mississippi and serves on the National Board of Directors. He is qualified to speak on finances, membership and lobbying," and "Jean Sloan, former regional vice-president of Region 2. She is qualified to speak on all phases of the Mental Health Association Program." Even speakers who do not specifically address organizational issues but deal more with policy automatically spread the word about the organization that sponsors their appearances.

Groups Cooperate

Advocacy groups work together in a number of ways. Communication among different groups is practical, as well as polite. Reasons for cooperation range from recruiting constituents to learning about policy campaigns.

In a section called "OWL and Other Organizations," the Organizing Manual stresses "to move our own agenda forward, we must create linkages, networks and coalitions." The book goes on to encourage members to reach out to other groups that concentrate on aging and women's issues as well as broader groups like professional associations, the YWCA, etc.

"A good number of people working in these programs, and some recipients of services, are potential OWL members," the manual states, "but equally important, this network has growing clout politically. All these organizations are potential allies on our issues."

The manual also states, "Working out informal and ad hoc working relationships between cooperating organizations is essential. . . ."

When asked about the proliferation of environmental groups, Betsy Reifsnider said of Los Angeles, "I don't think there is competition among environmental groups here. As far as we're [the Sierra Club] concerned, we would always like the environmental movement to get bigger. We're glad for all the support we can get, and if we can coordinate things with other groups, then that's just great."

Using the different styles of a variety of groups can be very effective. Reifsnider pointed out that "usually the Sierra Club likes to appear very moderate. We work with some other groups that do more outlandish things, though. We act like the three-piece-suit people. The groups have different constituencies, but we all work together."

To work together, OWL says, like the Sierra Club, the organization "must be very clear on what its particular role is in the wide spectrum of related organizations."

Coalitions are group cooperation taken one step further. Instead of loose communication, coalitions bind separate groups in a temporary but structured organization. Of all advocacy groups, coalitions are probably the most difficult to set up and manage. All of the information presented here about forming individual advocacy groups and keeping them together also serves for coalitions. The differences are that organizational members have structures themselves and know the group will eventually disband.

Groups need to have three common traits to form a successful coalition.

They need to have the same policy goal or be willing to compromise to achieve one. They should be committed to achieving the goal and have a philosophy of democratic decision-making.

All the better for the coalition if the groups have different styles, skills, set-ups and constituents. The more constituents attached to the coalition the better. And a variety of styles and skills will boost the campaign effort.

When representatives of the groups get together, they have to create the structure for coalition decision-making, funding and action.

The League of Women Voters, NOW, OWL and many other groups have formed rules and guidelines for working in coalition with others about common issues. In its Campaign Handbook, the League says, "Make sure everyone who joins the coalition — groups or individuals — understands and agrees to the rules of the game."

The OWL manual says, "Set positive ground rules early. Anticipate differences..." and talk about them at the beginning.

Other suggested rules of operations include the following: Each organization may act for itself, outside the coalition, but not necessarily in the name of the coalition. Plan the campaign together. Clearly define tasks. Decide who will pay for what. Decide how to communicate among member organizations.

Chapter Five

Caring with Clout:
Recruiting and Involving
Constituents for the Issues

In the world through the looking glass, as the Red Queen tells Alice, "It takes all the running you can do to stay in the same place. If you want to get somewhere else you must run at least twice as fast as that!"

So it is in membership country. The time will never come when you can relax and call the job done. Yet this endless race is well worth running, for the change and growth that take place in the process of gaining, involving and retaining members are the vital signs of a healthy organization.

— From "Membership Management,"
League of Women Voters of the U.S.

Without constituents — members of the general public who care about policy — issues and advocacy groups would be powerless. Constituents lend their names, their experiences, their voices and their time and energy, in any amount they choose, to the causes they care about. Constituents have the most to give to and the most to gain from advocacy activities.

Successful methods used to recruit and involve constituents in advocacy activities accentuate the dual motives of people who want both to gain from and give to advocacy efforts they believe in. Advocates recruit and keep constituents involved by showing them the two-way street advocacy offers them. They point out opportunities for positive personal and public change as they bring in and involve constituents.

Recruiting Constituents

There are three stages in recruiting constituents: identifying them, reaching out to them and getting confirmed support. Advocates follow these steps in order when they do a concerted membership "drive." More often, and in established groups, advocacy groups do all three simultaneously as they bring individuals into the fold.

Identifying Constituents

In order to recruit constituents, advocates develop some idea of who they are looking for and what characteristics constituents for their issues share. Most advocates can profile the constituents for the issues they work on.

For some issues, location is all constituents have in common. Groups that deal with problems isolated to a specific community look for supporters — who may differ in many other ways — within that community.

Citizens for Community Improvement reaches out to people who live in Des Moines, Iowa, because they deal with specific problems in those neighborhoods. Brenda LaBlanc described constituents by saying most people "are in lower or middle income neighborhoods where they already face economic problems."

LaBlanc reported CCI "concentrates on low and moderate income neighborhoods and people. Let's fact it, affluent people have fewer problems and can buy their way out of most. Their attorneys do their legwork. Less affluent people must do for themselves."

But, LaBlanc added, "Those of us in Des Moines get together with people from other cities in Iowa when we need to approach a problem at the state level. Six cities in Iowa have similar organizations and are affiliated with the network. Similarly, we are affiliated with National People's Action that unifies similar organizations throughout the United States."

Advocates can often identify constituents based on race, gender and nationality. Sally Mead knew for sure that the constituents for mental health services were all the Native Americans living in the North Pacific Rim of Alaska, and her employer, the native corporation there, defined that constituency for her. "Five extended families make up the entire village of English Bay. There's basically one ruling family at this time. There are thirteen children, and the oldest is forty-five and the youngest is twenty. The impact of any social problem of one person goes way beyond that one person and impacts the whole villge."

The Women's Rights Project Sandra Kurjiaka ran in Arkansas looked for "local women — black and white — and the issues they care about."

People who are poor, ill, abused, addicted, and victims of all kinds share characteristics as constituents for much needed services. And, in an unexpected category, people who share the same profession also share life experiences.

Advocates find people who share common life experiences at service agencies of all kinds and at particular places of work as well as in the general public.

"Every day women walked by us, pregnant, strung out with all kinds of drug problems," when Kattie Portis was in a traditional drug rehab program. The residential treatment program she started later served those women who are addicted, members of minorities and residents of the area. Portis said, "A lot come right out of jail or a mental institution. Sometimes they come to us with their nightgowns still on." The children of these poor, often single women, often "seriously neglected," are Women, Inc.'s constituents, too.

The brochure Charlotte Tropp's RSVP program gave out described their constituents in the first paragraph: "Retired Senior Volunteer Program (RSVP) is for anyone 60 and over who wants to use his or her experience and talents in useful volunteer service to others in the community."

Even if people do not live near one another share any birth condition or life experience, some of them care enough about policies and their effects to work on their behalf. This type of constituent encompasses the others. But people who share concern may not share other common characteristics. These members of the public develop concern for issues even though those issues don't necessarily affect them personally.

Constituents who are against a nuclear weapons build-up, for example, do not have to be hit with a missile or know someone who has been to believe missiles are dangerous.

The element of concern is illustrated by the actual membership of advocacy efforts. Many men have asked to join the League of Women Voters over the years, and they can. Whites work for black civil rights. Tish Sommers said of OWL, "We didn't start out with an interest in younger women, but many have come to us."

Carol Tucker Foreman pointed out an irony that is not unusual in dealing with poor and minority constituents' issues: "The success of welfare programs," she said, "is overwhelmingly dependent on a feeling of well-being among the middle class. It used to be that if the middle class is feeling comfortable and secure, the food stamp program and other welfare programs would have support. And if the middle class was feeling insecure, they would be hostile."

But in 1981 the tables turned. "So many people felt threatened—even those who had jobs," Foreman remarked, "if there was ten percent unemployment, thirty-five percent of the workforce reported feeling threatened. All of a sudden the hostility to the food stamp program diminished as people thought, 'Oh, Jesus, I might need them myself.'"

Although mental patients, their families and friends make natural constituents for the Mental Health Association of South Carolina, its manual

"Reaching the Public" says, "Public education programs help us identify all sorts of people who are interested."

The League of Women Voters' constituents are people concerned about all sorts of public issues. Often, local chapters analyze "present membership" and gaps in membership by giving out questionnaires and doing interviews.

Betsy Reifsnider said of Sierra Club constituents, "I think a lot of the American public is on our side; polls show eighty percent want a clean air act. Ninety percent or more want a clean water act. I think we at the Sierra Club try to show people how they can have a voice in changing things."

Where constituents live is a consideration of state, regional and national advocacy groups; they break down the large organization into smaller more manageable, more effective units.

These groups look for supporters on all geographic levels, and often do several types of recruiting—only one of which aims at people who live near each other. Branches on local levels recruit along with national and state affiliates. Where they live is the only common bond that can affect all types of constituents.

Although where constituents live is important to recruiting efforts— except in the case of specific local problems—location is secondary to other shared characteristics when advocates look for supporters.

Reaching Out for Constituents Directly

Based on knowledge of who their constituents are, advocates make efforts to reach out to them. Outreach for constituents does not necessarily cost a lot of money, but it requires constant expenditures of time and energy. Methods center on educating people about issues and emphasizing the rewards of getting involved.

Direct outreach efforts—those that ask for a specific response from people—are most effective at getting people to sign on to advocacy efforts. The request for a response is called a "hook." Most advocates use a variety of methods to reach out directly to and bring in as many constituents as possible.

Some methods are only useful when the outreach effort is localized— that is, when constituents share a local problem or advocates focus on a local area to recruit people with other characteristics in common.

The personal touch: The LWV says, "The personal touch is one of the most effective tactics for membership recruitment." OWL echoes, "Paper is fine, but personal contact carries far more clout."

"There's no substitute for face-to-face contact for including people and building membership," Lois Gibbs wrote in the CCHW Leadership handbook. "You can call people on the phone, send flyers, distribute leaflets and get lots of media exposure. But to build the relationships that will hold an organization together, you must meet and talk to people one by one."

The personal touch is easiest to achieve when advocates are dealing with local issues or larger issues "localized" for one specific area. Advocates who reach out to people with shared conditions and shared concerns who do not live near one another have a tougher time achieving the intimacy of direct personal contact.

Talking to friends: The LWV and OWL remind members of a common sense outreach technique. They advise people to mention their advocacy work when they get together with friends. The LWV manual goes on, "Take people to League activities . . . distribute information and be willing to take people's dues. . . . Think membership and be a salesperson for the League."

Doorknocking: Lois Gibbs, who nearly threw up the first time she did it, knows a lot about this difficult, but extremely useful technique for dealing with local problems. She describes the process in the CCHW leadership handbook:

"When you knock on a new person's door," Gibbs wrote from experience, "there's that awkward moment when the person is trying to decide whether to slam the door in your face. Your opening lines have to be clear, open and appealing. . . .

"The person you're talking to isn't stupid; she or he knows you want something, so what is it? Are you passing around a petition? A petition is an excellent door-opener. . . . Along with your petition bring a bound notebook . . . to collect information from people you meet. . . . Also make notes about the people."

The LWV "Membership Manual" describes one neighborhood outreach drive: "One League thought that a new development in its area might be a potential source for new members. They blitzed it with flyers describing something about the League and what it was doing in the community and set a date and time for a new member meeting, with an RSVP attached and a person to contact. Twenty members signed up at the meeting and a new unit was formed in their area within a few weeks, which featured babysitting, one of the needs expressed by the new members. Within six months it turned out to be one of the most active units in the League."

Sally Mead's mental health work in the native villages in Alaska was built on constant, sophisticated doorknocking techniques. "We started out intially looking at counseling in terms of an individual mode," she explained. "It didn't work at all. Then we started working more with families and finding in some ways that didn't work by itself at all either. What we've been doing ever since then is a method called 'retribalization' or 'social networking.'"

By going door to door Mead and other staffers identified who the natural helpers in the villages were. One staffer, Mead reports, "went through a long process of getting to the point where they accepted him. He spent nine months going into the village, arriving every week with his little suitcase going around talking to people and saying, 'Is there anything here that you want me to do?' and they not responding. Then he said, 'Well, I guess I'll go on over to the other village.' It took nine months of this before they finally came around to say, 'Hm. Maybe I'd like to talk to you.' And then it started happening."

Public speakers: The Mental Health Association of South Carolina handbook "Reaching the Public" says of public speakers, "Their special talent is the ability to move others to think and act. They are agitators in the best sense. They are concerned with public attitudes and motivations as well as the giving of factual information on mental health and mental illness."

Carol Garvin, president of the MHASC, described the effect of one speaker. "The director of a local chapter," she said, "asked me to go with her to the high school to talk to a psychology class. Burt Yancy, the golfer — a manic depressive — spoke to the class about his illness. The teacher thought her students would be interested in hearing him if they had some explanation before of what this was all about.

"They were very bright kids. They asked remarkable questions and were very quickly receptive to learning something about mental illness and to even do some direct service. "It surprised me how many of them were interested in mental health and some of them have volunteered to work with us since."

The Coalition for Basic Human Needs used a similar approach to recruiting welfare recipients. "We'd get ourselves invited out to talk to public housing tenant groups — all those kinds of groups," Janet Diamond said. "Afterwards we'd get them to sign petitions on the spot. We'd take phone numbers and tell them we were going to call them for help, and we did."

Conferences: Conferences can be designed to reach out to people who may come from a larger area than one town or city. The Women's Rights Project of the Arkansas Civil Liberties Union holds local educational conferences specifically designed to recruit supporters for women's issues from across the state.

"Basically we . . . go into a community," Sandra Kurjiaka explained, "and try to get an organizing committee in the community, you know, four or five women to identify what issues to address and what things trouble them in their town.

"Then we do a conference there — a big one-day informational thing — which is not a goal in itself, but is a way of getting people together. Mostly we've been able to attract working class women, black and white. We've been at this since nineteen seventy-eight and I guess we've been in about ten or twelve towns.

"It generally runs between fifty and one hundred people there for one day. I try to bring in people who have expertise in particular areas—battered women's shelters or a rape crisis center or people to talk about educational equity or civil rights law. Sometimes it's women's health issues, so we try to bring in some women's physicians who deal with those questions. We just try to get information to those people so they know what to complain about.

"Then we say the community should have a task force—people to receive complaints on discrimination. Then they feed it to us and we see if we get patterns and practices established.

"We think we've managed to organize the communities. During this legislative session when we had to get hold of people, they were there. I mean we had some two hundred fifty names on our mailing list, and they got those letters and postcards out. It seems to be working."

Tangible outreach tools: When advocates reach out to the public they use tangible materials to hand out, mail, post or distribute. Lois Gibbs calls these devices "props." (See Appendix: Tools of the Trade for sources of more information.) In fact, most advocates and advocacy groups are heavily involved in producing informative materials.

Petitions: Lois Gibbs, as she pointed out in the doorknocking section, frequently uses petitions as outreach devices. "Many organizations use petitions for just this purpose, to get people to open their doors and to collect names and addresses of concerned residents. The petition usually won't solve the problem . . . but they're great . . . tools." Gibbs says. (See Chapter Ten for information about petitions and policy change.)

Handouts: Lois Gibbs knows all about fact sheets, too. "Gather your facts," she says. "Distill them down into understandable form . . . getting that person interested in the first place means being short and sweet to begin with.

"Be sure to list your or your group's full name and how you can be contacted. . . . Many community organizers will not distribute a fact sheet unless it contains a 'hook' of some sort. . . . So your fact sheet would ask people to *do something* [come to a meeting, write a letter, something]."

Flyers and posters usually advertise, educate, excite and ask people to do something soon—usually attend a meeting or event. Fact sheets are also used to educate people about policy change. Flyers and posters are designed to be handed out, left at people's doors, posted in public places and even mailed. To grab attention, they are usually bold and simple to comprehend.

The content of brochures advocates make and distribute as outreach devices varies widely, but if a brochure asks the reader to respond in some way with name, address and phone number, it is definitely being used for constituent development.

"Don't Agonize — Organize," says the orange and black OWL brochure. Along with the purpose of the organization, a list of problems older women face and OWL's national agenda, a form is provided for people who would like to join or contribute.

"Need help?" That's the question on the front of the Mental Health Association of Aiken County (S.C.) brochure, which offers a classic example of offering services as a hook. Inside are listed almost 60 social service agencies and hotlines in the area. At the end, the brochure asks for questions and suggestions and invites people to join the Aiken chapter.

Letters: Outreach letters are often used by state or national organizations. They articulate issues and solicit support from constituents in any location. Often other materials, such as copies of articles, are included with the letters. Some letters are sent to people who have expressed interest but have not committed themselves yet. Many are sent "cold" from bought or bartered mailing lists from other organizations and publications.

The president of Common Cause sent a typical four-page bulk mailing. The letter, about the organization's "campaign to end the nuclear arms race," is full of quotes, information, offers of more information, and an invitation to the reader to join and participate.

Another form of the letter technique is to ask current constituents to give names and addresses of friends. "Mail us your friends," says the form from the Civil Liberties Union. "Mailing to the people whose names you give us produces ten times the results of any other mailing list we can use."

Audio-visual material: In addition to, or instead of, public speakers, other good recruiting devices to use with groups are slide shows, films and videos. OWL has a 17-minute slide-tape presentation called "Three Stories" that are for sale or for rent for only $10. The flyer that promotes the slide-tape says, "Want to increase membership? Now we have just the vehicle to tell what the Older Women's League is all about."

CBS did a program called "NETWORK: The Politics of Participation," and the organization has copies that it rents for $15 or sells for $100. NETWORK also has a slide-tape show that "offers some ways to become involved politically" which rents for $5.

Audio-visual recruitment can be expensive if paid for out of organization funds. Getting donations and using non-profit studios, student productions or programs already made by the commercial media are all possibilities.

The news media: Almost the only direct recruiting — recruiting with a "hook" — that can be done with news media is advertising, and advertising can be very expensive. (See Chapter Nine for usefulness of media in education about issues.)

On the other hand, television and radio stations are required by the Federal Communications Commission to do public service announcements (PSAs) periodically. Tish Sommers said of PSAs, "Since they are expensive to make and take valuable commercial time, they are not easy to get, but they do have a great deal of impact." She explained radio spots. "Because television is where the big money goes, radio is a lot easier to penetrate. . . . College or publicly supported stations are good bets."

The print medium offers a few alternatives to paid advertising, too. Occasionally organizations get donations to take out ads. Events can get listed in calendar sections with addresses and phone numbers for people to contact. Local papers might run brief "stories" which have direct recruiting devices at the end. And smaller papers may run public service "fillers" recruiting interested constituents for non-profit organizations.

Although coverage by the news media has limited usefulness in signing up supporters, positive publicity does seem to have an indirect impact on increasing public participation in causes. If nothing else, news coverage creates a backdrop against which advocates can do direct recruiting more easily.

Because the Civil Liberties Union receives a lot of media attention for its work, people think of the group, especially when they need help. The Arkansas chapter gets lots of phone calls from people who think they may have a civil liberties problem. Those people are candidates to join the organization.

Lois Gibbs and other individual advocates become media "stars" sometimes. The TV docudrama about Gibbs's life, plus numerous talk show appearances and newspaper interviews, "have made me well known," Gibbs said. "Because of who I am a lot of folks call me and say, 'How did you win Love Canal?'

"Many times they don't even know I've started the Clearinghouse. All they know is my name and my Love Canal association. So they call up and we say, 'Well, we actually have an organization that can help you.' We tell them everything that we do. People hear I'm in Arlington, Virginia, and they just call directory assistance and they look up my name and say, 'Well, I didn't know you had this big group.' It's all because of the TV show."

"Media coordinator was a new position we invented," said Janet Diamond, who went on to hold that position at the Coalition for Basic Human Needs in Massachusetts. "What we perceived," Diamond recalled, "was that through the media we could do electronic organizing. We could accomplish a lot of things we couldn't accomplish on our own one by one. We managed to get ourselves on the six o'clock news all the time. We got on special TV and radio shows. We eventually got ourselves on '60 Minutes.'

"A lot of times we just talked about welfare in general and about benefits. We became the recipients' voice on welfare issues to the press. It was very effective. Welfare recipients watch the news, and suddenly they heard what they were thinking about expressed on the electronic media or in print. We got a lot of feedback from people, people sending us letters saying, 'That's wonderful! Tell it like it is!'

"We got known across the state as a welfare rights group. People would call us not just with an individual problem, but they called saying they wanted to help us out. Suddenly we were real; we were tangible. We were a big deal even though we were still the same little tiny organization in one room. We became magnified because of the press."

Help from government and other groups: "Every time James Watt [Secretary of the Interior, 1981–1983] opened his mouth," laughed Betsy Reifsnider of the Los Angeles Sierra Club, "we got a flood of calls here with people saying, 'I want to help.' So it's wonderful. He was our biggest fundraiser and recruiter."

Ironically, government officials who behave badly actually drive members of the public into the arms of advocacy groups. Since this is not the ideal way to recruit constituents, and because some government officials are caring advocates themselves, it is more common for government people to cooperate directly with advocates in recruiting supporters.

Service providers sometimes refer clients to advocacy groups. Social workers often tell Boston women with drug problems to contact Women, Inc. State mental health officials and professionals in South Carolina sometimes direct patients and their families to the Mental Health Association.

Advocacy groups cooperate with other groups in outreach. The League of Women voters membership manual says, "A recruitment tactic used successfully by many Leagues is a personal letter aimed at certain target groups . . . here are a few possibilities for getting names: . . . organizations such as Welcome Wagon, Chamber of Commerce, PTA, retirement communities, welfare groups, NOW chapters, political groups, social clubs. . . .

"One League," the manual reported, "invited every women's club in the area to a city-wide membership coffee. One hundred seventy-five people came to the coffee and 25 ended up paying dues as new members. The other 150 went away with information about what the League was doing in the community, and the good public relations gained in the effort was icing on the cake."

"We didn't have the resources to organize everybody," Janet Diamond reiterated about CBHN. "We had two staff for the whole state. That's a lot of doorknocking we just couldn't do." She and the group expanded, as many do, the old fashioned notion that "organizing" is really a local neighborhood activity.

"There were organizations and agencies that we could work through, like CAP (anti-poverty) agencies," she said of their efforts directed at people who share life experiences across the state. "Those were very useful, the organizations that had already organized people. We would tap into those. The public housing tenants organizations were another great source. We'd work through them."

Reaching Out for Constituents Indirectly

Some methods advocates use to recruit constituents are more indirect because they contain all the educational elements of direct recruiting but no "hook" that tells people how to respond. Everything advocates do to educate the public serves the function of indirectly recruiting constituents. The specific impact of indirect recruiting is hard to document. Indirect outreach is used to reach out to harder-to-reach constituents when localized outreach efforts with "hooks" are impractical.

Confirming Constituents

"We put a lot of stress on membership," Carol Garvin said of the MHASC. "We're a membership organization, and the reason we do education is to identify people and to recruit people. If I give you five dollars for membership in the Mental Health Association, that means I have some general agreement with your reason for being and some general willingness to educate myself a little bit more about the cause. People come in with different degrees of involvement, but signing up members is the one way we know who supports us."

Advocates put "hooks" in their outreach methods whenever they can, because they want to confirm members of the public as constituents for the issues. It helps if advocates can document the amount of support for the issues, so they like to be able to count confirmed constituents they have identified.

Juanita Kennedy Morgan said, "When you say National Black Women's Political Caucus, we do have the power. Membership is all we have."

Signs of commitment: Name, address and telephone number don't sound like much, but if a person offers those basics in support of a cause, that person can be counted as a constituent. Everything else is gravy.

Some advocacy groups ask for money to show commitment, too. Membership organizations ask for dues in amounts that vary from $5 to more than $100 for professional organizations of some kinds. On the other hand, advocacy groups that serve poor people or whose constituents are mainly service recipients do not solicit money as proof of commitment.

Some groups ask constituents to give more than just basic information when they join. OWL's membership form asks people to list their "concerns" and their congressional districts. Common Cause wants to know names of other people in the household.

Contributions of time and energy are often requested of constituents. OWL's membership form asks people if they are interested in starting a new chapter. One of Common Cause's forms solicited people to sign up as a member of the nuclear arms alert network, letting people check "please send me Action Alerts and Legislative Bulletins whenever you want me to write to my representative or senators."

Lois Gibbs and CCHW stress work commitment. The Leadership Handbook says, "Whether you're selling brushes, vacuum cleaners or toxic waste solutions, the time comes when you have to close in for the sale. In organizing, the 'sale' is the person's commitment to *do something*. Signing a petition is fine for most people, but you will meet new people who can and will do more, but you have to ask them.

"Use your judgment to gauge what each person can 'afford,' to do," the handbook advises. "Everyone can do something unless they're either in a coffin or in a coma. Ask for concrete things such as, . . . Can you bring two other people to the next meeting? Can you give a ride to someone? Could you pass out flyers on the block? . . . And so on."

Sometimes the "hook" asks people to call or write or attend an event. They are then asked to give name, address and telephone number at the event.

Involving Constituents in Activities

Not surprisingly, constituents remain committed to working on issues for the same reasons they originally joined. Members of the group stay involved when advocates and groups continue to deliver on their first promises of both giving and receiving constituents' help. Once a person signs on with the cause, mutual support possibilities become richer, more complex and more specific.

Methods for keeping constituents involved also emphasize the double rewards of involvement in activities that bring about policy change and enhancement of members' lives. Constituents stay involved because of what they get out of their participation. They gain new skills and more education about issues. Often constituents receive direct personal help. And, by working with a group, individuals find themselves with more clout and power for which they get recognition.

Constituents Learn a Lot

In an interview, OWL president Tish Sommers said, "We try to make a balance between moving forward rapidly and involving people." OWL operates on the principle of "developing leadership through doing. In other words, somebody comes into this office and says, 'I want to help. My background is in this,' or 'I'm interested in learning that.'

"We let them do it and give them whatever help and support they need. That's the way you find leadership. A lot of people have done exactly that. We've found some very terrific talent that way."

She said a lot of OWL leaders "have come up through the ranks of direct experience. Laurie Shields, for example, is one of the people that hadn't done this kind of work before at all, but she was widowed and very affected by the issues. The same is true with many women in the Older Women's League. They didn't necessarily have organizational experience in the past, but they picked it up very rapidly."

"Once people have bitten the bait," offers the League of Women Voters's Membership Manual, "make it easy for them to . . . get involved. Be prepared to handle the influx of new members that should result from a concerted effort. The goal of creating a surge in membership . . . is a legitimate one, but make sure that as much time is spent on ways to keep those members as is spent on the membership drive itself.

"Follow through," the manual advises. "Send a welcome letter with a membership card immediately. . . . Find out why they joined and help them get involved in ways that fit their needs."

The League offers the following advice: "Make the introduction exciting. Many Leagues have found that the most effective way of 'orienting' members is to get them involved in a piece of the action. 'A Conference on the Farmworker in Florida,' 'A Day in Court in Kansas' and 'A Lobbying Workshop in Nebraska' were all first events designed to get new members involved in local Leagues right away."

Once involved in advocacy groups, members get a chance to learn much more about the issues than they already gleaned from personal experience or highlights presented when they were recruited. Presentations of more detailed, current information make them into experts on public problems and policies. Advocacy organizations use all of their communications techniques to disseminate the facts. (See Chapter Nine for more details.)

Newsletters and other mailings to members convey information about issues. "Is Bottled Water Enough?" asks a headline in the winter 1984 issue of CCHW's "Everybody's Backyard." Dr. Beverly Paigan, the writer, goes on to answer that question and discuss the contamination of well water by toxic chemicals. She uses language and everyday terminology readers can easily understand.

The Mental Health Association of South Carolina's newsletter describes upcoming television shows about mental illness as well as books containing information of interest. One newsletter recommended "'Children of Darkness,' an upcoming PBS special on the psychiatric treatment of adolescents," and a book about children and adolescents in need of mental health services.

CCHW, OWL and many other organizations send resource lists to members. Some of the many materials about issues that can be ordered cheaply from OWL are "Testimony: Pension Equity for Women" and "'Til Death Do Us Part: Caregivers and Severely Disabled Husbands."

Knowledge of the content of policies and programs is only half of the education offered to constituents. Training in organization management, methods for bringing about policy change, public relations and direct service delivery skills is also available to members. Many of those skills are useful, even marketable, in other areas of their lives. Members who receive training from more experienced people, combined with actual practice, learn while they work on the issues that concern them. Organizations offer written materials and training sessions of various kinds to teach these skills to their members.

"How to Manage an Organization" could be a course title, but for involved members it is an ongoing curriculum not taught in most schools. No matter what roles constituents choose to play, they definitely get practice in making decisions in a group. NETWORK offers workshops on mangement, advocacy, lobbying and how faith and politics are connected. The League of Women Voters publishes useful books on group management.

"We go out to the chapters and do training," Carol Garvin said of the Mental Health Association of South Carolina's management education. "We often go to the first meeting of a new board and run through some of the basic things they need to know about the organization. There are thirty different chapters, and each one's needs are different."

Probably the most mysterious skills involved in advocacy are those needed to change policy directly. Observation, training and practice give constituents knowledge about decision-making structures in government and about methods useful for putting them to work.

Kathleen Sheekey of Common Cause said, "We have a state leadership conference each year. Staff people from the state offices and others come to Washington for a series of workshops on advocacy. The state organizations also do some of their own advocacy training."

Carol Tucker Foreman recalled that in her "old Planned Parenthood days. . . . We traveled around the country meeting informally with groups in Planned Parenthood chapters. We provided them with good information. We even did training sessions for members on how to make effective presentations of various kinds to Congress. They were great constituents because they were very interested in the issues and were willing to become very knowledgeable of them and how to work for them. They became marvelous lobbyists, and still are."

Knowing how to publicize an event or issue or group is useful in many endeavors. Addressing publicity chairpersons, the MHASC manual "Reaching the Public" says, "Your job will be to present the news of your chapter to the public. All the information you give out should be accurate, complete, brief and timely...."

Advocacy groups that call their constituents "volunteers" usually train them in how to deliver services.

The lead article in one issue of the MHSC's *Bell Ringer* tells about Cecelia, who "moved in and out of mental hospitals for years." When she was released at one point, "she was introduced to Joan Williams, one of the several volunteers trained by the MHA and the S.C. Department of Mental Health to help returning patients make a more successful adjustment to community living.... Volunteers like Joan are trained to provide patients a variety of supportive services and information on community resources," the article states. "A volunteer is most effective because the recovering person needs to know someone cares. Anyone interested in the Community Connection Program is encouraged to participate in the training," the article concludes.

Constituents Get Direct Services

It is a wonderful irony that the same constituents who can get training in delivering services to others may also be service recipients. Association with an advocacy group puts constituents in contact with resources for help for themselves.

Cecelia and the volunteer who helped her are both members of the MHASC. Retired folks at RSVP are trained to help other retired folks do their taxes at workshops sponsored by Share/RSVP.

"Seniors, all this is for you: friendship, legal help, hot meals, transportation, home repairs, home health care, recreation, extra income and more..." an RSVP brochure says.

Gini Laurie said the people who subscribe to the *Rehabilitation Gazette* "talk across the pages. They meet across it. And I also feel it's a way for professional people to look over the shoulders of people who are disabled and see in the *Gazette* thoughts they might not have known of from the other white coats. I'm always very careful to put the diagnosis in the article so you know exactly what that other person is."

"We had two levels of conferences," Lotta Chi said of a program funded by the Women's Education Association of the Organization of Chinese

American Women. "One was for the people who are a little more settled here. Because we have such a variety and a scale of need, we try to have two different types of conferences. One if for those who have a career, have a job and want to better themselves. Then the other kind is for people newly arrived here and it's on how to get the first job.

"My area of interest," Chi said, "was the newly arrived immigrants. I was in charge of that one in Chinatown. It was quite gratifying because they were all so excited. You go in and they all say, 'Can you help us?'"

Constituents Get Clout

It's amazing. As soon as people join a group, their power as individuals expands. Suddenly their opinions, knowledge and activities have much more effect on the issues than they did when they thought, spoke and acted alone.

In meetings, one on one or in writing, constituents are asked to share their experiences, thoughts and observations. Members get to contribute information and ideas on specific issues in some detail.

CCHW sent out a questionnaire asking members to describe the hazardous waste problems in their communities. The note at the end says the survey was designed "to help us better serve you. The survey results will help us to focus our programs and design our publications around your needs and issues."

The League of Women Voters sent out an American Foreign Policy survey asking constituents where they get information, what they think of it, what sorts of activities by the League they would like to see and what they think are problems.

"Lest we forget — lest we lose our right to legal abortion and birth control," says a flyer from NOW, "We must tell our stories. . . . We must confront the opposition with our real experiences and the real women whose lives they seek to manipulate and destroy. . . . Write NOW and tell your story and join the movement for women's rights to make our lives livable."

In most organizations, constituents have a strong voice in identifying the issues that will be worked on and they have a say about how the policy campaign will be conducted. (See chapters Eight and Thirteen for more details.)

Members get a voice in the management of their groups, too. Not only can they vote about issues and elect leaders, but they can also become leaders themselves. "Elections are an essential part of any democratic structure," says the OWL Organizing Manual. "The person accepting the responsibility should feel the support of the chapter, and the ballot is one way to express that support."

Organizations offer members the opportunity to take actions that really bring results. Knowing they have helped someone or had a part in changing public policy motivates constituents to stay with groups. Whether they act as information resources for education or volunteer fund-raisers or make other contributions, constituents find the results of their actions rewarding.

"Everybody benefits from Share!" the brochure says. "Seniors can continue to make a significant contribution to their community by sharing with students the talents and skills they've developed through the years.

"I walk because I support Focus:HOPE," says Sandy Skinner in a newsletter about the major fund-raising spirit building walk in Detroit. "It realistically supports people in the community. I'm a clinical social worker. . . . Focus:HOPE has always helped in getting food to moms and children. . . . Many of these cases are not long-term problems, and Focus:HOPE has been a great immediate help."

A League of Women Voters recruiting brochure lists policy successes the League chalked up in Oregon, Denver and DeKalb County, Georgia, and says, "By now, you're probably wondering what role you can play in the League. Well, it's up to you. . . . There's a lot of work to be done. . . . It's there. It's important."

"By intervening, filing motions and testifying, and most importantly, involving low and moderate income consumers in the rate process," reports the Des Moines Citizens for Community Improvement, "the CCI Task Force has shown that organized people can make a difference in rate requests."

Constituents Get Support and Recognition

Working alone, a person is not likely to get much praise. But groups notice and express appreciation for individuals' contributions. The *Rehabilitation Gazette* offers almost constant support for its disabled readers. "It's like what the hell!" said editor/publisher Gini Laurie, expressing the magazine's theme. "So you're disabled. So what! Get on with it. It's inconvenient, sure, but you can conquer it with mechanical things. This is what they [people in the magazine] say to each other on a very human kind of level. And what the *Gazette* has done is let people read about somebody else, what they've done."

One of OWL's major purposes is to "provide mutual help in various forms" for its membership. For example, OWL has walking clubs to foster health and social contact for older women.

"There's also the question of changing our image," Tish Sommers emphasized. We have a national ad campaign one of the ad agencies gave us as a non-profit contribution. Everything we do provides role models of positive, energetic women getting together and taking responsibility for their lives."

The OWL manual encourages, "Finding ways to express recognition, to reward accomplishment and to signify group approval can be as creative as any aspect of organizational work. For example, the Louisville Chapter, first in the nation, honored its members who had accomplished something special at a large dinner, to which were invited numerous friends from other organizations.

In Arkansas, Sandra Kurjiaka reported, "We want to do a recognition dinner to give some awards to people who've worked in the area. The Arkansas Gay Rights group is giving it."

Another common way groups recognize people is by writing about them in their publications. Every month the RSVP/Share News features a section naming and thanking all new volunteers with an article featuring one person.

Chapter Six

Playing Politics: Creating and Monitoring Government Groups

You must get inside in order to become.
— Juanita Kennedy Morgan

Government is indisputably one of the three major segments of society that advocates find themselves putting together and guiding. Many advocates get involved in politics as a natural part of their work with other groups on behalf of issues.

Advocates who want to affect policy know they have to play roles in setting up and maintaining government groups, just as they do advocacy groups and constituents. They work to get people who support their positions elected, appointed and employed by all three branches of government. And they don't stop there; they watchdog officials and groups that deal with their issues and evaluate their performance.

Some advocates, during their careers, have worked inside government as well as outside. Others try to persuade government groups to become advocacy groups that generally support their issues. The goal is to get those on the right side on the inside where they can affect policy.

Getting Those on the Right Side Elected

"We try to tell people that unless they become involved in politics, they're going to be at the bottom of the heap," said Juanita Kennedy Morgan, executive secretary of the Black Women's Political Caucus.

"Our main thrust," she added, "is registration and voting. Electing black mayors is becoming more popular, for example in Chicago and Philadelphia and my hometown of Birmingham. After the dogs, hose fights and all of that! We, as black women, played a particular role in all of that. We feel we played a particular part in Chicago [getting the late Mayor Harold Washington elected]."

Voter Registration: Inspiration and Education

Morgan described the Caucus's voter registration and inspiration techniques: "We sometimes go from door to door. Sometimes we go to churches with speakers. They go up to speak with registration cards and that type of thing. So we go in and try to tell people how important it is to vote because they feel like, well, for example: 'Reagan is in there. He ain't done nothing for us. I might as well not vote.' Well, that's the wrong idea. And not voting leaves you kind of vulnerable. Many, many people here and there and yonder think like that. And it means you have lost."

"CAUTION: This election may be hazardous to your health. Protect yourself! Vote." This message is printed in large letters in the October, 1984, edition of the Citizens Clearinghouse on Hazardous Wastes Action Bulletin.

The July 1984 edition also had reminders: "Register and Vote. There's a lot of political news in this Bulletin by no coincidence, since the major election is only a few months away. As was the case at Love Canal, these upcoming elections present the opportunity for you to use your political clout to make progress about your issue. Politicians want to look good before the voters, but they will only respect you if your threats to use the ballot are credible. If you need help in developing a voter registration campaign, you can get help from Project Vote! [a project of a coalition of advocacy organizations]. . . . In addition to giving you general help, Project Vote is also running several specific voter registration campaigns in key target districts. . . ."

The League of Women Voters is probably the queen group for voter registration and inspiration. Since its founding, the League has focused a good deal of its efforts on what it calls "Voter Service/Citizen Information (VS/CI)."

The League handbook, "Making a Difference," describes that organization's finely tuned approach. Like Project: Vote! the League identifies groups of voters to target for registration: youth, blacks, Hispanics and other language minorities, Native Americans, institutionalized, handicapped and aged.

Some methods the LWV uses for publicizing registration are: "newspaper attention-grabbers, radio and TV spots, posters, flyers, bulletin boards, door-to-door canvassing, hitch-hike on neighborhood meetings, votemobile" and campaign themes.

Janet Diamond, formerly with the Coalition for Basic Human Needs, then with the Massachusetts Welfare Department, stressed, "Voter registration has to go hand in hand with lobbying and advocacy and grassroots work. A person who's not registered to vote is not a constituent [from the elected rep's point of view] no matter whether they live in the district. The more people that are registered to vote that you can get to become known to that senator or representative, the more likely they are to pay attention to your legislation."

Working in Election Campaigns:
Limitations and Freedoms

Advocates make sure the constituents for their concerns are registered voters. And many also take the next step to see that people who are already advocates for policies they support get elected.

How advocacy groups get involved in elections depends on two features of the groups they work with: the group's philosophy and the tax code. Groups commonly referred to as "volunteer," "membership," or "direct service"—501(c)(3) and 501(c)(4) organizations—are forbidden to take stands in elections under threat of losing their non-profit status.

The Internal Revenue Service (IRS) says that these types of organizations cannot "participate or intervene in political campaigns on behalf of or in opposition to any candidate for public office. . . . Such participation or intervention includes the publication or distribution of statements." (See chapters twelve and thirteen for more details about other limits.)

On the other hand, professional oganizations, called 501(c)(5)s, are not limited. Unincorporated, informal groups and pure political organizations are not constrained either.

Organizations publish caveats from time to time. The CCHW's Leadership handbooks warns, "Caution: Electoral politics are very tricky. Though your organizational fight is political and you will probably be dealing with politicians either as friends or enemies, you should be careful about how you get involved in elections."

The OWL Organizing Manual says, "[B]ear in mind . . . the restriction in the OWL national by-laws against OWL endorsement of any political candidate. . . ."

Although the IRS places limitations on 501(c)(3)s' and (4)s' participation in elections, there are four ways advocates associated with those groups have discovered they can legally work for their candidates.

Work as individuals. To the warning, the OWL Organizing Manual adds, "One of the fastest ways to build rapport between elected officials and OWL is to find members who will volunteer to work in the next campaign.

Members . . . as individuals and not as members of OWL, are free to work in any campaign."

Lotta Chi said she and others from the Organization of Chinese American Women work as individuals to help congressional representatives who support immigration legislation: "When a good congressman is running for office, Laura Chin and I donate our time. We try to do registration and send invitations out, then collect money—campaign funds. We helped with a fund-raiser for a congressman from California. I sat at the registration desk where he was at one of his receptions.

"So that's how we get our connections. Because we're doing it all for free. Also, we don't do it just for Democrats or Republicans. We are involved across the board, so I don't think anyone can complain. We say, 'We don't have money, but we have people with free time to help you.'"

Nancy Sylvester of NETWORK suggested work in lieu of money, too. "We urge people to get involved in election campaigns, not as an organization, but as individuals," she said, "because one thing we emphasize is that helpful congress people have a right to say, 'Would you help me?'

"We shouldn't be too cynical. There are trade-offs with everybody. We need to be politically conscious. Most of these elected people, the ones I think we'd really like to see in office, do not have money. We can give just pure individual labor."

Report candidates' positions. The Citizens Clearinghouse for Hazardous Wastes offers caveats, but told readers in its July 1984 "Action Bulletin" that they "may, however, tell your members and the public how the various candidates stand with respect to your issues. For example, in this issue of 'Action Bulletin' we're pretty clear about how the president has acted on issues of concern to our members. You can draw you own conclusions. The rule is: Just the facts, and then let people decide."

The CCHW handbook describes an informational technique: "[G]roups have for years only supported positions or 'platforms' and have then made it known to their members and to the public which politicians support that platform and which ones don't, without ever specifically saying that they support or oppose a candidate."

Kathleen Sheekey said of Common Cause, "No, we don't endorse candidates. What we do is to track campaign contributions very carefully and we distribute questionnaires among candidates on issues like nuclear arms control and campaign finance reforms."

Create a PAC or 501(c)(5). Some non-profit advocacy organizations have set up Political Action Committees (PACs) to deal with involvement in elections. Organized by, and accountable to, the advocacy organizations, these "connected" PACs can solicit and give out voluntary contributions only within the organization and cannot ask for contributions from the public. The advocacy organization administers and pays the costs of these PACs.

"Our fund raising used to be for the ERA," Janet Ferone said of NOW in the early 1980s. "We have switched it to Political Action Committees. Now we have taken a new course, which is to have as a first priority women who have been NOW activists. Then we know that they are not just telling us that they're for women's rights.

"We ran a woman in Easton, Massachusetts, who was NOW's former state coordinator. We really pulled together to run her campaign for state rep. She didn't win. A coach from the high school won the election."

Boston's NOW PAC later endorsed Michael LoPresti for state senate, and he won. A one-page statement about LoPresti's favorable stands on reproductive and lesbian rights ended by saying, "Boston NOW is urging its membership to vote for Senator LoPresti and to work on his behalf to ensure the success of his run for reelection."

"Politicians are always looking at the next election," Betsy Reifsnider of the Los Angeles County Sierra Club observed. "I think one of the best things we have ever done is to start to endorse candidates. We had an eighty percent success rate in the last election. Now when the staff goes to talk to legislators, the people we endorsed are very ready to see us and often call us to say, 'I thought you might like to know about this issue that's coming up.'

"One state senator made the Natural Resources Senate committee very pro-environment. Now I don't know if he would have been that way if we hadn't done a lot on his behalf. I do think our support had some effect. I would also say that the people we didn't endorse are now much more aware of our political clout. They think of the Sierra Club and have much more respect for our power than they would otherwise. Getting involved in elections was one of the best things we ever did."

Some advocates form non-profit 501(c)(5)s — professional organizations — to be able to work in campaigns and endorse candidates.

Endorse potential candidates. There's a huge loophole in the tax code that allows advocates to praise or criticize anyone who is not a candidate at the time for a particular office.

Even the League of Women Voters, so particular about not taking stands for individual candidates, takes advantage of the loophole. The LWVof Boston held a reception to honor Lieutenant Governor Evelyn Murphy, the first women to hold constitutional office in Massachusetts, rumored to be planning to run for governor, but not an announced candidate.

Especially when it comes to "tributes," advocacy groups can sing the praises of *potential* candidates in favor of their issues all they want, as long as the person is not involved in a campaign at the time.

Targeting Elections and Candidates

In addition to encouraging people to vote, the Black Women's Political Caucus, according to Juanita Kennedy Morgan, believes, "It's imperative that people know how to vote correctly. We try to teach women to learn to find out what a candidate has to offer them. What is he going to do for me in order for me to support him? We say, 'You must talk to him and you must get him on the line,' so to speak. To get them to say that they will do certain things for women or certain things in the educational field or on taxes and interest rates. Get him to say, 'I will see to it that black people and women in general are able to get some loans and I will see to it that they will be able to get some grants....'"

Choosing people to support can be tricky sometimes. Morgan said, "The one thing we try to do in this organization is not divide our women. We don't try to restrict our members. If we find that we can't basically agree on a person to support, then we will say all of us will go in the direction we feel best."

The Mexican American women Martha Cotera works with in Austin, Texas, function much the same way. "The only way that we have been able to get any kind of political power," Cotera maintained, "is to be very active politically. We get involved in political races at the local level—city council and school board—at the county level, at the state level and at the gubernatorial level and, of course, the U.S. Senate and House. So we get very involved in political campaigns. That means we're involved in campaigns all year long, except for three or four months a year for a breather."

"What we do is we target people who would be most responsive to our issues," she said. "We can't do all the races, but we can target maybe two races. Right now we're targeting the mayor's race and a woman's race, an Anglo woman who's very good. The sad thing about it is she's running against a Mexican American candidate, male, but he does not identify with the Mexican American community, so it's OK.

"We targeted the races and we went in to meet the candidates. We get other people in to meet them. We do fund raising for them. We do facilitating with them so they can meet a lot of groups. When the campaign starts, we work actively to get the vote out.

"We're telling the candidates that we want them to support the industrial development program. ... So all the candidates are supporting that issue now. It's good because whoever wins, we've got them down on record as supporting our issues. If we get in quickly and early and make sure we have some kind of say in structuring their platforms, we can get our issues through.

"There's been an ongoing issue about the hospital. The concern is whether or not the board would recommend to sell the hospital to a private entity. That is a recurring issue, so we pick our candidates. We have meetings with them, and we tell them what our issues are. We get commitments and positions from them on these issues, and then we support them.

"Like with the mayoral candidates. We made it very clear that the Mexican American community did not want to sell the hospital. And then they ran on that platform. And if they don't run on that platform, we do everything we can to defeat them. So both mayoral candidates are supporting 'no-sale.'"

The same technique has already worked with other issues. Cotera and her group wanted a school to be rehabilitated. Cotera said the candidates "knew they weren't talking to just one person. We said, 'We want Fullmore. We expect money for Fullmore. We will not have this bond money spent on any other school, and we want your commitment to Fullmore.'

"Some of the ladies were scandalized that we were doing this. But we said, 'If we don't do this, we're never going to get the school replaced.' So we went to the candidates before they got elected, and we said, 'We want you, and based on this issue we will support or not support you.'"

The politics of advocacy can become pretty sophisticated. "Sometimes," Cotera said, "you can keep an issue from a candidate if you know you don't like the person. In this case, the candidates we wanted were all supportive of the issue, and I tell you that two weeks after they took office they voted to spend the money to replace Fullmore Junior High after forty-five years of people trying!"

Fielding Candidates

"You must get inside in order to become," said Juanita Kennedy Morgan. "We want our women to become part of government. This is the way to get inside. So long as you're out running around, this one speaking there and that one doing that, you're not doing anything but beating tracks. So our method is to organize where there is a metropolis—where there is a mayor, a governor, that type of thing. That way our women have someone on the city council, for example, to be part of what's happening.

"Getting black women to run for office is not our main purpose. Our main purpose is to get them involved. Our secondary purpose is to run some of our women for office."

Martha Cotera agreed. "In order for women to stay involved politically they need to see some women up front in elected positions. We need up-front visual people. We do have one Mexican American woman in the state legislature from the Corpus Christi area. From our area we have no one in positions at the county level except a Mexican American woman constable."

Brenda LaBlanc ran for office in Des Moines in order to draw attention to housing issues. When Des Moines restructured its city council, it held a new election in 1968. "It was a big election," LaBlanc remembered, "and I felt that we still had a lot of things to say about this housing inspection thing. We hadn't been able to say very much because the newspapers always reported what the officials said and little about what we said. I decided I would run for council. I ran at large.

"It was a great experience," she commented, "but a terrible lot of work. I was running all over the place making speeches. There were about twelve contenders for the at-large positions, and I came in fourth, which I felt was pretty good. And there were four people that had to run in the final for two seats. I came in fourth again, but I really didn't want a seat. I was running so I could talk to people about the issues. I did get a plurality of votes in the Northeast area which made me pleased, because it is the area I live in."

Getting Good People Appointed

Once officials whom her group supports are elected, Martha Cotera explained, "They know us by name and face, and we can lobby them for appointments. We also lobby for economic contracts for minority business people. We lobby very strongly for that. So affirmative action and contracts are two big issues at the local level of government here."

Boards, committees and commissions are a few examples of government positions at local, state and national levels that are very important to public issues. Advocates try to get sympathetic people appointed to these usually unpaid positions in policy and decision-making groups.

Juanita Kennedy Morgan said, "We not only run black women for office but we also try to put some of them on some of these boards, so that they become a part of the zoning board or various other boards where the action is. Those are the people who determine what you are going to do. We say, 'How can you stand out there and not be a part of it?'"

During an interview Martha Cotera said, "Today I've got a meeting with the governor's appointment person. We're going to be lobbying for the appointment of Mexican American women to boards and commissions at the state level. That's to get participation in the political process, especially the policy making, because, you know, the positions are very limited, but through policy appointments you can spread your power and influence. It's the only way I know, and I don't know any easy way."

On the local level, Cotera pointed out, "We are very strong lobbyists for health issues, particularly health care for low-income people of all races, because women are most affected. We do that by having women on the boards. We have Mexican American women on the hospital board. We have women on the health advisory committees through our connections with city hall. We pressured, especially to get women on the public hospital advisory commission."

Cotera herself has been appointed to many groups. She recalled that more than a decade ago, "They put me on a committee about bilingual education. We were on it for three months, and we worked fast. We were the first ones to finish. We had a really exciting group. We worked good and we worked fast, and here we are again."

Carol Garvin, a member of the South Carolina Mental Health Commission, vividly remembered being notified of her appointment. "I was fixing salad dressing in the kitchen when the phone rang. And this voice said, 'Could you hold for the governor?' I said, 'Yes.'

"So I stood there and I thought: Now, Carol, you're a grown woman, and this is just the governor. I had thought this was in the works. I wasn't sure it was going to happen, but I knew why he was calling. I assumed why. So, anyway, I was standing there beating the salad dressing madly. It was the best-mixed salad dressing we ever had! And I was thinking: Now, just be calm. I heard this clicking on the phone. He said, 'Hi, there.' And I said, 'HELLO!'

"I've finished about a year of my five-year term," Garvin said in an interview in 1983. "It's a body that's in transition, because it has three relatively new members.

"I don't know how the commissioners were appointed, but I think there was a move in the governor's office to appoint some people who really did have some information and who cared about mental health issues, rather than someone who had some political clout, of which I have none. I think these last three appointments are definitely people who see themselves as advocates. There are a couple of us on there who have had Mental Health Association involvement."

The commission, according to Garvin, is a group "that delegates most of its work to paid people, so it's a much different set-up than I am used to. But it is very interesting, and it gives me a chance to express in some really practical ways some things I'm really concerned about. I'm pleased that my involvement has not just been window dressing."

Eleanor Josaitis of Detroit has been appointed to many groups over the years, including the U.S. Department of Agriculture's National Advisory Council on Maternal, Infant and Fetal Nutrition.

Getting Good People Hired by Government

The majority of advocates who participate in government are those who are employed there daily. Some work in the legislative and judicial branches, but most are administrators in the executive branch. Government-employed advocates have an important impact on issues, because they have control over such practical matters as dispersal of funds, information, and the daily operations and implementation of policies.

When Michael Dukakis was elected governor of Massachusetts for the second time, Janet Ferone said many groups in the state, including NOW, formed the Mass Coalition for Women's Appointments. "This is very exciting," she said, "because a bunch of strong, influential women's groups have all come together to work on a process where we can present the new Dukakis administration with recommendations, résumés and backgrounds on women to fill positions. We are not going to put up with the 'I-would-have-hired-a-woman-but-I-couldn't-find-a-qualified-one' routine. We have submitted over three hundred résumés, and they are on the Dukakis computer."

Lois Gibbs and Citizens Clearinghouse for Hazardous Wastes work with advocates employed by government all the time. Despite the presence of government officials who are no help at all, many help groups fight hazardous wastes.

The November 1983 Action Bulletin article begins, "Informed sources at EPA revealed to CCHW that three major policy shifts are in the works for the Superfund Clean-up." After detailing EPA plans not yet officially announced, the article ends, "Use this information in your negotiations with local officials...."

Lois Gibbs explained in an interview, "Many EPA employees are very frustrated about what's going on. They feed CCHW information. They tell us about dangerous toxic hot spots that EPA is trying to cover up." As if that were not enough of a contribution, Gibbs says, "EPA employees write many of our newsletter articles themselves. Notice that we never use bylines."

Lotta Chi said, "Some people in the Organization of Chinese American Women are now in government. Some are in AID [Agency for International Development] and are directors of programs for food for peace. And then there are people who are working for government now in all kinds of areas that affect us."

The organization had a friend in the Department of Education. "Three years ago we began a very good grant from the Women's Education Agency," Chi explained. Dr. Leslie Wolf is the director. We submitted a proposal and she gave us a three-year grant to produce conferences all over the country to help Asian women" adjust to the U.S.

Marlene Sciascia was employed by the city of New York in the mayor's office for the handicapped from 1977 through 1979. "I got in under Beame, and then Koch was mayor," she said. "My position was at several levels really. We dealt with city, state and federal regulations. In addition, the federal definition of disability encompasses people with mental illness, as well as people with physical disabilities.

"I was the administrative assistant to the director at a camp for physically disabled teens. He became the deputy director of the Mayor's Office. So it was through him that I found out about the job. The director was the person who actually hired me.

"My title was legislative coordinator. Obviously, we didn't have enough time to do all the work. It was me and two others. Once in a while I would get an intern. In thinking about this interview I realized for the first time that I was replaced by two people — one to do legislative work and one to work on regulations. I don't think even that was enough people.

"I liked the contact with the individuals on the social change level, which was one of my motivations. I was so very, very excited people would just get sick of hearing how well work was going. There was all this potential.

"We came in," she said, "and there was all this unorganized information. Files were all over the place. We organized everything. I could set up my own system, and we could keep track of all the legislation.

"I would call people in the community, and some of the providers and I would say to them, 'What would you like to see happen in the next year in terms of legislation?' They were falling off their chairs. 'Somebody wants to know what we want!' So I was gathering information, and I was in the right place to gather the information.

"It was wonderful. We put out our first legislative packet that year that was sent to Washington. The thing we put together for the handicapped was so visionary."

Carol Tucker Foreman, a food stamp and consumer rights advocate before she was made assistant secretary of agriculture by President Jimmy Carter, pointed out some of the advantages of being an advocate working for the federal government:

"As a member of the administration I had access to members of Congress. I also had access to editorial boards of newspapers and to television. I spent a great deal of time in 1979 going from one city to another trying to get editorials that, if they didn't favor food stamps, at least didn't attack them. Sometimes it was a success if the newspaper just said nothing. And I appeared on television shows to tell why the food stamp program had grown so much."

Watchdogging Government

Even after advocates get elected, appointed or employed in government offices, advocates in the field do not take it for granted that all will go well for the issues. Advocates evaluate the performances of government groups and individuals all the time. In addition to monitoring the progress of policies themselves (see Chapter Eight), they also monitor the people involved with them. Advocates keep track of what government officials are doing by observing them, keeping records and holding meetings with them.

Some League of Women Voters chapters have an "observer corps." Although their main function is to track issues, they also learn about the officials involved.

"Sometimes the benefits are immediately apparent," an LWV booklet says of observation. "The mere presence of a nonpartisan note-taker keeps officials on the public accountability track. Sometimes the 'payoff' comes in ways that cannot be foreseen at the time. One Southern League found that knowledge of personalities and procedure, both formal and informal, gained through observers' regular attendance at county board of education meeting made the League a formidable community force when it negotiated with the reluctant board about compliance with federal civil rights legislation."

Martha Cotera's group found out whom they can and cannot depend on in the city council through ongoing observation of meetings. She said, "We have a very good council person, but he just keeps going to his good friends for advice, and they are really sexist. He goes to them for recommendations, and they're never going to recommend any of us for anything. We constantly have to keep a white woman — I don't care what color she is — but we need to keep women on the council to have an inroad. This particular man is really super, but we cannot depend on him. His friends just don't think. So we work through our woman council person."

So, how did a public official actually vote or act? Advocates use many ways to find out, then tell people. Some organizations, like the League of Conservation Voters (LCV), keep a running record of politicians' votes. The LCV then provides the information to others, including the media. Both the Sierra Club and the Citizens Clearinghouse on Hazardous Wastes use LCV materials to educate constituents about elected reps.

When records are not compiled for certain issues, advocates compile them themselves. The OWL Organizing Manual suggests, "It is a profitable habit to begin a card file on the voting records of legislators within each chapter district, both nationally and within the state. Newspapers generally carry the reports of votes on specific bills, and district offices can always be phoned to find out how a member voted."

Although advocates can ask officials how they stand, many run into the same problem Marlene Sciascia had. "It's hard to get someone to say to you, 'Who cares about people with disabilities?'" she remarked. "Elected officials — city, state and federal — don't want to. So we check in. We watched the Social Security bill for example. We checked with [Senator Jacob] Javitt's office. The veterans' office let us know how the votes went."

The judicial branch is often portrayed as being least affected by "politics." But as Sandra Kurjiaka observed in 1983, "The courts respond to what they view as the political climate. You know, they're not so pure. We're getting losses on cases that should be victories."

In one case a popular, award-winning state park naturalist came under fire. "During the Republican administration here," Kurjiaka reported, "they passed a rule specifically aimed at this man. It said you have to have short hair to be a park naturalist. And we said, 'Oh, this is so silly. All this stuff has been litigated already, but we'll take the case.'

"You know, we thought we had this tiny little case. The federal judge ruled with us, saying basically just what we did—this is silly to have litigated. It is the law that you cannot impose this standard.

"Well, the state appealed it to the eighth circuit court of appeals and they decided, in all their wisdom, that a park naturalist has the same duties as a police officer and could, therefore, be forced to have short hair.

"I'm finding a rule like that, given the previous rulings from that circuit, to be very bizarre. I really think it's a response to the Reagan program."

Another approach to tracking elected officials' records, recommended by CCHW, is to hold regular "accountability sessions" targeting the group's major concerns and examining officials' responses to those issues.

Working with Specialists

Advocates create, tap into and cooperate with a variety of special groups in our society. They try to persuade specialists to join their efforts, just as they do other groups in society. Finding and working with each of these expert groups can be tricky. Both advocates and specialists end up learning from each other.

Process Experts

Employing a process expert—a lawyer or policy campaign consultant— is necessary for advocacy groups sometimes. It is extremely important in both cases that the group be the expert's boss and not the other way around. The group should know exactly what it wants the lawyer or consultant to do and make sure whoever they choose is respectful of the group's decision-making process.

Lawyers are helpful in structuring groups and in carrying out court actions, if a group decides litigation is necessary to change a public policy. (See Chapter Ten.)

The CCHW "Start Up Kit" for new groups answers the question, "Should we hire a lawyer at this stage?" this way: "Why? Most of us were brought up to believe that the system works. When it doesn't work, hire a lawyer and she he will make it work. That's just not necessarily true . . . . If you don't have a specific and concrete reason for using a lawyer, then perhaps you should wait until you do."

Experienced advocacy groups are careful to seek out and use lawyers that respect group decision-making and know how to use the resources an advocacy group can provide. Attorney's fees can vary from high to free, so advocates also try to get the best attorneys for the best bargains.

The summer 1985 installment of "Organizing Toolbox" in CCHW's *Everybody's Backyard* was called a "Guide to Lawyers." What are lawyers useful for? According to the article by Will Collette, they are good for legal advice, representation in court, getting a temporary restraining order and filing for damages.

But Collette stresses that groups should not use lawyers for anything but legal advice and representation. The group should do its own research, represent itself everywhere but the courtroom and manage its own publicity efforts.

The way Sandra Kurjiaka worked with lawyers illustrates the way legal expertise and advocacy needs blend. She said the Arkansas CLU "has a panel composed of six volunteer lawyers, wonderful attorneys, plus others on call who volunteer to take specific cases.

"The panel can get enmeshed in just the law," she reported. "I meet with them twice a month and bring them all the cases and they'll say, 'But the law says' and 'My stand is.' I say, 'It doesn't matter what the law says. We're here to make it say what it should. So the law says that! What do I care? They make laws so we can challenge them.'"

As the lawyers advise and educate, so do the advocates. Kurjiaka pointed out, "We're doing lawyer training projects in June about challenging the constitutionality for a state to have sodomy statutes. Some training is necessary because the challenge is a very difficult piece of law to do. You have to do it very meticulously. The director of the National Gay Rights Project has put together a five-hour workshop for attorneys at the end of June."

The same issues hold true for public policy consultants as for lawyers. Groups have to know exactly what type of consultant they need and exactly what they want the person to do. The consultant needs to have a respect for democratic decision-making. Most important, the group should do its own research and represent itself in public. Consultants can be very expensive; groups should be sure the lobbyist can do what members can't before they hire one.

Issues Experts

Physicians, scientists, academics and many other professionals in a range of areas lend information and expertise to advocacy efforts to mold good public policy.

The medical and scientific experts learn from advocates, too, of course. Gini Laurie reported that at the *Rehabilitation Gazette* Post Polio conference, which 439 people attended, "The togetherness was extremely important. I think of the balance and the sharing and the learning between the professionals and the disabled who were there. I think of the contacts that people made with each other.

"One of the things that will come out of the conference is a handbook for physicians. It's pretty well along the way now. It will be the best possible handbook you can get for physicians—something very simple that will get distributed all around this country and, if we're lucky, translated and sent around the world."

The *Gazette* itself, Laurie said, offers a way for professional people to "look over the shoulder of the people who are disabled and see in the Gazette thoughts they might not have known from the white-coats."

Institutions

Churches and universities are tied into advocacy work in a number of ways. Juanita Kennedy Morgan and the Black Women's Political Caucus try to educate ministers and members of congregations on the importance of getting involved in the political process. Morgan said, "We try to do education through our churches, and really the church is one of the main strengths for this type of thing. We educate our ministers to the point where they recognize that they too must become a part of this thing in order to bring black people together."

Brenda LaBlanc said Citizens for Community Improvement in Des Moines, gets its funds to pay staff "mostly from local churches. The staff is forever sending in proposals. One church group pays for the tenant-landlord thing and another pays for the anti-crime."

Barbara Reed described another way churches are useful—this time for housing issues in Atlanta. "I started working with Interfaith, Inc. in 1972. I went on their board as advocacy chairman and I've been there since. We have fifty churches that are members of this organization and have some representation on it. When we arrive at a stand we call the representatives of these various churches and try to get them to get people within the churches to contact people on the city council, or the Fulton County Commission or the state legislature or congresspeople."

Business

Probably the most obvious way advocates work with business is to use donations from them to support advocacy work. Eleanor Josaitis's Focus: HOPE does just that. But they also work with them in more complex ways. Their Industry Mall is a private-public corporation designed to train and employ local people.

And, Josaitis noted, "We have been able to get corporations to move back into the city — corporations which left the city years ago. We did it by showing them that we could help them get tax abatements where they were fulfilling a social need, and we said we could help them find qualified people who could work for minimum wage and produce what they needed to produce. We told them it would be to their advantage to move back to the city. And they've done it. Two corporations have moved back into the city because of our persuasion that they have something to gain from it."

"Insurance Companies Boycott Hazardous Waste," reads the headline of the May 1985 Action Bulletin of CCHW. The article says that "The insurance industry is pulling out of pollution coverage. . . . Nearly all insurance underwriters have decided to drop or reduce coverage for 'sudden' and 'non-sudden' incidents. Policies still being written are going to cost 2–5 times more for less coverage. In addition to Bhopal [the chemical poisoning case in India], your pressure and lawsuits are also major factors."

Media

Although newspaper and television coverage are only mildly important for publicizing organizations and attracting constituents, they are critical for educating the public about issues and goals. (See Chapter Nine.) Advocates, therefore, try to get to know people and outlets important to them.

"First, find out who you will be dealing with," advised Tish Sommers in the OWL Organizing Manual. She suggested keeping lists of all local outlets, plus names of people who cover related issues.

"Second, adopt the mind set of a media professional. For example, deadlines are important to all of us, but to media people they are more demanding. Learn the relevant deadlines, and add them to your card file. Think of yourself as an ally to the news people, providing the information they need, but don't waste their time. And when the press does a good job, express appreciation.

"For ongoing public relations, the print media are still number one," Sommers continued. "Put energy into using them effectively" because, "besides using important press statements as handouts, there are many other uses. Once something appears in print it takes on more importance."

The Mental Health Association of South Carolina's booklet "Reaching the Public" says, "Newspaper editors are important to you. . . . Editors are interested in getting to know you as a news source.

"You must learn to recognize and use for publicity only those things that interest others. Ask yourself this question: Will this story interest others than those in our group? If it will then it is worthy publicity. If it won't then it's not.

"It is said that the difference between amateur and professional publicity is the amateur thinks of his story while the professional thinks of his audience."

Carol Garvin of MHASC recalled, "Once in a while we've had some success in bringing something they could use to the attention of the press. I think part of the real trick to working with the media is to know they have requirements, too. They're not really interested in every little nitty thing that we're interested in. So we have to figure out which things are really useful for them."

The League of Women Voters emphasizes that an important element of an issues campaign is to "analyze positions of all relevant newspapers, TV and radio stations and get names of sympathetic reporters, publishers, producers; use them for advice and help in getting the proponents' story across. Work on those elements of the media that are sympathetic."

Part Three
CHANGE FOR THE BETTER

Chapter Seven

Not Behind Closed Doors:
True Stories of Policy Campaigns

*"For years I have been learning about public policy. Now I am
wondering what I can do to help make it."*
*"Why, nothing! Public policy is made by big-wigs behind closed
doors."*
— Recent exchange between a graduate student
and a political science professor

Poor professor! He clearly didn't know what's going on in the realm of
public policy.

Lucky student! He took a course in another department of the university where he learned how citizen advocates resolve public issues. On
top of that, he also had a hand in changing a public policy before he graduated.

"Public policy" sounds like a big deal. But a public policy is just a decision made by one of the three branches of government—executive, legislative or judicial—at local, state or federal levels.

After looking at hundreds of policy campaigns carried out by dozens
of organizations, a pattern emerges that can be translated into five basic
steps every policy campaign goes through regardless of the issue. After
identifying a problem, advocates do more research, formulate a policy goal
and strategies for achieving it, carry out those strategies and, finally, review
and monitor the effects of their efforts.

Advocates always employ education—of the general public, group
members, government officials and generally everyone possible—as a critical strategy in every policy campaign. The three direct strategies—
negotiation, legislation and litigation—correspond to the branches of
government. If advocates want administrators to act differently, or if they
want to influence regulations, they employ negotiation. To get a new law

or change an existing one, advocates work with the legislative branch or sponsor voter referenda. To question and clarify an existing law or activity, advocates enter courts with their issues. Formulating public policy in an open democracy is a challenging and complex business, as the following stories show. Reports from advocates all over the country and in the nation's capital illustrate what happens to real public problems that go through policy campaigns. (See chapters Eight, Nine and Ten for details about stages, methods and techniques advocates use as they conduct these and other policy campaigns.)

Making Local Policy

On the local level, advocates educate members, area residents and government about the issues. They employ the strategies of negotiation and litigation with city and county agencies charged with administering laws and in the lower level courts. Local laws are usually made by city councils, boards of selectmen, aldermen and other groups.

A piece of legislation is called a "resolution" or "ordinance" at the local level. Another way to get legislation enacted in a city or town—just as it is on the state and federal levels—is to put a referendum question on the ballot so that voters can speak their minds on the issue directly.

Protecting Homes from Government

Brenda LaBlanc and Citizens for Community Improvement in Des Moines, Iowa, have dealt with government policy regarding their homes for many years, carrying out campaigns on several fronts.

She explained that the city of Des Moines "had a deal where they said if a person wouldn't let them come in to inspect their house there was a one hundred dollar fine or thirty days in jail. We said we'd go to jail. There are a lot of old people in the neighborhood. They said, 'We'd just as well sit in jail as sit in our houses.'

"It happened at the time there was a lawsuit from California over a similar situation. They said inspections are unconstitutional, because there's a basic law that you don't have to permit anybody in your home without a search warrant. It had already reached the Supreme Court, and we held on until the decision came out. The result was that it was declared unconstitutional. So long as everybody in the neighborhood agreed that they wouldn't let an inspector in, the city couldn't do anything."

The housing problems were not over for LaBlanc and CCI. "As a team," she reported, "we fought against the housing inspection department all the time. We became the champion of the poor landlord, because they picked on a lot of homes where some elderly person had moved into a nursing home and it was being rented for very little. Usually it wasn't in very good shape. We went to a lot of those city Housing Advisory Board meetings as a champion of people in homes that weren't in too good a shape, but what the hell! We actually fought against the housing code, and we got a lot of extreme things taken out of it.

"Now they say they're only interested in inspecting rental properties. People who are renting places where they're satisfied with the way things are and where there's reasonably low rent don't want to be forced to pay rent for something better. It really isn't anybody else's business.

"We've told them that renters have the right not to let anybody in. It isn't just the people who own their homes who have that right. So we've been able to prevent them from condemning some rental properties, too. The reason they brought in this inspection thing was to be able to condemn property more freely for developers and we have stopped them from doing that."

Legitimate Female-owned Businesses

"It is common knowledge," Connie Spruill said of programs that require female- and minority-owned businesses to get contracts, "that some of the subcontractors have been set up as front companies. In other words, they aren't a legitimate minority company or a really legitimate female-owned company. It's a company that a man owns, and he puts it in his wife's name or his secretary's name or something like that.

"What we are going to do about that is to have the definition changed of what is a legitimate female-owned enterprise. The city of Columbus [Ohio] has done that for us now. A lot of companies that are husband-and-wife-owned are now excluded from the program, because those aren't the ones who need help. Also, companies where a woman owns it and her husband owns a similar company will be excluded. We got women put back into the title of the minority and female business development program. Now this is on the city level. We got a victory here.

"For example, we have a project here in Columbus called 'Capital South.' The construction is a private job, but, because of the way the city ordinance reads, they are expected to enforce the goals of employing women on the job sites and also seeking out women-owned companies to supply subcontracting. That's the way it reads now in the city ordinance.

"We got a victory on the city level. Now we want to get it at the state and at the federal."

Campaigning for Mass Transit

Before Dorothy Ridings was president of the League of Women Voters, she was an advocate in Louisville, Kentucky. "One success we had," she said, "was the Mass Transit Referendum. We used old-time political strategy to win the campaign. . . . I had never been involved in a political campaign before, because they were usually candidate-oriented, candidate-driven. But for the new mayor of Louisville, this was the first public issue.

"He turned his whole organization over to us—all his lists, his phone books—the whole bit. We ran a 'political' campaign, and we used all the tricks. We got the bus drivers and the bus drivers got their wives to set up a speakers bureau in addition to those of us who went out and said, 'We think mass transit is good for this community.' We put together a broad coalition of business interests, labor interests, black interests, women's interests, you know, handicapped. . . . It was a good coalition trying to sell people mass transit.

"A bus service is not a real sexy topic. But we won that vote and got people to vote themselves a tax increase, which doesn't happen real often. The referendum passed by a phenomenal majority.

"I helped run the campaign. It was just like working for a candidate except that in this case it was a public issue. We got them to vote to tax themselves for something which we thought was very vital to them and to other people. It was awfully satisfying."

Raped, Then Fired

"One of the cases I'm working on," Sandra Kurjiaka of the Arkansas CLU said, "is a woman who was raped on the job, and she ended up being fired by a co-worker of the guy who raped her—all security guards with this company. The company ended up saying things like 'A woman doesn't need to be doing work like this,' etc.

"The woman called the office and said, 'I don't know who else to call. Is there anything I can do about this?'

"The police—oh, this is cute!—and the prosecuting attorney said there wasn't enough evidence to charge the guy. We have positive identification. This woman saying, 'C.B., the man I work with, raped me at three fifteen this morning.' And she went to the hospital, and she had all the tests and everything.

"The man was a police chief. And the prosecuting attorney says we don't have enough evidence to charge! We probably can't do anything about that. See, she waited so long to come to us that the prosecuting attorney is no longer the prosecutor. It made that all very messy. Prosecutors and district attorneys have total discretion as to when they will and when they will not charge.

"So what we have done is we've sued the alleged rapist. We've sued him in civil court, as well as the company she worked for, for sex discrimination for her firing. And also for the violation of her civil rights. The ultimate sexual harassment on the job is to be raped. So we're suing everyone connected with it that we can lay our hands on. We just filed, and we received from their attorney motions to dismiss."

What a Dump!

"There is so much garbage generated in the city of Los Angeles you wouldn't imagine," Betsy Reifsnider of the Angeles Chapter of the Sierra Club began her story. "And there is no place to put it. So the city council has decided to dump it in Griffith Park. Colonel Griffith gave the park to the city about 100 years ago. People go hiking there, and it's just a beautiful sight. I found out about the city council's plan when a Sierra Club member who never got involved in anything before called us up and said, 'Here's what's going on. I think this is outrageous!'

"We did too, because we have had a long-standing policy that there should not be garbage dumps in city parks," Reifsnider laughed.

"The member wrote an article for the 'Southern Sierra.' A few people called here and said they would like to get involved. We gave them his name. He started learning more. He gave a presentation to the conservation committee.

"Soon I'm coming into the picture," she paused to explain. "The process is typical, because it shows the chapter structure and where I usually come in it.

"The conservation committee approved of his stand, and then the executive committee voted to approve any actions the conservation committee might take to stop this project. That's when I come into it, because I am the person who can coordinate things or at least be a repository of information.

"I found out that a member of the city parks and recreation commission was very interested and outraged, too. I talked to the attorney for the group that represented the Griffith family to get a lot of information from them. Then I talked to a lot of members of the group to let them know. I asked those with a background in solid waste management to go lobby the city council public works subcommittee. I learned that the city council still plans to go ahead with the plan to dump in the park.

"Now I keep calling city hall to see when it's coming up on the agenda. At the same time I'm writing letters to the city council members to make them aware that there are alternatives to landfill and what they can do. From the information we have, the city council, which is very pro-development and anti-environment, will probably go ahead and vote for this, because they can't see any alternative.

"What we're doing is getting a group of people together to initiate a lawsuit. We certainly hope that the threat of a lawsuit will have some impact. There is no environmental impact report on this at all. The Griffith family is involved in the suit. They're very upset. We hope this suit will be a bargaining chip, and the city council will start talking to us. They should know they are on shaky ground. They listen now, but it's more like pat-pat on the head, and they say there is no alternative. Letting them set a precedent like dumping garbage in a city park would be ridiculous."

Parking for the Disabled

As a legislative coordinator in the New York City Office for the Handicapped, Marlene Sciascia found herself using negotiation and legislation to get parking permits for disabled New Yorkers.

"On the city level we have a councilman, Ruth Messenger, whose record is great. We worked with Ruth and her people on one issue which was the Special Vehicle Identification Permit. . . . We wrote a bill, and she sponsored it, and it still has to get re-introduced. It didn't pass.

"There are other places, like Minnesota, where this is a state level issue, but the state of New York means nothing in NYC. It was very, very odd. We were trying to figure out why this city agency was making it so difficult for people with orthopedic difficulties to park their cars.

"We sat down and had a meeting with them, and we had a meeting with representatives from different agencies that had influence on this, and it turned out to be this very strange personal issue.

"The doctor who's supposed to oversee people who get these physicals thinks that you can recover from some of the things people have. So it's sheer incompetence at issue here. Post-polio is a condition that someone develops after they've had polio. It starts at a later date. The doctor didn't recognize that. You had a doctor that didn't have expertise in the area.

"They had a set of regulations they used to decide on people's disabilities. The doctor was employed by the city and the state. So people would have all these problems with parking because the law says you can park in most standing zones if you have this permit.

"Plus, it was like they were giving money. They were interested in 'limiting the number' of permits they were giving out. This made me wonder if there was power tripping involved. People in the community said that some people who had those permits had connections and didn't have disabilities. Were they holding out permits so they could save some for their friends? It was the only explanation I could think of."

Making State Policy

At the state level, policy-making tends to be done in the capital, with input from all over the state. Laws are made by referendum and in state legislatures. State courts deal with litigation, and negotiations with officials of departments and agencies produce new administrative decisions.

A *Tale of Two States*

Stefan Harvey, from her Washington, D.C., headquarters, described two efforts to establish WIC (Women, Infants and Children) nutrition programs in two states and the two different outcomes. "The WIC program," she said, "would have never gotten started in Wyoming if the Children's Foundation had not poured an enormous amount of time into it. In Michigan we failed miserably. The same staff person did both. There I set up the contrast.

"In Wyoming we were trying to get the program started. In Michigan we were trying to get the state to spend the money that had been allocated. I think the primary reason we succeeded in Wyoming and failed in Michigan was that in Wyoming there were people who could be convinced to work on the job of getting WIC implemented. There was a young guy, a professor, who was very interested in getting the program started. He took it upon himself to be the chairman of the statewide WIC committee. There were a number of people—a nurse, a minister, a social service type and a nun who worked with this guy and spearheaded the campaign to get the program started. So we had a group of people to work with. They knew Wyoming politics and they knew the needs of the state. Our staff person was able to describe the program and tell about her experiences in other states. Between them they got members of the state legislature in the program and got them to take a stand on it.

"In Michigan, while there were people actively involved in anti-hunger issues (there was an office of nutrition in the governor's office) the staff person was unable to find people who were willing to take on the objective of seeing that the state health department allocated its money.

"So there are examples of a success, where in eighteen months Wyoming got a statewide WIC program. But the state of Michigan never spent millions of dollars that had been allocated for nutrition."

No Nukes in South Dakota

In her work on nuclear-related issues, Norma Wilson has been affiliated with several organizations and tried various strategies. "There was a Black Hills Energy Coalition," she said. "At the time the Black Hills Alliance was formed this was formed. They drew up a Uranium Choice Initiative which we voted on in the fall of nineteen eighty.

"I was active. My husband was active. Lots of people in the Vermillion area were active in circulating petitions and later going around and talking to voters about the initiative telling them it was to prevent any aspect of the nuclear fuel cycle being initiated in the state. No uranium mining, no milling, no nuclear power plants, no dump unless the people approved it in an election. The people of the state would have to approve any of those steps to initiate it.

"But the measure failed. It was on the ballot in nineteen eighty and it failed by only a two percent margin — fifty-one to forty-nine percent. That's very small. And of course we had only a tiny fraction of the money to spend on this compared to what the corporations had. They spent a fortune to defeat the measure.

"They were largely successful in the West River. The people in the Black Hills area make their money from mining. And they were afraid if we didn't permit uranium mining without a vote of the people that they would suffer economically."

There was another problem with the initiative. "It was called 'the uranium choice initiative' and we're afraid people thought if you voted yes you were voting for uranium mining. So a lot of people may have accidentally voted no. We have talked about trying to put a similar measure on the ballot but have it worded better and expanded."

Cleaner Cars — Cleaner Air

Betsy Reifsnider, Conservation Coordinator of the Los Angeles County Sierra Club, described a legislative campaign in California that resulted in cleaner air in that state.

"In the last session of the California State Legislature," she began, "a bill called Senate Bill 33 went through—the Vehicle Inspection and Maintenance Bill. We introduced the bill. Senator Presley authored it. It took the whole legislative session two years to get through.

"This bill should cut air pollution from cars in the L.A. area, for example, by twenty percent. It is a great step forward. The auto club lobbied heavily against it, but it was probably the one environmental bill that went through the last session of the state legislature.

"We had a lot of people going up there, as individual Sierra Club members, after getting a little bit of background from our state lobbyists in Sacramento. We went into our state legislators' offices. We also had a phone tree of the air quality people set up. People would call and say, 'Please call or write your state senator and have them vote for this bill.'

"I remember I called my brand new state senator and I said, 'Hello. I'm one of your new constituents in Pasadena. We have a smog alert today. I'm hoping that you'll vote for S.B. 33.'

"I think we were successful because the club in California really zeroed in on that as a major bill, and we put a significant amount of volunteer time into it. We made it a top priority."

Pro-choice/Anti-makeup

Sounds bizarre. Sandra Kurjiaka described the rather unusual ways women in Arkansas prevented the legislature from enacting anti-abortion policy. "The women's community here really did prevent the legislature from putting more of that anti-abortion stuff back in the law. In about four days we got out several thousand postcards that the NOW folks use. They say, 'I'm pro-choice and I vote.' Women sent them to the legislators and they didn't put that anti-abortion vote in.

"What really bothered them was all the women that had been there for another issue earlier in the session. All the while, I mean all through the negotiations and meetings and everything, they just kept saying, 'If we would just keep those women away that were here last time.' They said they'd do anything not to have the halls filled with 'those women.'

"What the legislature did do was pass a bill saying that it's unlawful to sell fetuses in Arkansas. Somehow it was very important to the anti-abortion movement that they not sell fetuses," Kurjiaka explained. "I don't know who they think they sell fetuses to, but I couldn't care less if the medical community uses them. They amended the law to say they couldn't sell fetuses.

"This legislator decided that truckloads of frozen fetuses are sold to pharmaceutical companies to make makeup. He decided that if he couldn't 'stop the slaughter of those innocent babies,' he could at least keep their bodies from being sold for makeup. I figured fetal tissue is not the feminist issue here. What they do with the fetus is not my concern. My concern is that they not interfere with women's right to free choice."

Clothes for the Kids

Janet Diamond related a legislative process from several years before that is a fascinating illustration of how a bill really became a law. She worked with the Massachusetts Coalition for Basic Human Needs (CBHN) at the time of a welfare funding campaign.

"The clothing allowance bill was written by a group of lawyers for us. Meredith Associates filed it. Dale Mitchell of Meredith Associates is a lobbyist.

"Getting sponsors for the bill involved more strategy than it seemed on the surface. There are certain people on the hill that will always sponsor poor people's legislation. However, because those people will sponsor any liberal cause, their effectiveness is somewhat diminished. We wanted to find a middle-of-the-roader, somebody with some seniority, particularly on the relevant committees, because the first hurdle was to get the bill out of committee.

"So we got people to call up committee people and visit them. They said, 'I live in your district, and there's this really wonderful bill.' We all did some of the phone work trying to target people. I can't remember how many sponsors we got, but it was quite a few. It was actually pretty popular, because it was so visual and because it was cheaper than a blanket cost of living increase.

"Dale worked out the mathematics. We worked up a fact sheet to go along with the legislation. We brought enough copies to pass around. We started to build our argument right away. They liked it. We got some good sponsors. We got Joe DeNucci, who was House chair of the Human Services Committee.

"The bill got out of committee. We testified at the hearing. We were trying to pack the hearing room. It would be nice if we could pack it with welfare mothers with every single soul's life depending on the bill. But we couldn't. So we packed it with whomever we could get in the room, because a packed hearing room is a packed hearing room.

"The bill went to the floor. We double-teamed the legislature the entire time it was in session. We had at least two people at the statehouse the whole time. If you've got a buddy with you, then you can make jokes about the whole process. You can whisper about the guy who's picking his nose or falling asleep. Two people were up there at all times.

"Now that doesn't sound like so much until you realize that in Massachusetts there's a budget season. The budget starts picking up towards May or June when it's actually being debated. The legislature can be in session sometimes until midnight every night for a week. So when we say we had people up there every minute of every session we mean every minute. I can remember sitting in the gallery of the House or Senate until three or four in the morning going home as the sun was coming up.

"As the budget moved along, things really heated up. I went there just about all the time coaching people on the things they had to say. They [legislators] always knew they were being watched. When our bill would come up, we'd perk up and look over the edge.

"The clothing bill passed, and then it had to go through the joint committees — the conference committees. We sat in the halls because the meetings are behind closed doors. The statehouse publishes daily the record of all bills to be heard that day. So Dale would let us know and sometimes we got called on a minute's notice. You know, 'My God, they're going back in session in an hour!' We'd just get whoever we could to go. We had baby-sitting networks for people who got called suddenly to go.

"After the bill passed the legislature, the next problem was to get Governor Ed King to sign it. He had never signed a welfare help bill before, but with special lobbying applied, he signed the clothing allowance bill into law.

"The bill came out in September on schedule. The welfare department didn't like it but it was law." CBHN then had to work out the snags with the department. The bill went on to develop and expand each year as advocates went back to expand the program. "Now it's a permanent law," Diamond said in 1983. The clothing allowance fell victim to budget cuts in 1991.

Married Woman's Property Bill

Elizabeth Cady Stanton, a women's rights advocate more than a century ago, wrote in her autobiography:

In 1852, the same year as the Women's Rights convention, the Married Woman's Property Bill, which had given rise to some discussion on woman's rights in New York, had passed the legislature. This encouraged action on the part of women, as the reflection naturally arose that, if the men who make the laws were ready for some onward step, surely the women themselves should express some interest in the legislation. Ernestine L. Rose, Paulina Wright (Davis), and I had spoken before committees of the legislature years before, demanding equal property rights for women. We had circulated petitions for the Married Woman's Property

Bill for many years, and so had the leaders of the Dutch aristocracy, who
desired to see their life-long accumulations descend to their daughters and
grandchildren rather than pass into the hands of dissipated, thriftless sons-
in-law. Judge Hertell, Judge Fine, and Mr. Geddes of Syracuse prepared
and championed the several bills, at different times, before the legislature.
Hence the demands made in the convention were not entirely new to the
reading and thinking public of New York—the first State to take any action
on the question. As New York was the first State to put the word "male"
in her constitution in 1778, it was fitting that she should be first in more
liberal legislation.

Vulnerable Women and Health Insurance

Tish Sommers' organization, OWL (Older Women's League), is a national organization that works on local, state and national policy issues.
OWL, like other national groups, works on similar policy changes with
different states.

"You take the question of access to health care insurance," she said in
an interview several years before her death. "We've developed a model
state health bill because states regulate health care insurance. This bill
would make it possible to convert an insurance policy from a person who's
been a dependent to an individual policy. Right now, if they're divorced or
widowed or if their husbands are older than they are and retire and go on
Medicare and they're not yet sixty-five themselves, these women are not
eligible for health care insurance except as an individual. Nobody was doing
anything about this.

"What we've done is develop the model state bill to bring the problem
out in the open. We use it as a means to bring the problem to the attention
of the public and the lawmakers. We're working in several states now—
California, Michigan, and Louisiana. Oregon passed one, but we're working
to improve it.

"There are four million plus women without any health insurance—
many of whom are dependent. We want women to recognize ahead of time
how vulnerable they are as dependents and that they better do something
about it. It's like getting credit in your own name.

"The issue is one we can win. I wouldn't say we will win easily because
the insurance companies are dead set against it. But it's winnable because
it's so obvious that a person should have a right to health insurance in this
country.

"Once it gets passed in a good form in one state, it's much easier to get
it passed in others. The people can go and say, 'Look, they have it in California, and it's worked. The insurance companies haven't gone bankrupt as
they said they would.'"

Suing for a Skill

Martha Cotera of Austin, Texas, knows the importance of bilingual education. "Bilingual children have a right to be bilingual," she says. "My child scores ninety-seven percent on English, so they don't put him in a bilingual program. The problem is that Mexican Americans — Hispanics — are expected to be bilingual as adults, but are not educated bilingually. You would be very disappointed if that Hispanic you wanted to hire were not bilingual. They are not training them in schools, but many employers need and expect bilingual Hispanics they can hire.

"At one time the state was trying to do away with bilingual education, so we went to court at the state level. And we got the state to formulate a policy. It's not very good, not very strong, but it's on the books now."

Making Federal Policy

Federal policy is important to advocates working at all levels — local, state, and national. Many advocates conduct national policy campaigns from Washington, D.C. Others stay in their states or cities. And a few travel back and forth.

High Lobbying

Women, Inc. is a neighborhood drug rehab program and education center in Boston. Director Kattie Portis described what she used to go through to get this local program funded. "Before Women, Inc., was state funded, it was federally funded. When it was federally funded I spent three months out of the year in Washington. Every day. We had to work miracles to get out of school (the Women's School that I ran for women) so we could lobby in Washington.

"We were funded by the Community Services Administration (CSA), and when we first tried to get in to get funded they wouldn't even talk to us. They said we should go to ABCD (Action for Boston Community Development, Boston's anti-poverty agency) and things like that. We never went to ABCD because we felt that what they were doing was good for some people, but wasn't good for our people — women who had a history of drug abuse, sketchy work history, no education or minimum educations. There had to be some high lobbying done for them.

"Now how that got done was really amazing to me. I didn't think I could do it. When we first wrote the CSA in 1979 the Carter administration did not respond. They felt that they were putting enough money in here to educate everybody and everybody would fit into this little mold that they had.

"So I started talking to some of Senator [Edward] Kennedy's staff from Massachusetts. As a matter of fact, one of them used to be my kids' counselor in Boys' Club. So I started talking to Peter Parham and telling him what was happening. We wrote Senator Kennedy a letter, and Peter called me back the same day and asked, 'How soon can you get down here?' He wanted us in Washington the next morning.

"OK. So I went to Senator Kennedy's office to be there at nine o'clock in the morning, met with Peter and he introduced me to this woman from Senator Kennedy's office. They gave me a staff person from the senator's office for one day. And that's how we got into CSA.

"When we got to CSA, the doors were open. The thing that I was most proud of was when we got into the meeting, we ended up in a meeting with about thirty women (CSA staff) to talk about some of the things we were trying to sell them. Service.

"As it turned out, in that particular meeting it was Maureen and myself. Maureen's white, and I'm black. All that busing craziness was happening back in Boston—that white folks weren't talking to black folks and here are Maureen and I hand in hand. I think that made an impact, too.

"So we started a dialogue. And we kept running back and forth to Washington. And it was crazy because we would get back here (we just left Washington two days before) and we'd get a call and have to go back down there. It would get killed in the bureaucracy somewhere. We'd follow it and bring it back alive.

"I think what really got us funded was all the work and sleepless nights and writing and phone calls. I think it was the courtesy and respect we gave to programs back here. But I think the biggest part was Jimmy Carter.

"Jimmy Carter's administration started to move really fast. This was right in the middle of the transition [from Carter to Reagan]. We had been working on this for a long, long time before this. But they called me up in the middle of everything and said, 'Guess what. Your funding will be in Boston tomorrow, and there will be a presentation with TV cameras. We want this and we want that.'

"They came with the new director, Russo. He came to Boston that day. And Jimmy Carter came to Boston. And Senator Kennedy came to Boston. All of these heavies came to town. Russo showed up with check in hand with his entourage of people. It was political time, but then I was getting what I wanted. So they showed up, and this city was rocking that day.

"The other thing that was requested of me was to be where Jimmy Carter was, and he went over to be where Senator Kennedy was, and I became one of the guys somewhere along the line. So Russo came, and he made the presentation for one hundred thousand dollars to do a vocational program especially designed for women. Shortly after he got back to Washington Russo called me up and said, 'You've got seventy-five thousand more dollars coming.' And they got it all out of there before Ronald Reagan came in."

Making Them Enforce the Regs

"I had to fight for one job I was low bid on," Connie Spruill said about her construction company in Ohio. "They took that job away from me, and I fought it for two months. Then I won the case with the fact that: 'OK. This is a woman of business. She can help us meet our goals.'

"You see, I complained to the Army Corps of Engineers. I mean I legitimately had that job. I was low bid. And that was the first time that I had to use the fact that I was a woman to get my job back. If the goal of using women-owned business had not been there and the government had not put it in writing, I wouldn't have a leg to stand on. We do have an opportunity if the regulations are enforced. But the problem is they weren't being enforced by the Reagan administration. He's blind to what's going on."

Correcting a Social Security Mistake

The Mental Health Association of South Carolina cooperated in a national effort to correct a federal action. According to Carol Garvin, "In nineteen eighty, the General Accounting Office told Congress that twenty percent of the people on disability might not be really qualified still. And so Congress instructed the Social Security Administration to take a look at these people. But it was supposed to be done over a fairly long period of time. What happened was that the Reagan administration saw this as an opportunity to throw a lot of people off disability to cut back costs.

"The Social Security people were instructed to speed up this process tremendously. What they do is sort of farm out their 'look' at people. The process of reviewing is done through state agencies. In South Carolina it's vocational rehabilitation which has the disability determination division. It became apparent fairly soon that a lot of people who were chronically mentally ill—who were quite sick—were being thrown off the rolls. This came to us through the national Mental Health Association; they alerted us.

"We decided if we wanted to talk about it, we needed some statistics. We wrote to all our members and said, 'Please send us some examples of case histories that you know about in a capsule form, not identifying the person but saying what happened to this person and why you think it was a mistake.'

"We also talked with a facility in Columbia [South Carolina] which is a transitional living facility. They knew quite a number of people who were having problems with this. We also talked with the Department of Mental Health to give us some statistical information.

"The statistics the national association put out said that when this review process started, eleven percent of the people on the rolls were chronically mentally ill, as opposed to those having some physical handicap. But as recertification went on, twenty-eight percent of the people thrown off the rolls were chronically mentally ill. We started getting reports from the mental health centers, and they gave us some really good information.

"That's when we started telling our chapter members about the issue, so they could talk about it to their congressmen, and we started going to the media. We started contacting the South Carolina delegation. We did an awful lot of this! I talked to Butler Derrick—the representative from my district—on the phone. I talked to him at a dinner one night." Garvin laughed. "I think he wanted to drink his coffee and be left alone.

"We contacted Senator Hollings frequently. Finally, in December we were told that the lame duck session was probably going to look at some revisions. We wrote and called Senator Hollings so many times that we got at least six of the same computer letters from him. It rather amused us.

"So there were some revisions made, but they were temporary. We thought we might have to go right back next year and do the same thing all over. The lame duck session of Congress did vote to slow down the reconsideration process, at least."

Talking Books

"We wanted to get the talking book program spread from just people who are blind to people who couldn't turn pages because they had no use of their hands," said Gini Laurie, publisher of the *Rehabilitation Gazette*. "This was done with the greatest of ease because I spread the word from the Cleveland polio ward to all the other polios around the country. There were seventeen respiratory centers like ours in Cleveland, and I got those mailing lists. Some people sent me their Christmas card lists. So I had polios all over the country whom I knew and we were becoming very close friends. They were getting the *Gazette*.

"So it was really very simple. All they did was just write a letter to other polio survivors in every single state. We asked them to write to their senators and representatives. You know, they pay attention to letters that say, 'I am writing this with a mouth stick, dear Senator.' And so they created quite an uproar in the Senate and the House. The bill was eventually passed. Talking books are now for the physically disabled as well as the blind."

El Salvador Certification: Teeth Needed

"At one point we had a success," said Nancy Sylvester of the Catholic lobby NETWORK in outlining the developments of the El Salvador Certification law. "As you remember, we got the certification conditions for El Salvador passed. The president had to certify that certain things were happening there before aid could continue. We had the more radical position of wanting to cut off all military aid, but we positioned ourselves then to push the compromise position. I think the Congress people understood that they could not go to their constituents without having done something about the situation. That was clearly a success.

"However, the Reagan administration certified — in the face of much evidence to indicate the contrary — that conditions in El Salvador were being fulfilled. It had not been written into the law that Congress had the power to veto or accept certification. So right now, what was just accepted in the subcommittee and will be facing a committee vote and a floor vote, is another amendment to the law that would tighten those conditions in the certification process. It would also give Congress the power to put some teeth in the process. It is not likely to pass because the Congress does not want to — Get this! — 'tie the president's hands on foreign policy.'"

Asbestos Disease and Bankruptcy Law

Carol Tucker Foreman was in the process of a getting an amendment to the bankruptcy act for asbestos victims — a policy she is working on as a public policy consultant — when she was interviewed.

"I represent a group of attorneys whose clients are victims of asbestos-related diseases. They all have suits against the Manville Corporation. Last summer the Manville Corporation took bankruptcy in order to stop paying, by their own admission, future claims or to set a ceiling on how much they would pay out on future claims.

"There are twenty thousand asbestos-related cases against the Manville Corporation right now. In the next twenty-five to forty years there may be twenty thousand or there may be one hundred twenty thousand. We think it's possible that the nineteen seventy-eight bankruptcy law does preclude them from declaring to avoid paying those claims. There's legislation pending in both the House and the Senate to reform the Bankruptcy Act to make it acceptable to the Supreme Court.

"The bill, as reported by the Senate Judiciary Committee, has provisions that would resolve most of my clients' problems. The bill being considered in the House of Representatives doesn't do any of those things. And neither of them deals with the future claims problem.

"My biggest problem is that I am representing a small number of attorneys against several very large corporations — not just Manville, but its co-defendants and insurance companies and a lot of other people. Plus the fact that what we're interested in is a very, very small piece of a much larger issue — the bankruptcy code. So almost no one will ultimately vote against one of these bills because of how it affects the issue that I'm interested in," Foreman pointed out.

"So it was a matter of lining up support, of getting included in a bill that nobody really wanted to include us in. We're in the Senate bill just by the nature of the way it's drafted. We're not in the House bill at all. The House bill was reported out of committee before I went to work for these groups.

"Actually, in this case it's marvelous. I'm not doing anything about the Senate bill because it's one of those few times when your interests are probably best served by letting the debate take place on grounds that have nothing to do with us. We will benefit if the bill passes.

"We worked with some of the senators who drafted that bill. We urged them to help out these victims and their lawyers. And the Senators happen to have a pre-existing interest in personal injury litigation work and didn't want to see it cut off by bankruptcy.

"We have other issues that deal with future claims. Those will be heard in a hearing soon in the Senate, and for that hearing we will try to present witnesses who will speak to the Manville Corporation's financial ability to deal with future claims. We will try to present evidence that they inappropriately used the bankruptcy statute. And that it's conceivable that the loophole that they used will, in fact, be upheld by the court and that, therefore, Congress ought to act to make sure that others don't do the same thing.

"Before the hearing we will go door to door to the members of the subcommittee and the members of the full committee generally discussing this issue with staff people who work on committee business. I will do as little of that as possible and depend on the lawyers for much of that," Foreman said.

Get Those Local Laws Off the Books

The Civil Liberties Union of Arkansas is concerned with basic issues of constitutionality. Naturally, the group does litigation regarding local cases and laws that involve interpreting federal policies.

"Homosexuality," director Sandra Kurjiaka pointed out, "is not just illegal in Arkansas; seventeen states have sodomy statutes. We just recently did a case defending a man who was charged with sodomy, and they gave him ninety days in a federal penitentiary. And we thought no, no, no. We really can't have somebody going to jail for ninety days for this act. This is insane!

"So we went to court to defend this and raised the constitutionality of the sodomy statute. Well, the 8th Circuit Court of Appeals said, in one of their more bizarre decisions, that since he could have been found guilty of violating another Arkansas law about public decency they were going to uphold his sentence. And they wouldn't consider the constitutionality of the sodomy statute in the case.

"The Texas folks last year won one," she said. "They challenged a similar sodomy statute. They got a bunch of plaintiffs and went in and said the law has a chilling effect. It violates our right to equal protection. And the district court agreed. And wrote a brilliant opinion. But the state is now appealing that. That's in the 11th circuit—whether or not it's a violation for a state to have a sodomy statute. Now if their circuit upholds the decision, we will immediately file another suit here."

Chapter Eight

Five Steps to Change:
The Process for Making Policy

We can't just hope for things to miraculously change for the better. It takes a lot of work.

—Norma Wilson

Most policy change campaigns are so complicated, take such a long time and involve so many people that at first glance it appears there is no particular order to the process. Sometimes it seems that each policy campaign is conducted in a unique way. Putting together and working with groups of people—a challenging task—looks easy compared to actually changing public policies.

But there's good news. Beneath the superficial confusion about how advocates and groups mold policy, patterns emerge. All policy campaigns follow five distinct steps from beginning to end. Groups that identify the stages in a policy change campaign see the steps much the same way, although they may use different words to describe it and emphasize some steps over others. Advocates follow this basic process to bring about policy change:

1. Identify an issue. Advocates uncover problems and choose issues to work on.
2. Research. Advocates gather more information about the issue and the people involved.
3. Review and plan. Advocates set policy goals and answer the questions: why, what, who, where, how and when.
4. Carry out strategies. Using education, along with either negotiation, legislation or litigation, advocates go after the policy change.
5. Follow through. When a decision is reached, advocates evaluate the campaign, let people know the result and continue to track the policy.

Keeping these five steps in mind as action campaigns go on can prevent the process from getting mired in everyday details.

Taking an issue through the five steps of a campaign requires people, information, resources and time. It also takes patience, courage and perseverance.

Step 1: Identify an Issue

Discovering problems and—when there are many—deciding which ones to work on are the two components of the first step in a policy campaign.

First Signs of Trouble

"What a problem!" That, in short, is how most policy change begins. A problem surfaces. How are those problems discovered? There are several patterns that emerge, depending on whether an advocacy group exists or not.

When an issue comes up and there is no organization to deal with it, a group usually forms. This happens often when local crises arise.

In March 1978, 800,000 gallons of cancer-causing chemicals from the Stringfellow Acid Pits flooded the small rural community of Glen Avon, California.

CCHW's "Everybody's Backyard," reports: "The nightmare began when heavy rains caused the 25 acres of open lagoons elevated in a canyon above the community to fill up and overflow. The main dam holding back the 32 million gallons of chemicals began to leak. To relieve pressure on that dam, a local government agency decided to release chemicals into the community. It 'forgot' to alert the people.

"The run-off," according to the newsletter, "traveled through a natural dirt wash and cut across yards, pastures and public roads. For five days the children played in the washes. . . .

"When the people in the community finally found out, what frightened them almost as much as the chemicals was the fact that the very government agencies people looked to to protect them were the ones responsible for exposing them to the danger. That their government deliberately withheld information from the people most directly affected by the situation added to the anger, frustration and disillusionment that led to the formation of Concerned Neighbors in Action (CNA)."

Lois Gibbs's CCHW Leadership Handbook explains what happens

when people discover a problem for which no advocacy organization exists: "Organizing starts when one or two people become convinced that something is wrong. Do you think you have a problem? Are your kids sick? Have your neighbors told you they've seen barrels or dumping? Observing what's going on around you and talking to your neighbors is the first research step in forming an organization."

Although Gibbs was addressing hazardous waste sufferers, the same types of questions are asked of anyone who thinks they have a public problem.

Fortunately, when some problems come up, advocacy groups to deal with them already exist. Organizations learn about issues from the public and from their own members.

Issues Come In

The Civil Liberties Union, like many other advocacy groups, is so well-known people often contact the organization when they have a problem. Sandra Kurjiaka of the CLU of Arkansas, said, "That's how cases come to us."

The CLU took the case of a woman who was fired after saying she was raped by a co-worker. (See Chapter Seven.) Kurjiaka said the victim "had been very frustrated by the law and how things worked for months. She read some little thing in the paper about something else we were doing and thought, maybe those people will help me. So she called."

Sometimes the phone call actually comes from a government official. Washington, D.C., lobbyist Carol Tucker Foreman said, "There are those rare cases where a member of Congress has gone out and developed his or her own idea and has decided to pursue it and wants to carry you along with it. It is usually a combination of a member coming up with something and then calling in some key outside advisers to see if they think this is a good idea."

Sometimes issues are identified by specialists. Lawyers, scientists, social workers and other professionals often contact advocacy organizations when they run into patterns of similar policy problems.

Advocates Reach Out for Issues

Most advocacy groups actively look for issues using a variety of methods to find out what members of the group, constituents for the issues and the general public see as problems.

Calling: Connie Spruill calls other women in construction in Ohio to solicit their ideas. "I am always on the phone saying, 'What's your problem? What are the problems that you're having? What do you think we need to work on? What areas?'"

Doorknocking: Doorknocking is useful for identifying local problems. A fund-raising proposal for Brenda LaBlanc's CCI in Des Moines, stated: "CCI's method of door-to-door organizing has been very successful. One reason for this success is that residents themselves define what the problems are, and are involved at every stage in resolving those problems."

Polls and surveys: Sometimes doorknocking is used to take surveys about specific local issues. In another proposal, Sally Mead described information she got about sensitive mental health problems in the North Pacific Rim of Alaska: "The child abuse and neglect problem has had limited documentation in these villages due to lack of access and follow-up by state child protection services. But village members say they are quite concerned about the problem. In 1980, a family services needs assessment was completed in the villages to assess their view of the status of family life. In the three villages, 70 percent, 100 percent and 75 percent felt there were serious family problems. Similarly, all three villages pinpointed alcohol abuse as the most severe problem. The problem of child abuse and neglect was linked directly with the alcohol abuse and great concern was voiced about this issue, though this subject previously had not been discussed openly."

First-hand experience: Sometimes organization staff and leadership uncover problems. Stefan Harvey, formerly of the Children's Foundation, discovered problems herself. "I got tired of traveling, but on the other hand, I believe if you want to be an effective advocate you've got to know what's going on," Harvey said. "The best way to know that is to be able to travel and see first-hand. Short of that, you pick up the phone and have very long conversations with people. It's very easy to understand what's going on if you've been to that community and you know the person you are talking to. There's an added advantage to actually going to a WIC program or just having a meeting with the staff. They may say they have no problem getting people into the clinic, but you may visit the clinic and see what goes on and be totally horrified. It's a matter of perception. I think that if you're going to be the best advocate you can you have to have as many first-hand experiences as you possibly can."

Eleanor Josaitis of Focus:HOPE said, "Issues come from many places — certainly from Father Cunningham [the director]. But the people who have worked with us for a long time, the managers, for example, are more than welcome to say, 'You know, I've got an idea. We ought to do this.' And we'll sit down and talk about it. It usually deals with something the person has been experiencing."

The staff of the Center for Budget and Policy Priorities and NETWORK in Washington, D.C., find many of their issues by reading. Stefan Harvey and her colleagues at CBPP spend a great deal of time pouring over government budgets, policies and laws to find out what needs to be acted upon.

Monitoring: Monitoring, according to In League, "is usually aimed at the administrative process. . . . Monitoring can determine whether both the letter and the spirit of the law are being carried out. Often, monitoring points up the need for revisions in the law or in regulations."

Advocacy groups often end up, like the League of Women Voters, doing a lot of monitoring "to assure that civil rights provisions are enforced . . . that clean air requirements are being met . . . that public officials comply with food stamp programs or school lunch laws," etc.

Monitoring, as will be seen later in this chapter, is also a research technique (Step 2), as well as a follow-through device (Step 5).

Deciding What Issues to Tackle

When many problems vie for attention, existing groups have to decide which ones to pursue. In the second phase of Step 1, advocacy groups use a variety of methods for choosing the issues they will work on. This phase of the campaign is critical.

Smaller, local groups usually use a single decision-making method. Groups that operate at national and local levels often employ one or two ways to determine policy change priorities. Common methods for choosing issues include local group decisions, board decisions, polls, conferences and conventions.

Phone calls: Connie Spruill said she calls people on the telephone to determine what their priorities are. "That is basically how the decisions are made—by finding out where the majority of the problems are and then concentrating on them. And if we make some headway, we go on to other problems."

Membership polls: Common Cause is a national organization with a quarter million members. Kathleen Sheekey said, "We poll our membership every year and we ask them which issues are particularly appealing to them, which ones they want us to continue on and what new issues they would like to see us get involved in. That's how we got involved in the area of nuclear arms control. Seventy-six percent of the members polled said not only should it be an issue for us, but also that it should be a priority issue."

Conferences or conventions: Juanita Kennedy Morgan said the Black Women's Political Caucus had a conference "every May on Capitol Hill where we determine the things that are happening or should happen. We have from two to three thousand women from all over the country attend."

Boards of directors: Some organizations let their boards choose issues.

In the Civil Liberties Union, for example, state boards, elected by the membership, determine issues to which the group will pay attention. Individual or specific cases may come to staff. Whether they are taken on depends on decisions by boards and attorneys.

After she finds out about a problem, Sandra Kurjiaka said, "I write it up. I go to my panel of attorneys and say, 'This is one of the cases we have.' Then we talk over things to do with it, if it fits our bill. Then I have to go and recruit an attorney who will volunteer to do the litigation for us, because we don't have a staff attorney here. That's the process we go through on every case."

Local, State and National Mixes

Multi-level organizations use different decision-making methods. Local groups and boards of directors can meet together and talk on the phone easily, especially about local issues. But state and national bodies of the organization use membership conferences or polls or boards of directors to decide the issues on those levels. Important internal communication is the exchange of information about issues identified at each level. Many groups pride themselves on their "grassroots" decision-making techniques.

The Mental Health Association of South Carolina's (MHASC) president, Carol Garvin, said frankly of the process, "It doesn't always come down to a neat little package." Basically chapter boards decide issues on the local level and the state executive committee looks at statewide issues.

"When you start a chapter," Garvin said, "you have to pick some things to work on. It's usually in the local board meetings where the issues come up. People get hot about working on them there. One of the functions of the state division is to cross-fertilize—let the chapters know what the others have done.

"Our state executive committee discusses issues. Sometimes things come up fast, and our director and I might discuss it and we might develop a certain approach. Then maybe we'll call around and do some checking out with some of our key people, because we have to respond right away. What we do comes out of trying to understand basic principles and approaches and then try to say, 'Well, how does this fit in with what we usually think and do?'"

The Sierra Club decides issues to work on "starting at the grassroots level," according to Betsy Reifsnider. "Our positions are determined by the Sierra Club volunteers. People talk about conservation issues in the local chapters. Their representatives go to the regional conservation committees— the next level. They talk about it, then it goes to the board of directors who finally vote on it, having the input of all these groups. The board is also all volunteers. We, from that, set club policy."

For national and state environmental issues, the process varies a little. "Usually our offices in Washington and Sacramento see the issues there and let us know. The people in Washington set goals two years ahead. I don't know how far ahead the state people do it."

Brenda LaBlanc reported, "Citizens for Community Improvement" is also "truly a grassroots movement. . . . In our city, each group is autonomous. They make their own decisions, deal with their own problems in their own way. When a state-level action is required, we participate only as we choose, and get together to determine our action in consensus.

"On a national scale," LaBlanc added, "the National People's Alliance canvasses groups across the country about their main concerns, and at our yearly convention, these are the concerns discussed. The exchange of information among people from different communities, dealing with similar problems, is immensely helpful to each of us."

The Older Women's League (OWL) has two levels—local and national. "We have six issues on our national agenda," president Tish Sommers said—social security, pension rights, health insurance, caregiver support services, jobs and budget cuts. We had our first national convention in Louisville last year. We started out with three issues and voted on three additional issues."

OWL calls its local issues process "Chapter Plan of Action." The handbook of the same name says deciding issues is a "vital process. Collective action begins with collective planning. The Chapter Plan of Action provides an opportunity for each member to voice her interests or needs, thereby incorporating the concerns of all members of the chapter. . . ."

The League of Women Voters (LWV) has a very sophisticated, long-standing process for identifying issues at the first stage in what the group calls "League Program." Dorothy Ridings, president of the U.S. League, described the process in an interview: "The word 'grassroots' is often overused, but indeed, that does typify the League in that our decision-making on issues is very definitely grassroots. Issues selection by the League is driven by member preference." At the local level a variety of methods, including chapter meetings, are used to determine the issues the groups will work on.

For national issues, "We have a convention every two years," Ridings explained, "at which time we adopt our programs—that is, our issues—our program for study and our program for action. Through a long process known as our program-making process the members make suggestions to the board and to the convention delegates who come from all thirteen hundred Leagues. The delegates vote on them at the convention. And they caucus and lobby. They send out materials trying to persuade the delegates to support this or that, whether it's for new study or for an action position on something we already studied. Now the traditional way of our coming to agreement is the consensus process. Consensus is difficult to determine in quantitative terms. Consensus is one of those things you know if you've got it."

The League has provisions for "emergency program." "Emergency procedures (in by-laws) are used only when the issues is of such a serious and urgent nature that members believe it must be dealt with before the next regular program adoption time," according to "In League."

Step 2: Research

Kattie Portis of Women, Inc., said of women she's worked with, "There's one thing I know—when they go at something, they have done their research!"

The word "research" sounds forbidding, boring and academic. But in the public policy world, when citizens learn about real problems and people, research is not only an important step but an exciting one.

Two main types of information are sought at the research step about the problem itself and about the people affected by it or with some influence over solving it. Research is critical in order for the organization to decide how to go on with the process and to use in the campaign for change.

In the Leadership Handbook on Hazardous Wastes, Lois Gibbs points out two approaches the advocacy group may take toward research. "Some leaders feel more comfortable researching the whole problem before they begin organizing people. Other leaders will simply do enough research to confirm the problem and then recruit people. They use research later as a group project that gets people involved. We favor the latter approach, since an organization is only as strong as its members, and research helps develop strong members."

Time Out: Managing the Policy Campaign

When the advocacy group takes an issue to the research stage, a smaller group is formed—if one has not emerged already—to take charge of the day-to-day management of the process. All the methods and techniques and detailed work are too much for the entire group to contend with. The composition of management groups varies. Some are made up of organization staff or officers. A management group can be a board, a committee or an informal cluster of concerned people. In a coalition, representatives of different groups manage the campaign.

The management group oversees the process, step by step, brainstorms methods to use, determines group resources and needs, keeps records and evaluates progress. At each step, the management group stays in communication with the larger group, making sure to include members in making major decisions and in carrying out the work needed.

At the research stage, the management group gets some idea of what the organization needs to know about the problem and people involved, then suggests a variety of methods and tasks to the whole group.

"The oversight function of management is vital," says the League's Campaign Handbook. "Good management cannot try to do all the work as well as direct it. Management must make sure responsibility is delegated. . . ."

Exploring the Problem

"The Children's Foundation got accurate information," Barbara Reed said. "I think it's important to be really accurate and do research and to make sure you are giving people accurate information. I also think figuring things out for yourself is a really important part of any kind of effective advocacy. It took me a long time to become an expert on the Women, Infants and Children nutrition program, and that's just one small program. I knew certain basic kinds of things, but I had to be able to provide the specifics and to pinpoint problems. To do advocacy you have to have some kind of in-depth knowledge." That knowledge can come from a variety of sources.

Ordinary people: A lot of information comes from people's experiences. "Because of our identity as Catholic sisters," Nancy Sylvester said of NETWORK, "when we advocate for the poor, we have had experience. Our members work with the poor. We're not an IBM printout with every piece of data known on it. But we bring our experience."

The Sierra Club also uses people as resources. Betsy Reifsnider reported, "We have a lot of people out there paying attention. We talk to each other. We do a lot of networking. If something comes up and I don't know anything about it, I don't look in a journal. I'll call a person I know is an expert on that. Then I get the up-to-date information."

CCHW mailed a survey to various local community groups with hazardous waste problems asking the type of problem, responsible parties, types of health problems, environmental testing and income of the community in order to understand problems better.

Specialists: The Mental Health Association of South Carolina gathered information about social security benefit cuts for national action. President Carol Garvin said, "We tried to get data and to relate it to local conditions so the local congressman would see some relevance to the district and to also try to get people here to understand what it's about. The national organization, working with the mental health law project in Washington, got some capsule case histories from here and from other states."

In national organizations, the national office can help the local groups with research. Garvin added, "We rely on the national Mental Health Association to provide us with some data. That's part of their job—to act as information resources. And sometimes we try to work up information ourselves. We also try to get information from professional people who do this for a living—that's really their job—to do assessing and counting."

The Garden Chapter of OWL in New Jersey took an interesting approach to research. Tish Sommers wrote in the organization handbook, "They have chosen the health insurance conversion problem as a priority endeavor. First they examined their own personal health insurance shortcomings and prepared questions for clarification. Then they invited two people from the state Department of Insurance to explain what the state is currently doing to both regulate insurance companies and provide equity for women.

"At a subsequent meeting, members heard from representatives of the Prudential insurance company and a broker who has had 50 years' experience in the field."

Printed material: Advocates also read up on their issues. Carol Garvin said, "I try to read through the professional magazine on community psychiatry, after a fashion. I read it to get a sense of trends. That's all."

Surveys: A survey sponsored by Focus:HOPE served several needs. When suburban housewives couldn't understand why inner city blacks complained of high prices, Eleanor Josaitis had them do a price survey of food and prescription costs in downtown Detroit. They learned fast.

Monitoring: Monitoring government, in addition to turning up problems in Step 1, helps advocates conduct research about them in Step 2.

Monitoring, according to the LWV, is "structured to provide orderly, well-supported data that could, if necessary, be used as the basis for any future remedial action you may decide is needed. . . . When you mount a monitoring project, you are usually acting on an educated guess that something in government could and should be working better than it is."

When the League watched how federal revenue-sharing funds were spent, it uncovered "some serious flaws in the formula for allocating the funds." Later, the LWV "capitalized on that data analysis to recommend changes in civil rights and citizen participation features, when the program was up for renewal in 1976." The information gathered in the monitoring process was used in a legislative campaign that year to revise the existing law.

Getting to Know the People Involved

"Good groundwork is essential for successful action," says the LWV. "Know your community inside out." This includes officials, constituents, other groups—everybody with an interest in the issue.

Getting to know the powers that be: Before any other research is complete, advocates familiarize themselves with the individuals and groups that affect their issues. They learn names, addresses and telephone numbers and the records of pertinent officials and government groups. (See Chapter Six.)

CCHW identifies two "key questions to ask when confronted with a problem: Who's responsible? and Who's got the power to give us what we want?"

A NETWORK newsletter says, "To lobby successfully you must have a thorough knowledge of your congressperson . . . in addition to the issue analysis provided by the national office. This information will help you strategize on how best to influence your congressperson's voting."

Betsy Reifsnider said of the L.A. Sierra Club, "We do keep in contact intermittently with certain people who have worked with us and are now aides in legislators' offices. I can call up people because they're old friends. We are developing an old girl network, for heavens sake! On the other side, they call me, because they know that the Sierra Club can generate a lot of people for a lot of things."

Getting to know other groups: One of the most important research tasks is to find out who else is working on the problem—if anyone—and what they are doing. (See Chapter Four.) While brainstorming about caregivers who said they need help and respite, an OWL chapter decided to find out what was available in the community and what was "currently undone but needed to be addressed." They decided to contact local human service agencies and other advocacy groups to find out. They also decided to ask about current pending legislation, if any, that related to the issue.

Lois Gibbs advises local people to contact state and national groups with the same questions about problems they are working on.

The reasons advocates contact other groups are obvious. Minimally, the groups want to share information and to make sure goals do not conflict. In the best cases, advocacy groups can form coalitions to share resources needed for conducting the change campaign.

Researchers' Rights

If the information advocates need about people or problems is in the hands of government, there are two important mechanisms that give average citizens access to facts. The LWV and the CCHW describe them.

The Freedom of Information Act, according to the League, "gives the public the right (with certain exceptions) to examine the written word to ascertain what the government has done. The Government in the Sunshine law lets the public observe meetings of government agencies to see and hear what is currently underway or planned," a League pamphlet explains. Like the federal government, many states and cities also have "sunshine" or "open meeting" laws.

Step 3: Review and Plan

"If you haven't drafted a plan of action and some data to support it, your chances of success are not great," Washington lobbyist Carol Tucker Foreman said in an interview.

After advocates have compiled information about the people and the issue, they move to the next task—sorting it out and developing a plan of action to solve the problem. They draw a line—the shortest distance between two points—from the situation as its exists to the point of change.

Midway through the campaign, the management team formulates specific answers to six basic questions. Like journalists, advocates answer the questions, *why, what, who, where, how* and *when* to determine how they will conduct the rest of the campaign.

Why? The Theme

"When you strip the issue down to bare facts, remove verbiage and confusing side issues and succinctly explain why [the policy should be changed] you have the basic ingredient to any successful campaign—the theme," the LWV Campaign Handbook says. "The theme is the tie that binds. It must be stated and restated throughout the campaign. It is your way of sticking to the issue and will help you avoid becoming sidetracked by issues raised by the opposition."

What? The Goal

At Step 3 the group also articulates the specific policy goal—the exact aim of the campaign. "No matter how much money you have or how many constituents [the two currencies of advocacy], if you don't know what you want to accomplish, you will fail," Carol Tucker Foreman said, speaking from years of experience on Capitol Hill.

"The group must have goals!" CCHW's Leadership Handbook on Hazardous Wastes stresses. "What do you . . . want to accomplish?" the handbooks asks. "The group should pick realistic goals, ones you can win. One or two are enough . . . three or four are really the maximum. Other goals can be added to a 'wish list' for the group to work on later. . . .

"The best indication that you know why the goal is important is that you can describe the goal briefly," says the League of Women Voters' Campaign Handbook.

The LWV's "Politics of Change" says there are two kinds of goals: long-range and short-range. A long-range goal is "the ideal toward which the group is working": clean air, decent affordable housing, etc. "Short-range goals . . . involve reasonable steps toward achieving long-range goals," such as an ordinance to prevent the sale of nonreturnable bottles, etc. Short-range goals are the ones advocates actually pursue, one by one, keeping the long-range ones in mind. Each campaign works toward one specific goal.

Planning Program says, "Positions should be ones on which the League can act effectively. . . ." The management group "prepares a short wording of the position and a longer statement that outlines in greater detail." The book offers this example: "The simple support statement could read: 'Support of a new central library which provides for expanded services.' The statement of position then, would include both the details and the rationale."

The CCHW handbook adds: "Goals should be stated in clear language, starting with the words, 'We want. . . .' Some groups are tough and call these goals 'demands.' Others feel that this is too strong a way to put it and call their goals 'needs of the community.'

"Be sure your goals do not contradict each other," the handbook warns. In communities in Connecticut, Tennessee and North Carolina, it says, groups, "[worked] through the internal hassles over goals and adopted the single goal of 'no landfill.' They did not say 'If there is a landfill. . .' as well. Industry and government were faced with a clear position and a united community and gave up."

"Research about the problem and who caused it, plus your discussion with people, helps you refine the issue," says the CCHW handbook. "When the group is finally ready to move, you should have an issue that you can define in clear terms. The issue [goal] should have the following six qualities: 1. It's immediate. . . . 2. It's specific. 3. It's winnable. . . . 4. It's 'targeted.' This means that you have identified 'who's responsible. . . .' 5. It's actionable. This means that the step or actions that can be taken are obvious and logical. . . . 6. It's unifying. You can express the issue in such a way that it rallies together all of the people who need to be rallied in order to win."

Janet Diamond of the Coalition for Basic Human Needs (CBHN) in

Massachusetts described a meeting where a management group decided on a specific focus for getting a welfare payment increase. They knew the state legislature was the only place to get it.

"The clothing allowance bill was something that did not exist," Diamond remembered. (See Chapter Seven.) "The idea was conceived in a strategy session we had with Massachusetts Law Reform Lawyers and Meredith Associates, a new lobbying group then. One of the women was talking about the cost of living increases and the infeasibility of getting any cost of living increase under the current administration. Because it is a very abstract concept, it just meant more 'bennies' [benefits] going to those 'terrible welfare mothers.' We talked about how legislators would view it as more money to spend on booze or that sort of thing.

"Also, the problem with a cost of living increase is that with AFDC [Aid for Families with Dependent Children], the increase is considered a change of eligibility for all benefits, particularly food stamps. We talked about the phenomenon of when you get a cost of living increase of ten dollars in your AFDC check, you get your food stamps cut by eight dollars. And maybe you lose fuel assistance money, and you end up with a negative gain.

"Why bother, we wondered, when it's just going to take a lot of effort and energy, and we'd just have to listen to more insults again about our inability to manage money and what a burden we are on government?

"We got to talking about how we would visualize an increase. How do you make it real to legislators? And what do we really need it for? We need it for clothing.

"And from that we reached the idea very collectively: well, why don't we have a payment once a year called a clothing allowance instead of a cost of living increase. And let's have it come in the fall, because that's when people need to purchase the most expensive clothing for their children. Why don't we call it a 'children's clothing allowance?'

"And we started getting excited about it, thinking, well, wait a minute, a one-time payment won't be counted against our grants, so we can ask for less money in the budget and actually accrue more real money, so we can argue it's fiscally responsible.

"And if we call it a 'children's clothing allowance' and have it given out on a per-child basis. In fact, recipients will spend it on whatever they want to spend it on—the first winter fuel bill or back rent if that's what they want to spend it on—but we decided to call it the 'children's winter clothing allowance.'"

"Start by defining, in 25 words or less, exactly what it is that you want," says CCHW's Leadership Handbook. Remember when you write a flyer or talk to a new person at her doorstep, you've got to be clear, brief and to the point.

Once specific positions are formulated, position statements are used throughout the campaign. The most common use for the concise position statement is in carrying out the education strategy of the policy campaign later at Step 4. (Also see Chapter Nine.)

Where? The Locus of Change

After the group has decided on a specific goal it must be decided where the power to achieve it lies. In order to answer the question, advocates consider the level of government to approach and even the branch, if one is not obvious. They also look at the political climate. They can formulate some ideas based on the research they did at Step 2.

When the CBHN sought a clothing allowance for welfare families, the answer to "where" was simple. The committee knew that the state legislature has responsibility for allotting new funds for welfare recipients.

Sometimes where to go with an issue is not so clear. As the League points out, "Sometimes it is possible to apply positions reached on an issue at one level of government to the same issue at other levels of government."

For the CCHW, finding out where to go with a hazardous waste problem can be difficult. The Leadership Handbook asks, "Is it industry? A government agency? A body of elected officials? The banks that provide the financing?"

In order to pinpoint the best forum for change, advocates do more research, if needed, by using standard directories or by asking government agencies for information.

Local action has many advantages—people can meet together; they share elected representatives, etc.—but restricting action to the local level is effective for local issues only. Disarmament activists, for example, work mostly for policy change to take place in Washington, even if they live far away and work locally. Letters, phone calls and affiliation with a national organization help local groups participate in state and federal policy efforts.

Who? Help Wanted

All three major groups advocates work with—the advocacy group, constituents for the issues, and government, plus some special groups—will probably be needed to get the policy enacted. At this point advocates have to identify the specific groups and individuals who will influence the outcome of the campaign.

"Member involvement must be a special focus of any action plan," says the LWV. "The management group analyzes the human resources in the group and how they can be used."

"Who are the chief supporters/opponents?" asks the League.

"What is the name of the lowest level person whom you think has the power to give you what you want?" asks the Citizens Handbook on Hazardous Wastes. "The reason for naming the lowest level person is that he/she is usually easier to reach and easier to pressure than the higher-ups. Besides, if you take it 'straight to the top' and Mr. Top Dog says 'no,' where do you go next?"

At this time the management group looks at other groups that are interested in the issue. Can you get together as a coalition? And what experts, if any, will be needed? Lawyers? Scientists? Local institutions? Media?

How? Choosing Strategy

Half of every policy campaign strategy is education. Members of the group, government and the general public are told the policy goal and the reasons behind it. Advocates choose the specific second half of the strategy from the three choices that correspond with the three branches of government: negotiation, legislation or litigation.

The management group looks at the information about the issue and the people with responsibility for it, then reviews the group's resources — time, money, energy and people power. The three different strategies require vastly different kinds and amounts of resources. If resources are lacking in some areas, other groups might be asked to join to complement the effort. At this step, one strategy usually emerges as the natural route to effect change.

The League says, "Often, the problem can be solved through improved administrative procedures [negotiation]; at other times, corrective legislation is needed. . . . If these avenues are unproductive, the third action tool — litigation — may have to be called into play."

For each goal, advocates choose one strategy that matches the branch of government to be approached. Negotiation is done with administrators in the executive branch. Legislation is done through elected representatives. And litigation takes place in the judicial branch. In case a particular strategy is not obvious, advocates look at the advantages and disadvantages to each of the three.

Negotiation: One advantage of informal negotiation is that advocates have an equal say about where, when and how the negotiations are conducted. The negotiation process doesn't usually take a long time or cost a lot of money. On the other hand, advocates who sit in small sessions have to make sure they are representing the whole group and sometimes have to check with the group before they make final decisions. Another disadvantage is that negotiations themselves usually don't generate official, public records of agreements, so advocates have to publicize the results themselves as part of the next step, Step 5, in the campaign. Commenting on regulations, another kind of negotiation technique, is formal and more similar to legislation in terms of needed resources.

Legislation: If a legislative campaign were made into a board game, it would be ten times more complicated than any other. Legislative change requires the most people, time, energy and other resources to achieve. Because of the complex procedures of most law-making bodies, the large number of government officials involved and the length of legislative sessions, getting legislative change is extremely difficult. Snags can surface everywhere, so the process can be frustrating and disillusioning. Hence the humorous admonition repeated by many advocates, "Never watch sausage or laws being made." Massachusetts is similar to other states; fewer than 10 percent of the bills filed every session get passed.

"Be prepared for the long haul," NETWORK's How to Organize says. "Many of the problems we seek to alleviate legislatively . . . have been with us for centuries and will take years to eradicate. The legislative process is slow and often frustrating, so our expectations must be geared accordingly."

Litigation: Litigation differs from negotiation and legislation because a legal expert is necessary. The group directs, advises and helps the expert prepare, but does not actually carry out the campaign in the courtroom. Litigation can be expensive, although there are ways to avoid expensive legal fees. Like legislation, court action can take a long time as it goes through various steps and delays in the judicial system. Court proceedings are fairly much out of advocates' control. A court ruling is very official, recorded policy, unless and until it's changed on appeal.

When? Timing

When to pursue a goal depends on the issue, the strategy and the political climate. The organization decides when it has accomplished enough research and gathered enough people and information to move. In addition, government processes and procedures will affect when the action proceeds.

After the strategy is decided, the management group develops a flexible calendar that spells out specific actions to be taken at various steps along the way.

Step 4: Carry Out Strategies

At this step, knowing the goal and having mapped out a plan, advocates carry out that actual strategies on the course to success. Throughout Step 4, the management group watches very carefully. If a snag develops or an unexpected change occurs in the situation, the group may have to go back to Step 3 and revise the plan. Every policy campaign has two strategy components—education and either negotiation, legislation or litigation. (See chapters Nine and Ten about methods for carrying out strategies.)

Education

Education of the public, members of the group who will actually carry out the action, and of government is half of every strategy. The public needs to know exactly what the group wants and why. People need to know what they can do to bring about change.

Education about the policy goal is the foundation of all campaigns for change. And that means rapid, meaningful communication—in writing and speech. Education about the goal is usually done against a backdrop of ongoing general education advocates conduct all the time.

In general, educational activities are geared up at the launch of the campaign, at various high points (hearings, court sessions, meetings, votes) and, finally, at the resolution of the issue at Step 5.

The Big Three

At Step 4 advocates come to a three-pronged fork in the road where they focus on carrying out one of three specific tactics. Each specific goal for policy change is matched with one major strategy at a time: negotiation, legislation or litigation.

Negotiation: Negotiation is probably practiced the most and talked about the least. In advocacy, negotiation refers to communication between advocates and government officials who have the power to change things directly through their offices. Negotiation may be in meetings or in official hearings when regulations are being formulated.

Government officials involved in negotiation are usually members of the executive branch who work for departments, agencies and commissions at all government levels. Sessions with elected executives—mayor, governor, president—their cabinet members and their staffs are considered negotiations. Dealings with legislators are not considered negotiations, per se, because individual legislators do not have the power to officially change policy by themselves.

Negotiation is an extremely important strategy because it is used to affect how existing public policy is carried out and how money is distributed. Government regulations—policies developed by the executive branch to implement laws—can only be affected by the negotiation strategy.

The suggestion that a group plans to pursue legislation or litigation sometimes precipitates negotiation that results in the desired change.

Legislation: Legislation is the strategy most people think of when they think of policy change. "How a Bill Becomes a Law" is a common chapter in many civics textbooks. To get a new law enacted, to change an old one, and, sometimes, to get permanent funding, advocates stage a legislative campaign at city, state or national levels. Occasionally they stop proposed laws they don't want.

In addition to work with legislatures, advocates also get laws passed by the public in a referendum on the ballot. This process—the only one where citizens vote directly on policy—is used when advocates believe their elected representatives are not responding properly to public desires.

Litigation: Litigation—the strategy that corresponds to the judicial branch of government—is practiced when advocates believe existing laws and regulations are not being followed or are being applied incorrectly or are in conflict with other laws. Litigation is usually the last resort after negotiations with officials don't bring about change.

Part of the initial stages of pursuing a lawsuit involve deciding to which court the case can and should be brought. Planning the litigation strategy often requires consulting a legal expert in order to know just how the case might proceed, so the advocacy group can make final decisions and choose methods.

Step 5: Follow Through

The bill is now law. The judge has issued a ruling. The administration has agreed to change its ways. At Step 5, advocates pause, shift gears and continue with the campaign. If advocates stopped at this point, without following through, all the work they did on education and legislation, negotiation or litigation at Step 4 would be in jeopardy.

At Step 5 advocates evaluate the results of carrying out the strategy. If they succeeded, they tell the public and people directly affected. They also monitor the policy to make sure it is carried out in future government actions.

Evaluating the Results

It's fairly easy to tell if a particular policy change strategy was successful or not. When there has been a victory, advocates have to do a lot more work. Even a loss is not a loss, when advocates seize the opportunity to learn from it. The same small management group that took the policy through the first four steps of the campaign oversees the last one.

The LWV booklet on program planning says, "Reaching a goal . . . can take a very long time. Be sure to evaluate the campaign's successes and shortcomings. . . . The results of such an appraisal, whether or not the League succeeded, can assist in designing a better, more sophisticated effort the next time."

Barbara Reed said victories advocates achieved in getting the Women, Infants, and Children nutrition program established and functioning created the climate for more wins. "There were measurable successes," she said. "It's one program that has not been severely cut back. It's a program that is generally well regarded. . . . It provides benefits to people."

After a victory, according to the OWL Organizing Manual, advocates should "make it a cardinal rule to thank those who made it possible. It doesn't hurt either to write to those who may have voted against it — a brief, kindly note of regret that we were unable to adequately communicate our needs but hope to work with him/her in the future on other issues of concern to older women."

According to a NETWORK handout, "NETWORK occasionally does enjoy a victory, and when that happens, the national staff is sure to have a party to celebrate! Frequently, the party will include other groups with whom we've worked in coalition on the issue. The positive spirit and sense of solidarity generated at these celebrations are enough to sustain us as we begin our next project."

What if the court didn't rule favorably? The bill never passed. Negotiations broke down, and the administration went back to its old ways. It happens, and it happens to the best. If advocates quit every time a campaign didn't work, there would be no advocates today.

Step 5, for an unsuccessful campaign, is a time for intense learning, and the management group, along with the organization or coalition, reviews all the previous steps to see what did and did not work. (See Chapter Thirteen for tips on what may have gone wrong.) It is also a very sensitive time for the group.

Getting the Word Out

A policy victory is not worth much if no one notices. Advocates, who are used to doing education at every other step, once again let everyone from the inside out know about the outcome of the policy campaign. Communication at this stage serves two critical purposes: directly helping people and nailing down the policy in the public mind. It also, of course, brings positive attention to the winners.

The most important people who hear about the new policy are those who will be most affected—the constituents for the issue who benefit from the change. Advocates work very hard to see that constituents for the issue learn about and understand policies that affect them.

Advocates make sure the general public knows about policy changes, too. There are several reasons, aside from pure pride, for advocates to shout about their victories. First, they want to identify more people who might benefit from them, in order to inform them of what they are entitled to. Second, they want to chalk up the victory in the public mind as extra insurance that it will get implemented. Third, they want to build clout for the organization and the importance of the issue itself, so next time the public and government will know more and perhaps look more favorably on similar issues.

Articles: When Focus:HOPE won a huge settlement from the American Automobile Association (AAA) for practicing discrimination, the advocacy group went to great lengths to get media attention, partially because beneficiaries of the class action suit—approximately 12,000 workers—had to be informed. Of an award of about $5.35 million, $1.5 million was especially earmarked to subsidize low-interest mortgage and auto loans to blacks forced to move from Detroit to Dearborn to keep their jobs. The remaining money was to be paid to the 12,000 black plaintiffs in the suit.

Gini Laurie said of the *Rehabilitation Gazette*, "We comb the Rehabilitation Act of 1973 and study it and get it down to the bare bones, so people know exactly what they are entitled to. I give information out on the laws and regulations. Then I get people to write articles about them.

"For instance, I found out that some people who are disabled had counted their work while they were disabled to earn disability payments. So I put that experience in. Got them to write it in their own words that could get themselves two or three years' credit towards disability while reporting their earnings while they were disabled."

Using straightforward language in the *Gazette* helps people understand policy. "I've got a quad who works for Social Security," Laurie said, "to translate Social Security–ese into plain English and write it with case histories, so that people could relate to it. So readers know all the Social Security laws. I keep track of everything that is current."

Telephone: When a federal court in California said that residents didn't have to allow housing inspectors into their homes in Des Moines, Brenda LaBlanc and others began calling their neighbors. "We called a lot of people who are renting houses—people who are satisfied with the way things are and where there's reasonably low rent. We called them and told them they have the right not to let anyone in. It isn't just people who own their own homes who have that right. So we're able to prevent the city from condemning some rental properties, too."

Conferences: "In the community of Magnoli," said Arkansas CLU Director Sandra Kurjiaka, "the women were having some problems. The sheriff's department has a trained guard group that rode about on their horses and they rode in rodeos and this sort of thing. They wouldn't allow women into the sheriff's horse guard or whatever they called it. It was a men-only kind of thing."

A call from a woman who was upset about that alerted Kurjiaka that women there didn't know much about their legal rights in general. "We talked about not only what you might be able to do about that but also what we might be able to do in general in the community.

"Some of the women were amazed when they found out they could have their own names on their checks. So we did a conference down there—a one-day thing dealing with race and sex discrimination, almost kindergarten stuff. We identified what illegal discrimination is. What things that have been remedied. Just that basic information. We told them about civil rights laws and what they can do about them. What things are illegal discrimination. What we found was tremendous ignorance. People don't know they have rights, let alone begin to do something about it."

Flyers: Diane Roach and the St. Paul Indian Center distribute a lot of flyers. "Adoption Subsidy in Minnesota," published by the Department of Public Welfare, tells people how laws that offer subsidies work. Another flyer Roach passed out tells about a new law and new rights for adopted people and their birth parents.

Monitoring the New Policy

Monitoring a policy change success is an important activity, because court rulings, new laws and administrative decisions are especially vulnerable to action that might erase—or improve them. By continuing their involvement after the win, advocates ensure that the policy isn't reversed, build on the win and see that the policy is implemented correctly.

Mexican American women have achieved policy victories in Texas, so they do a lot of monitoring. "We used to be much more structured and used to have a monitor at every meeting," Martha Cotera said. "We don't do that anymore because we have people involved in the process who monitor the different issues. We have more people on these boards and commissions who let us know what's happening.

"Now we monitor issues instead of meetings. It's much better to track issues. For example, we have certain people that are interested in bilingual [education] who track that. We have somebody from the hospital who naturally keeps us informed and involved about health issues. People interested in affirmative action track that. It works a lot better issue by issue."

After the clothing allowance bill for welfare children made it through the Massachusetts legislature one year, advocates were able to build on the success to get the bill expanded.

"We had set the amount per child very low—fifty dollars per year," Janet Diamond recalled of the first bill. "We went back the next year to put it through again, but that was OK because we had our foot in the door already. By then it had a track record. It would be something they would have to take away from people the next year.

We got seventy-five dollars per child the next year. Then the next year Michael Dukakis became governor and he adopted the cause as his own. He upped it to one hundred twenty-five dollars when it was supposed to go to one hundred dollars. Now it's a permanent law in existence more than five years, and it would be unthinkable to pull it out now."

New policy, whether in the form of a regulation, administrative decision, law or court ruling, must be implemented correctly in order to be effective. After the decision, the policy often goes to another branch of government, usually the executive. Monitoring is necessary as the policy enters the new arena. If signs of trouble appear, advocates have to mount another campaign.

Monitoring administrative decisions: Negotiated policy change— including regulations—runs the highest risk of not being implemented if the results are not broadcast widely. Advocates who obtain a victory using negotiation take measures to be sure agreements are implemented.

At the conclusion of a successful negotiation session an accountability meeting is often scheduled, so the group can talk to the administration to be sure agreements are being lived up to. If all is well, the group has its victory party.

After the last session with administrators, many advocates send a letter of confirmation listing the agreements reached and the date, time and place for the accountability meeting.

Monitoring new laws: Usually, legislation goes to the executive branch for implementation, where regulations are proposed for carrying it out.

"We are working on setting up a citizens committee on earning sharing—the concept that the combined earning of husband and wife during the marriage should be divided equally and shared between them for Social Security benefits purposes," Tish Sommers said of an OWL monitoring activity.

"A bill that was just passed in Congress mandated the Department of Health and Human Services (HHS) to come up with ways to implement earning sharing. But we cannot leave it to the current administration to both monitor the activities of HHS and to make sure the law is not implemented at the expense of women.

"Earnings sharing has been around as a concept for a long time and could address some of the fundamental problems women have with the Social Security system. However, it could also be implemented in such a way that it could turn out to be a Social Security cost-cutting measure. Therefore, we're very interested in seeing that doesn't happen."

When the clothing allowance bill for welfare children passed the Massachusetts legislature (see Chapter Seven), Janet Diamond said, "The Welfare department didn't like it, but it was law. That's the advantage of going for the legislative change versus the regulatory change. The welfare department had no choice. They said they were worried about how this was going to impact their error rate and setting up the computer system to put it in place.

"There were a million little details to follow up on. We had to meet with the implementers and have them put their cards on the table. Find out their concerns. We offered our help. We put out fact sheets on eligibility so they could cut down on their error rate. We didn't want them to testify the next time the budget came up that the clothing allowance jumped their error rate one point or something. That would kill it."

Barbara Reed said of follow-up to legislation that WIC advocates got through, "We were very successful in expanding participation and in improving the overall operations of the program. We made the people who ran the program accountable for what they were doing. The advocates did the monitoring. We knew the people we were monitoring — the people who administer the programs — and they knew we had a constituency. I don't think people pay that much attention to you if you do not have a constituency."

Federal laws that must be applied on the state or local level need special vigilance. "Monitoring to see if Minnesota complies with the Federal Indian Child Welfare Act is one of the key parts of my job," Diane Roach said of her work at the St. Paul American Indian Center. "Monitoring the courts is very important because one of the things we want to start doing is have these Indian children become aware of their heritage.

"The counties and the state have to notify the tribe to find out if the child is of Indian heritage. If the child is enrolled with an Indian tribe or if they're not enrolled and they are eligible for enrollment, it puts a whole different aspect on the proceedings.

"Now when a tribe is notified of a court action, the court transfers jurisdiction so the tribe can take control of the case itself, or the tribe can intervene. When a tribe can't come down for a hearing, they write a letter asking me to appear. Then I make my report to them. They go according to my recommendations usually."

Monitoring court decisions: One issue Common Cause lobbyist Kathleen Sheekey worked on at the U.S. Congress was to try to stop "court stripping" bills that would serve to "overturn Supreme Court decisions in the areas of abortion, school prayer, busing, social issues—the Jesse Helms bills. We got quite involved in that congressional battle, because we thought they were trying to circumvent the process. If you want to overturn a Supreme Court decision you need to amend the constitution, not pass a bill by majority vote of Congress."

In the Focus:HOPE/AAA lawsuit settlement, the court agreed to monitor the AAA's compliance with an affirmative action program for eight years. That program called for the company to hire blacks for 50 percent of all clerical job openings in Detroit, 15 percent out of state, 23 percent of professional/technical job openings and 13–15 percent of all management openings.

The League of Women Voters warns, "Be prepared to monitor the court order in the suit. The court will issue an order directing the parties to take certain action in accordance with its ruling in the case. If, as a party to a lawsuit, you have reason to believe that an opposing party is not in full compliance with the court's order, you may, through your attorney, petition the court to find the noncomplying party in contempt of court."

Chapter Nine

Education: The Policy Change Power Tool

I think we should congratulate Congress for funding the WIC program. But we should also congratulate all the people across the country who continue to remind Congress of the need for it.

—Stefan Harvey

"Information is power," as the saying goes, so advocates do a lot of public education as they conduct policy campaigns. Carrying out the strategies — Step 4 — always includes educating the public and members of all groups.

Specific education about policy goals during a campaign is built on general public education about the issues that advocates conduct over time.

Creating the Atmosphere for Change

General education is the one activity that does not have a specific place in the campaign sequence. Advocates constantly spread information about their issues.

Some organizations — the Civil Liberties Union and the Mental Health Association, for example — state that public education is one of their main reasons for existence. These groups and others work to increase public awareness of problems and solutions as an ongoing consciousness-raising device. That way the stage is always set for the specific issues campaigns connected to particular policies.

Teaching

One way advocates create an atmosphere for change is by teaching. Norma Wilson uses her classroom not only to teach literature but also to increase the social awareness of her South Dakota students.

"I'm teaching people primarily of European ancestry about Native Americans and about their own traditional oral literature, which was the first literature of North America. I'm teaching them about Native American concepts of land.

"Freshman composition is a course for people just coming into college. It's an important time to reach those students, to shake them up a little bit, to show them some other ways of looking at the world different from the way they have been brought up, to open their eyes. This a real isolated place."

In Ohio, Connie Spruill worked in grade school programs to educate kids about women in construction. "Part of our whole problem," she said, "is that women have been programmed from the time they were born that construction is not what you do. Little girls don't play with trucks; they are supposed to play with dolls. If we had started many moons ago and switched it around, the little boys would be playing with dolls and the girls would be out there building the buildings. It's just the way our society has programmed each person.

"So we're out to re-program. We've started here at the grade school level to introduce them to all the things that girls can do besides be a nurse. We have some local programs that the women in construction go to and speak. We speak in the elementary schools all the way up to high school."

Public Speeches

Speakers bureaus are a common device for spreading information about issues. The League of Women Voters brochure on establishing speakers bureaus says, "A well-presented speech can raise the public's consciousness — or conscience — about an issue."

The Mental Health Association of South Carolina (MHASC), in "Reaching the Public," describes speakers in its bureau: "Their special talent is the ability to move others to think and act. They are agitators in the best sense. They are concerned with public attitudes and motivations as well as the giving of factual information on mental health and mental illness." The bureau fills engagements to speak, and provides discussion leaders and panelists to all sorts of groups in a variety of settings.

Printed Information

Organizations publish brochures, fact sheets and leaflets to distribute to the public just to inform them about current problems. The National Organization for Women, for example, puts out brochures on various issues that affect women. Although there is always a form at the end people can fill out if they want to join NOW, the primary purpose of the brochures is general education.

A brochure distributed in 1984 called "Women's Rights, Reagan's Wrongs" detailed administration policies in areas such as employment, health and foreign policy that NOW felt were detrimental to women.

The *Rehabilitation Gazette* was the major advocacy work of Gini Laurie. The international journal for disabled individuals provides education not only to disabled readers but also to many professional and government people.

The OWL newsletter devoted more than five pages in two issues in 1983 to an in-depth analysis of how the Reagan budget affects older women. Entitled "Inequality of Sacrifice," it covered topics from health to jobs. Designed only to enlighten readers, neither the article nor the newsletter contained a specific hook, suggesting actions an informed reader might take on the issue.

The News Media

Tish Sommers, in the OWL Organizing Manual, wrote, "News leads to attention, leads to changes in the climate, leads to making reform possible." The media—both print and electronic—are very useful for conveying general information about issues.

Carol Garvin described an MHASC media education program: "We did a ten-minute radio show about common emotional problems every week for maybe a year. The shows are still running. It's a good way to reach people.

"We had a conversation rather than an interview. I wrote a script and then, if some of the other chapters wanted to use either the script or the tape, they could take their choice. I wrote about fifty-two, and then I ran out of time. It was a lot of work but it was fun.

"The station owner said to me one day, 'Do you realize we're reaching ten thousand people with this program?' I was floored! I thought, well, if half of them turned me off, I'd still reach five thousand, which is wonderful. It did impress me with how many people you can reach with the radio with comparably little effort."

Homemade Educational Tools

Advocacy groups create their own educational devices—videos, books and demonstrations to make the climate fertile for change. Focus:HOPE in Detroit produced a video, "Broken Promise," about the consequences of growing old and hungry in that city. The organization has its own video issues education program. It took the group four months and $22,000 to make "Broken Promise."

The *Rehabilitation Gazette* sponsored the Second International Post Polio Conference and Symposium on Living Independently with Severe Disability. It educated disabled people, the professionals who attended and the entire St. Louis community. Gini Laurie, the *Gazette*'s publisher, also write a book, *Housing and Home Services for the Disabled*, which received wide review.

Although most public events are specifically used to getting attention for a specific policy campaign, sometimes demonstrations and other events are held to keep the issue fresh in people's minds. On the 10th anniversary of the Supreme Court's ruling upholding women's rights to abortion, dozens of Boston organizations joined NOW in a widely publicized "Rally for Abortion Rights." Anniversaries and observances like Gay Pride Week, which brought out more than 50 for speeches and a rally in Arkansas, give advocacy groups a reason to do public education about their issues in general.

Homemade Devices Plus Media Attention

As if the devices mentioned above were not educational enough in themselves, all of them got media attention. These days, many educational efforts benefit from a double whammy: the device itself is educational, and if the media cover it, the effect is even greater.

"Broken Promise" was shown on a local television channel, then positively reviewed in the *Detroit Free Press*, where the sad information about the plight of the city's elderly was repeated.

The *Rehabilitation Gazette* conference generated newspaper articles and a ten-minute feature about polio survivors on "Sunday Morning with Charles Kuralt" on CBS. This further increased the span of Gini and Joe Laurie's general public education efforts.

Of course, public events draw lots of media attention. The gay rights and pro-choice rallies were covered on television and in the daily papers. In the past, these demonstrations were directed toward members of the public who might view them in person; nowadays they are almost always held for the prime purpose of getting media attention.

Focusing Facts on a Policy Goal

After the public has gotten lots of backgroud information on the issue over time, specific goal-oriented education is critical at Step 4.

The strategy the group has chosen — negotiation, legislation or litigation — is unrelated to which education methods they use to back it up. Education techniques work well in combination with any of the three alternate strategies.

When advocates focus the facts on the goal, they educate the public, their members and pertinent government officials about the policy specifics and the strategy being used. After the policy change goal has been achieved, education continues to be a vital part of the campaign in Step 5 as advocates make sure everyone knows what has happened (see Chapter Eight).

Carol Garvin summarized the education part of a campaign for national legislation. "First you get some data. Then you tie it to local conditions so your congressman will see the relevance to their districts. Then you get your people to understand, so they contact their representative."

As advocates carry out specific strategies at Step 4, the education campaign goes on simultaneously. In general, educational activities are timed to match two steps in the strategy: the launch of the campaign, high points (hearings, court sessions, meetings, final decisions) and the result.

Information from research at Step 2 and the position statement drawn up at Step 3 in the campaign are very useful when it comes to educate people, especially officials.

Stefan Harvey explained the differences between communications with government officials, advocates and constituents. "In written materials to congressional staff people and people at the Department of Agriculture," she said, "we communicated differently than we did with readers in the newsletter. Not only were things written in a different style, but also different information was provided.

"It was a subject of great debate at the Children's Foundation," Harvey added, "if the publications we sent out to WIC participants were written as they should have been. Publications specifically for the participants were written differently from the WIC newsletter that we sent to advocates and administrators across the country. The question was, how do you communicate in writing with people with limited reading skills? We tried to use oral communication with participants, and I think we were successful."

Galvanizing the Public

The methods advocates use to get information to the public about their specific goals are often innovative. Advocates use the media, speakers, printed material—the same devices used to do general education—to get attention for specific policy campaign goals.

"Using the Media to Work an Issue" is the title of one section of the OWL Organizing Manual, and that's just what advocates do. The League of Women Voters Action manual says, "In taking action, PR [public relations], particularly press coverage [because it generates clippings that can be copied and used], plays an integral role in letting the community know . . . what you want." The manual goes on to say that use of public relations techniques gives "even the most recalcitrant public officials pause when they know that your point of view is reaching the voters."

"Suppose your [OWL] chapter has decided to work for passage of a health insurance rights act," Sommers suggested. "The key times for exposure area: introduction of the bill, hearing in committee, vote by the legislature. But continuing exposure will be needed to mobilize pressure all along the way. Media coverage will be crucial."

Advocates develop media timetables to coincide with major events in negotiation and litigation. Sommers went on to describe a press conference, feature stories on affected women, talk shows with legislators and women, regular news releases (each with a specific news hook), and a collection of facts, figures and case histories of women around the state.

"A major tool we used is media," said Janet Ferone of the ERA campaign. "I've been doing public relations for the past two years for the Boston chapter of NOW. A lot of that involves getting on talk shows, getting on TV programs, and using the newspaper to talk about the ERA. We tried local angles—Mass. residents go to Utah, etc. We had an ERA Awareness Week where we ran ads giving the text of the amendment."

Carol Garvin reported: "The director and I have made a few helpful media contacts. For instance, last year when we were talking about the disability issue he was on one of the Columbia [South Carolina] television stations and I was on another telling people about the problem. I was also on a radio program, and we were interviewed by a reporter from the state's largest newspaper. The reporter wrote a very good article which was then picked up by the AP and was in papers all over the state."

Stefan Harvey spread the word about WIC through media contacts in Washington, D.C. "Once the major networks became interested in WIC and we got our first five-minute piece on it, the next time the subject came up and we needed to use the press as part of our lobbying effort, we could always pick up the telephone and talk with the press people, because we already had a relationship with them," she said. "We've always used the press as extensively as we could."

Letters to the editors of local newspapers "can be an effective tool for calling public attention to key issues," Nancy Sylvester of NETWORK pointed out.

It sometimes pays to advertise. Although the League of Women Voters is usually very non-controversial, according to Dorothy Ridings, the group took an ad to promote passage of the Clean Air Act in Congress. "The member of Congress from the Cincinnati area was a key pressure point," she remembered. "He was doing some things we disagreed with. We had tried our usual approaches to him on the Hill, through his staff, through one person in Cincinnati and through our state League in Ohio. He was opposed to the Clean Air Act. We felt his constituents would not agree with him if they really knew what his position was.

"So, in order to give broader exposure to his stand, we ran ads in the Cincinnati area newspapers saying, 'Congressman Lucas, we disagree with you, and we think your constituents do, too, and here's why.' We ran a little tear-out clip-and-mail thing with it. There was a tremendous response." (See Chapter Eleven.)

Common Cause used the same technique. It paid to put two open letters in the Tennessee and Washington state newspapers to congressmen Gore and Dix, appealing to them to reverse their votes on the MX missile, according to Kathleen Sheekey, because "they were two of the leaders of the effort to go along with the administration."

"Generally, most [officials] don't want their stuff in the papers," Sandra Kurjiaka stated. "The anti-gay resolution—the man who introduced it, Dowd, said in the committee hearings, 'Listen, I didn't expect all this fuss and publicity. I just wanted to quietly pass this.'

"And that's what it's really all about. They [officials] just want to do their business and be left alone. And when you can get the press to look at what they are doing, that can have tremendous impact."

Kathleen Sheekey described two more common media devices Common Cause used at a crucial juncture of the MX debate. Letters to the editor were written by members in districts of swing Congress members. And the group sent out a press release listing how legislators had already voted on previous nuclear freeze issues, pointing out that they voted for the MX and reversed their positions.

Another technique, called "actualities," has also proved effective. Sheekey gave an example: "If you were the chair of Common Cause of Massachusetts, I could tape a 30- or 60-second spot for radio distribution asking [then House Speaker] Tip O'Neil's friends to turn him around on this issue, and then we would phone it in to the radio stations and ask them if they are doing an MX story this weekend.

"Actualities aren't PSAs. They're a little more actual. But it's not a paid radio ad either. It's more like an interview. It's worked quite well. We've done it in three key districts in the last week, and most radio stations are eager to take it. In Maine, we had Archibald Cox, our national chairman, do the actualities as a summer resident of Maine."

In court cases, the media is also used often, but media coverage has to be carefully planned. Sally Mead said she and others working on the Carolyn Brown case "did not want to publicize it too much. If there's a lot of information out, that can prejudice a jury. Then they might need to move the trial."

Carol Tucker Foreman said that when she was in the Carter administration she had "access to editorial boards of television and newspapers. I spent a great deal of time in nineteen seventy-nine going from one city to another trying to get editorials that, if they didn't favor food stamps, at least did not attack them. I appeared on television shows to tell why the food stamp program had grown so much."

Advocates can exploit media coverage of public events. "I'd say the best, not the most outlandish, but the most fun thing we've done, was gathering one million signatures against James Watt," said Betsy Reifsnider of the L.A. Sierra Club. "At the local level we had a big party at Olivira Street. We stacked up all the petitions that were gathered in Southern California. We invited the news media and had a big party. We had lots happening and we had a band. Some of the local legislators came to the party. Then they trucked all the petitions to the train station for delivery to Washington and took off."

The main purpose of most public events is getting media attention. Lois Gibbs calls these public demonstrations "direct action." "The media is a very important part of any action. Alert the media a few days in advance.

"Actions should always be fun," she said. "They should clearly express the facts of your issue and tell the world how you feel about them."

Public demonstrations are useful at any step of a campaign. Sandra Kurjiaka and the CLU of Arkansas used a rally as a public education tool at a different stage in the process. "In nineteen eighty-one," she remembered, "there was an anti-gay resolution introduced in the state legislature. I got a phone call asking me to come and testify against it."

In June 1982, a headline of the *Arkansas Gazette* read, "Gays Proclaim Pride, Resolve at Capitol Rally." At the rally, sponsored in part by the Civil Liberties Union, "only a few participants wore paper bags on their head," the article stated. Several people were quoted, including Kurjiaka who "chastised homosexuals for remaining silent when the state's sodomy law was enacted in 1977."

The event received a great deal of media attention in Arkansas. "It was exciting," Kurjiaka commented, "because it was the first time we got people out. The papers kept saying there were fifty or sixty, but there were one hundred fifty folks out. It's a very closeted non-political community here.

"People still ask us, 'Is it OK if I do that? I feel real chicken because my father is going to lose his job. He's a minister, and if everybody sees me he'll lose his job.'

"Right. In Arkansas he sure would. Anyway, this year when they introduced the annual anti-gay resolution, the room was full. And there were hundreds of letters and phone calls from all over the state. It was wonderful!"

OWL chapters all over the country got involved in various "Motherhood and Apple Pie" actions in 1983, designed to call attention to women's rights to Social Security. Rosemary Bizzell of the Southern Indiana Chapter gave this description of their protest outside the local Social Security office to the "OWL Observer," May, 1983:

> We really had a fantastic time! About twelve members participated, and we had terrific press coverage with an advance story in the New Albany paper and a large feature story on the front page of the Indiana section of the Louisville Courier-Journal. The NBC station used it . . . and CBS carried it the following night.
>
> The people in the SS office were very supportive. We didn't bake pies—we bought day-old ones and told everyone we didn't have time to bake pies any more.

Then-president of OWL Tish Sommers said the events were "media oriented and got a lot of publicity. Now since the passage of the social security legislation, the problem is no longer in the news."

Thirty members of Citizens for Community Improvement protested at the 1981 meeting of the Iowa Power stockholders, while other members participated in Commerce Commission hearings on a requested rate hike. The result? Iowa Power was ordered to refund $10 million to customers.

"The ERA Countdown Campaign was very successful in organizing rallies in a lot of different states," Janet Ferone reported. "Rallies are a real visible way to get people in tune with the issue."

"The Washington, D.C., League stationed members outside the main post office to buttonhole hundreds of last-minute taxpayers filing their nineteen seventy-six returns . . ." according to the League Action manual. "Picketers with signs asking for full voting representation for the nation's capital were covered by four television stations, eight radio stations and the major TV networks."

Demonstrations don't have to feature people. Cows can also participate. When there were a lot of legal attacks being made in the courts against the administration of food programs, Carol Tucker Foreman said the Consumer Federation "got together with a bunch of cattlemen from South Dakota and brought one hundred head of cattle from South Dakota to Washington and put them on the Mall to try to emphasize that farmers who had made good profits in nineteen seventy-three and seventy-four were really having hard times by nineteen seventy-five thru seventy-six. Consumer prices hadn't dropped, but farm prices had."

A conference can serve as a public event that interests media in policy campaigns, too. When Lois Gibbs and 700 other people gathered to mount a campaign against toxic chemicals, they received heavy television and newspaper coverage. Speakers announced a "bill of rights" that would be introduced as laws to protect the environment. They also described an upcoming lobbying effort that would extend from every congressional district to Washington.

Kattie Portis and medical professionals testified before Congress about the horrible effects babies suffer when they are born addicted to heroin because of their mothers' addiction. They were trying to win increased funding for programs for women addicts. Many newspapers picked up on the story, thereby spreading the information even further.

Sometimes advocates use brochures to alert the public to specific issues. Sally Mead helped the Carolyn Brown legal fund put together a "Position Paper" in brochure form to explain the obstetrician's legal case against the right-to-life group who called her a "baby killer" for advocating free choice in abortion. At the end, as most of advocates' specific educational tools do, the brochure suggested ways the public can help, including calling a number to volunteer, contributing money, speaking to legislators, writing to newspapers on the subject and talking to friends and neighbors (the latter being educational tools themselves).

"I think at the bottom of everything," Sally Mead said of Carolyn Brown's lawsuit, "is that education is probably the most important issue for her.

"We're going to have a booth at the fair this summer. We hope to present a lot of literature and information and be available for people who would like to discuss abortion rights."

Informing Constituents So They Can Help

In addition to educating the public, advocates make special efforts to inform group members and other constituents about their policy change goals. Members, after all, are the people who will actually work to bring about the change.

Elected government officials and administrations are primarily concerned with counting votes and money, so advocates teach sympathetic voters about the policy campaign and how they can help.

Information About Campaign Goals

"Members want to be where the action is," the LWV points out in "In League." "Besides encouraging member involvement in the study phase of an issue, the [management group] should provide ways for members to 'get in on the action' once a position is reached. In planning any action strategy, the board should identify specific areas of the plan which can be carried out by members directly and which utilize 'member power' effectively. Managing elements . . . in this way enables members to experience participation firsthand."

"Send for more information," is a hook used to get constituents more directly involved in processing a specific issue. Sometimes, along with the information, advocates provide a sharper hook by suggesting a specific action the person can take in the campaign. The direct hook is necessary to get help from those people the advocates feel are sufficiently prepared to express themselves on the specific issue.

Carol Garvin of the Mental Health Association said, "We do a lot of alerting of our people in lots of different ways to issues on these occasions and asking them to something specific."

Newsletters and special bulletins: The Citizens Clearinghouse for Hazardous Wastes "Action Bulletin" usually contains all three elements of constituent education about advocacy campaigns: information, offers of information, and directions for what the reader can do.

The "Action Bulletin" is a subscription newsletter, one of several regular publications from CCHW that contain updates on various issues campaigns.

"The first phase of CCHW's campaign to phase out land disposal of hazardous waste and the phase-in of positive alternatives is beginning this week. Check your mailbox or call for action on the national landfill moratorium. As a first step, we are asking you to send a postcard to EPA Administrator William Ruckelshous and President Reagan asking them to follow their own demands on us — stop being emotional and take the lead from the scientists . . . ."

The November 1983 "Action Bulletin" says, "The next two phases of the campaign will include: model resolutions you can work to enact at the local, county and state level modeled on legislation that has already been passed by the state of California and suggestions for church sermons and pastoral messages that we suggest you take to your local and statewide church organizations for adoption. . . . You'll be getting a lot of mail from us over the next few months on these efforts and we're asking you all to do what you can to help. . . . Contact us if you need more information."

CCHW later topped itself by issuing a general sign-up sheet for an entire year, asking people to indicate what sorts of things they would be willing to do for legislative and negotiation campaigns.

The Center for Budget and Policy Priorities in the nation's capital sends out a mailing for which it charges a subscription fee. These mailings contain extensive updates for WIC administrators and advocates about pending

federal legislation, regulations and other administrative actions affecting
WIC (Women, Infants and Children's nutrition program) nationwide. Like
the "Action Bulletin," sometimes the newsletter gives information, sometimes it offers more and often it suggests actions readers should take.

This example comes from the WIC newsletter from Stefan Harvey's
group, the Center for Budget and Policy Priorities, October 12, 1983: "The
U.S. Conference of Mayors Forms Its Own Task Force on Joblessness and
Hunger." After detailing which mayors are on the task force and what the
group's purposes are, the newsletter advises, "WIC advocates and administrators in these cities should contact their mayors and let him or her
know the benefits of the WIC program and the degree to which WIC is
unable to meet the total need in the community."

Carol Garvin of the Mental Health Association of South Carolina said,
"Our director sends out an excellent newsletter giving our viewpoint, especially on state legislative issues. It also says, 'and this is what we'd like you
to do.' Sometimes, if we're in a hurry, we send out a particular notice.

"It's really important to get in touch with people. And to use a lot of
different ways," she pointed out. "We've got a newspaper we send out to
members every quarter besides the legislative newsletter."

Although many of the materials advocacy organizations distribute offer
general information about issues, some are useful in specific campaigns.
OWL puts out a "Respite Care Packet," for example, that includes commen-
tary, analysis and a model state bill members can use for state advocacy
campaigns on the respite care issue.

NETWORK, the Catholic social justice lobby, puts out a long newsletter labelled by the congressional session at the time. "NETWORK News
Review" describes issues of interest currently before Congress and sometimes asks for member action.

Its May-June 1983 issue, in the legislative update on Central America,
says, as many of the updates do, "The NETWORK staff continues to dialogue
with legislators. Members are urged to keep concern for El Salvador before
their representatives and senators."

The Sierra Club newsletter, according to Betsy Reifsnider, always tells
what legislation is hot and "what readers can do to bring pressure on their
representatives. On the state level we get a publication called 'the Planning
and Conservation Lands Lobbying Network.' It lists every single bill and
where it is [at] any time in the state legislature. It gives background on each
bill, with who supports it and who opposes it." For information on federal
legislation, the Sierra Club has a 24-hour Washington hot line.

Common Cause issues action alerts. Kathleen Sheekey said, "In the
case of the MX vote, we sent a first-class mailing to every Common Cause
member in a hundred key districts, asking them to write to their representatives."

Phone calls and fax machines: Advocates talk frequently on the phone with constituents during Step 4 of the process, letting them know what's happening and suggesting actions to take, no matter how things are going. Sometimes an unexpected event occurs, forcing advocates to act speedily. The telephone is the only tool that gets the information out quickly enough for people to be able to respond.

Betsy Reifsnider of the Sierra Club said, "Most of my time is spent getting volunteers to have enough knowledge, letting them know what is happening on a given issue, putting people in touch with one another. Then it's like chemistry.

"That's what a lot of my work is," as conservation coordinator—"shuffling people together and putting them in contact with one another and giving them proper information. It's very easy for people to contact me at the office, and I, in turn, can contact them. I am a conduit and repository of information. Then I give it out to other people." The group uses a phone tree to get the word out to people quickly.

Common Cause also has telephone networks. Sheekey reported 40 to 50 volunteers in Washington "who connect with volunteers in the states."

About intervention in El Salvador, NETWORK reports in its newsletter that "the national office initiated a general phone alert to members and met with congressional staff to support the Leach-Hatfield Bill. NETWORK continues to oppose military assistance to the conflict there."

A fax is handy if many members or volunteers have them where they work. Stefan Harvey said that in her days as a child nutrition advocate in Washington, "Even after achieving many successes, we never relied any less on people across the country. In fact, it is more accurate to say we relied more on those people, because we knew who we could call, and who, in fact, could generate pressure.

"We knew we could call Georgia Mattison in Massachusetts and she would know exactly how to proceed. All we had to do was tell you what was going on in Washington.

"Similarly, across the country over the years, people came to know they could rely on us. . . . It was a very nice relationship when people who were terribly concerned knew they could be kept up to date, and we knew who was interested in lobbying."

Janet Ferone reported Boston NOW did "periodic phone banking. Groups lent us their offices—unions, companies—let us use their phones. We get on the phones with a set script. . . . Through the phone banking we urge people to contact their legislators. So we are using the phone banking to do what we really need to do—get the grassroots support out against this amendment."

Telephone trees or phone chains—systems by which members alert each other—are often used to get the word out to constituents. OWL says such methods are "one option to ensure greater member response regardless of the time element."

NETWORK uses phone chains as "the basic vehicle" to "communicate quickly about pending legislation." The chain is updated frequently, and the last person called lets the originator of the chain know it has been completed.

Letters: The Citizens Clearinghouse for Hazardous Wastes sends out letters periodically, in addition to its newsletters and bulletins. One from Lois Gibbs in 1983 describes President Reagan's latest statements and actions regarding landfills, then quotes experts on the dangers of toxic wastes in landfills. Readers were asked to send an enclosed postcard to President Reagan and EPA Administrator Ruckelshous or write letters, send copies of responses to CCHW, encourage friends to do the same and send a tax deductible donation.

Ten different advocacy organizations in Washington, D.C., including NETWORK and SANE, joined to send out an "Arms Control/Military Spending Alert" in 1983 explaining the status of legislation concerning the MX and nuclear freeze resolutions. Specific instructions followed telling people how and where to write, call or send telegrams, adding the number of the Nuclear Arms Control Hotline.

At the bottom was a tear-off slip on which recipients were to indicate which representatives and senators they would contact, whether they would ask two other people to do the same and whether they had enclosed a list of other people interested in receiving alerts. The slip also included a box to be checked to request more information.

Organization gatherings: Meetings and conferences are natural vehicles for sharing information about specific issues and enlisting the aid of people already involved.

Seven hundred people from around New England gathered to kick off a national citizen campaign against toxic chemicals in the environment. At the rally Lois Gibbs and other leaders let attendees know how to help in the policy campaign. Representatives from local, state and national environmental or citizen action groups ranged from individuals concerned about a specific toxic waste dump in their neighborhood to representatives from such national environmental groups as the Sierra Club.

Betsy Reifsnider said, "I spend most of my time between the office and going to our regional groups and various meetings to let the volunteers know what the issues are."

Kattie Portis, director of Women, Inc., belongs to the board of the Massachusetts Human Service Providers organization. "We stay on top of laws that have to do with our budget. So as we are doing research, I keep feeding it back to the staff. I do that with everything anyway, because I feel that in order to run this agency everybody should know what I know.

"I make sure that happens and I take people to different meetings with me, too. When it comes time to lobby I tell them the week before. I even tell the clients, because it's important to make them struggle a little harder, to find out that ain't nobody giving us this money."

Working on location: Gay rights advocates in Arkansas used an unusual but effective method of alerting constituents to pending anti-gay legislation. "It was exciting to get folks out," said Sandra Kurjiaka. "We did it mostly through the bars. We called the bar owners and said, 'This is what's happening.' We gave the information about the legislation and the rally to the bar owners in places like Fort Smith and Fayetteville and all around. Then they got the word out to the folks and the folks got the word out to their members that they didn't want this anti-gay legislation going on. Also we did mailing to the gay rights list."

Campaign Training and Support

Advocacy groups provide training and materials to members and constituents to help them carry out the specific tasks needed in the policy campaign. General training programs include workshops, conferences, printed how-to material, and resource lists (see Chapter Five).

In addition, the group that is managing the policy change campaign often ends up coaching constituents as they go along. Most training focuses on how to carry out legislation, rather than negotiation or litigation.

The foundation of the training includes providing support for constituents, as well as information, so they will feel comfortable and competent as they lobby their legislators.

The OWL manual assures members that although the legislative process sounds formidable, "It can all be learned. The whole of the experience with the displaced homemaker legislation was accomplished, for the most part, by rank amateurs in the political field—quick studies, though, and stubbornly committed because it dealt with their problems."

"Welfare recipients do not have a sense of entitlement—just the opposite," Janet Diamond said. "They feel guilty. They feel ashamed and embarrassed. They feel disenfranchised. They feel they're wrong.

"So a Coalition for Basic Human Needs person would go with people for the first time they went up to the hill. We'd introduce them," she said of the management group for particular legislation. "We'd make sure they had an appointment [with the legislator] and we'd introduce them to the legislator or aide."

Betsy Reifsnider said she too went occasionally with Sierra Club volunteers, "especially when people feel afraid. I will give them some background information and tell them to talk to the official with another person who has more knowledge on the issue or who had done it before, so the person who is afraid can just listen and chime in whenever they feel they can. Volunteers learn by doing."

"What we do," Connie Spruill said, "is educate the other women construction business owners on how to communicate with their legislators, how to let them know what's going on out in the field. The legislators are not being made aware of discriminatory practices, so they have no idea unless we tell them."

NETWORK sponsors weeklong legislative seminars in Washington where lectures about the congressional legislative process and tours culminate in attendees visiting their representative or aides on the Hill.

At the training session, trainers "highlight the problem of fear," Nancy Sylvester noted. "It's that sinking stomach when you walk in and see this huge desk and possibly this huge fellow sitting there.

"We do role playing before; I never send anybody up to the Hill without role playing. After they've had a chance to prepare the information, I'll role play a variety of kinds of personalities and have them present their spiel. Then when they encounter the real experience they can get through it.

"Afterwards we always do a debriefing. I think it's really important that they have a chance to hear and talk about what kind of visit they had, how they feel and what they could do differently next time. Sometimes I think people think they have to put on a different kind of air which is self-defeating. One has to be oneself and be comfortable with that."

Sometimes constituents testify before congressional committees, and other advocates coach them. Janet Diamond said constituents need "extra support because they are so scared." Many give excuses at the last minute for why they can't testify. "They say, 'Well, I don't have bus fare'—or give a million different reasons."

Kattie Portis prepares constituents to testify about program funding using role play, too. "I tell them, 'You can be strong, but you always have to be respectful.' And we do role play. 'OK, this is the committee, and this is the audience back here. Don't worry about the people in the back 'cause they are there for the same reason you are. You need to get committee members' attention. Even if you see them nodding out, say, 'Excuse me, don't you understand, I'm talking my heart out.'"

Making Government Aware

Policy campaign education efforts eventually narrow their focus to responsible government officials. Much of the communication between advocates and officials could easily be called education (see Chapter Ten).

"Certainly today you need technical information," Carol Tucker Foreman said. "Congressional staffs, no matter how large they get, are always too small to have a member of Congress informed sufficiently on all the things they should be informed about.

"Lobbying is overwhelmingly an ability to do staff work for a member of Congress, so he or she can go forth with an idea—remove the purchase requirement for food stamps, create a consumer protection agency, amend the bankruptcy laws. It's a matter of going to Congress with an idea that's backed up with a fair amount of information to show it's not crazy."

Several years ago Kattie Portis, director of Women, Inc., was asked to speak to 14 Massachusetts judges about sentencing women addicts. "One of the things that happens," she said, "is they try to set women up. Guys get an opportunity to go into treatment when they're sentenced. I think because women are parents, they leave them out there too long, until they're in real bad shape. Then the women have no place to turn.

"Then there's the female who's violent. She might hurt herself, other people or her kids. For some reason they don't do anything about those women. They send them to prison for 30 days; they don't treat them.

"A woman shows up—a dope fiend, an alcoholic—and everybody's just trying to protect her kid. There are some women who don't need to be in prison. They need to be somewhere with some resources and education. Otherwise they go back on drug charges all the time."

During the welfare rights campaign in Massachusetts, members of the Coalition for Basic Human Needs took fact sheets when they went to visit legislators, according to Janet Diamond. "We started to build our argument right away. The cost of living increase would cost $20 million, and only this much of it would reach the people, where this would cost $20 million 'but every penny of it will reach the people, so you're saving blah-blah dollars.' They liked it."

When Stefan Harvey was first hired by the Children's Foundation in the 1970s, she went to work to try to save the Commodity Supplemental Food Program, which the Department of Agriculture planned to discontinue. The group did two things to convince Congress that it should be spared the ax.

"We wrote a fairly major report," Harvey said, "which no one had ever done. I traveled and visited local programs and talked to people and put the report together. That report was then distributed to key congressional offices and a few people across the country."

The second component of the education phase was a press release, which, Harvey said, "surprisingly enough, got a fair amount of coverage. We tried to bring attention to the USDA's decision." The program was not discontinued.

Harvey accounted for the fact that the WIC program has received an increased appropriation every year since 1972 by saying, "I think they give money to WIC for two clear reasons. First, the program has worked. You read editorials and stories in the *New York Times* and the *Washington Post* about the success of this particular program. Studies have presented concrete evidence that this program works. That makes Congress vote for it—even those Congress people who think poor people are riding the shirttails of the dole.

"Second, despite the size of the program, it still cannot serve all those who are in need. As an advocate at the state, the community or on the national level, you can continue to present data to indicate there is a need. If you take that data and put it beside the research that shows WIC has some real bearing, and, if you look at what will happen to people who don't get adequate nutrition, it all adds up to a very convincing collection of information. Congress buys that.

"I think we should congratulate Congress, in part, for funding the WIC program. But we should also congratulate all the people across the country who continue to remind Congress of the need for it."

Some advocates invite government officials onto their own turf in order to educate them. "We would always urge the Planned Parenthood chapters to invite a member of Congress to come and address their annual meeting," Carol Tucker Foreman said. "The member would almost always agree, and we would suggest the congressman be asked to speak about his position on the proposed family planning and research bill.

"And, of course, the member of Congress had likely never heard of that bill. And where would they call to get information? They call Planned Parenthood. And we would say, 'Well, if you would like us to send you over some materials we have prepared, it might save you some time.'"

Chapter Ten

Reaching the Goal
Using Negotiation,
Legislation and Litigation

*We have to counter a lot of people who have money and not
much else with citizen interest and activism.*
—Carol Tucker Foreman

Getting a favorable administrative decision, a law or a court ruling is
the main prize in advocacy. Yet carrying out negotiation, legislation and
litigation involves the most specialized, complicated activities advocates
perform. At Step 4 in policy change campaigns, when strategies are carried
out, skills and information about people and policy are at their sharpest.

Education about the policy (highlighted in Chapter Nine) is a constant
strategy. The three direct strategies—used in the executive, legislative and
judicial branches of government—call on advocates to employ a variety of
resources, methods and techniques, depending on which one they choose.

Negotiating with Administrators

The negotiation strategy, as advocates describe it, involves communication between advocates and government officials or business administrators who have the power to change things directly. Government
officials involved in the negotiation strategy are usually members of the executive branch at local, state or national levels.

Sessions with elected executives (mayors, governors, etc.) and their
employees, comments on regulations and all appearances before appointed
commissions and boards are considered to be negotiations for change,

173

because those groups have the power to make certain policy decisions themselves.

Dealings with individual legislators are not part of the negotiation strategy, because individual legislators—or even groups of them—cannot deliver final policy changes independent of the entire legislative body.

Negotiation is used to affect how existing public policy is actually carried out and how money is raised and spent, as well as to influence government regulations—specific policies and procedures developed by the executive branch to carry out laws.

"Making a Difference," the League's voter education handbook, says, "Negotiation with officials about improvements may be all that is required to effect a change. . . . You may come away with guarantees of better publicity for registration, training sessions for polling place workers or other advances."

In all matters of change—not just voting rights—advocates often find that negotiation may be "all that is required" to affect policy. Informal meetings between advocates and administration officials are used frequently when advocates want to change the way existing public policy is actually being carried out.

No official format exists for common negotiation sessions with administrators, so advocates get a say in creating the rules for how sessions are conducted, which can help the cause right away. At these informal sessions, either the entire group meets with the administrators, or advocates represent a group when they meet with the official(s).

Local hazardous waste groups—and others—often find themselves involved in face-to-face negotiations as they try to prod correct action from government and industry about laws and regulations already on the books.

Groups Meeting with Administrators

In the CCHW Leadership Handbook Lois Gibbs tells how to conduct negotiations in large "action meetings" between local groups and officials:

> After you've thought through what you want and who can give it to you, your most likely next step is to set up a meeting with that person. . . . An action meeting should involve as many of your people as want to attend. Everyone's angry, everyone's got a stake in the issue, so it's only fair that everyone be able to participate. And, let's face it, your strength is in your members.
>
> Where should the meeting be held? Generally, it should be on your territory. In sports, they call this going for the "home advantage. . . ." Pick a location that is convenient and meets your needs. Give timely notice.

Tell your "guest" where the meeting will be, when you want the "guest" to arrive and what the purpose of the meeting will be.

Another vital part of pre-planning is the agenda. . . . Think through all the possibilities. . . . What if he/she doesn't come? Make sure that you have handled the invitations properly. Never allow the blame to fall on the organization or its leadership.

If the official does show up for negotiation with the advocacy group, Gibbs advises,

Be well prepared. Have the list of things you want posted up on a chalkboard or large piece of paper in front of the room. . . . Be ready with people who will ask the pointed questions to your "guest." Will you or won't you do X? The leaders at the front of the room should keep "score."

Your guest will try his or her best not to give you a straight answer. For every yes or no question, your guest will try to say "maybe." Don't fall for that! Any answer that isn't a yes should be scored as a no.

An effective tactic to close the meeting is to insist that your guest signs the scoreboard at the end of the meeting. By signing, the [official] is simply certifying that those are indeed the answers. . . .

Citizens for Community Improvement filed a charge against a savings and loan in Des Moines. "We asked to have a pre-hearing meeting with them," Brenda LaBlanc related. What happened next shows how officials will negotiate settlements sometimes rather than go through the time, expense and potential trouble a formal government setting might cause.

"That was kind of a fun meeting we had because I know they expected a bunch of rabbly people to show up. And we ran the meeting," she laughed. "They were very defensive, etc. And we said, 'We don't want to get you into any trouble and file a charge against you. We want you to do these things.'

"And they agreed to all the things we asked them to do. They also offered to deposit this money we had been given by State Farm Insurance, and they would handle low-interest loans. And they agreed to take the money and administer this loan program that only asked for eight and one-half percent on home improvement loans.

"So when we went to the public hearing with them, instead of having the hearing, we just announced that we'd reached agreement and read the terms of the agreement. So that worked out very nicely."

Advocates Bargaining with Officials

Sometimes practical considerations dictate that representatives of advocacy groups negotiate with officials on behalf of the whole group. LaBlanc went to Washington as such a representative from Iowa to talk to the head of the finance administration about red-lining. "I've gotten together with National People's Action several times," she reported, "to talk to Paul Volcker because we were trying to get him to make some special concession on interest rates for home-buying for low-income people—something that he consistently refused to do. We did get him to consider it." Because interest rates fell, she said, "People are beginning to buy again, so maybe we'll get active in trying to help people buy homes."

CCI uses the negotiation strategy frequently and won millions of dollars for consumers from utility companies in the '80s using that strategy. A funding proposal reports, "The group has intervened in three utility rate requests, [held] numerous public meetings and negotiation sessions, resulting in tangible victories."

The Energy Task Force was organized in 1980 "in response to a 30 percent electric and 14 percent gas rate hike by Iowa Power and Light. CCI formally intervened with the Iowa Commerce Commission," the proposal states, "and began a series of public meetings with Iowa Power officials." There the CCI Energy Task Force demanded withdrawal of the rate hike, funding for weatherization programs and another forum—"a meeting with Iowa Power chairman of the board for negotiation."

The proposal says CCI will continue to use negotiation to get what it wants in the energy realm. "Through public meetings, negotiations and being made part of the decision-making process, disconnections can be lowered. . . . The project will work for including a process of negotiation on payment arrangements and plans include an 'ability to pay according to income' clause."

In an interview, Lois Gibbs described how, at a bargaining session with administrators, Citizens Against Landfill in Lake Charles, Louisiana, got the money to pay for expert help. She attended one of the group's early strategy sessions.

"One of their biggest problems was that they were going to have a permit hearing about the landfill site. For an expert to testify on their behalf would cost them $50,000. I said that we have some at CCHW who are willing to write up comments, but they don't have the national expert aura about them. They wanted to have the best to stop this landfill, so they tried to define how we'd get the money. They decided the county commissioner and the state legislators should pay the $50,000, and they should not, especially since government was pushing to have this landfill expanded.

"Consequently, we put together some state legislators with Shirley Goldsmith, the leader of the group, and gave a presentation to the county commissioner on why they should fund the expert, how much it was going to cost, who she was going to hire. She clearly laid out all the things that were discussed at the group's strategy meeting and presented it to the commissioner.

"I also gave a small rap about how it's in their own behalf to support citizens and how it's going to be much cheaper in the long run if they do this now. She won a major victory.

"They didn't agree to appropriate fifty thousand dollars. They said that sounded like too much of a made-up number. So the group went after about forty-eight thousand nine hundred sixty-three, or something like that, which was also a made-up number, and they got it."

Lois Gibbs gets many of her approaches to negotiation from the National Training and Information Center. In "A Challenge for Change," published by that group, Shel Trapp gives advice about how to conduct bargaining sessions where representatives like Goldsmith bargain for the entire group:

> A critical point in any . . . drive comes when the organization gets to the bargaining table. It is at this point when the [official] has admitted that he must recognize the power of the organization and allow it into the decision-making process, that the organization's credibility is on the line; does it have the ability to negotiate . . . ? Can it bring back the bacon to the community in the form of a victory?
>
> Once the organization has developed enough power . . . that it has forced its way to the bargaining table or negotiation session there are usually three stages.

Stage 1 involves deciding the terms of the session itself: where, when and how many people the group can take. The group also decides on specific demands and who will present them. As they form their demands, according to Trapp, the group decides which are "throw-away" and which are "bottom line."

As part of preparation Trapp suggests role playing and making sure the negotiators have all the latest facts and are prepared for alternatives that may arise. "When going to the bargaining table," Trapp advises, "it is important to recognize that seldom, if ever, in this world does anyone get everything they want."

At Stage 2, Trapp suggests having "as many people present as possible." He says all the demands should be presented, with different people as main negotiators on different points. "If the negotiation sessions can only take place in a closed session . . . the leadership should [go back to the group] to ask if agreements are acceptable."

Trapp recognizes the necessity of follow-up when negotiations are concluded. At the end of the final session, he recommends setting a date for an accountability meeting with officials to make sure they are holding up their agreement. He also says, "Let the world know. Hold a press conference or issue a press release. If it is a very localized victory, pass out a flyer."

Send a "letter of confirmation to the [officials] with the organization's understanding of agreements reached and the date, time and place for the accountability meeting," he continues.

Trapp offers some final thoughts about bargaining sessions between advocates representing groups and administrators: "Simple issues can usually be handled in one meeting. . . . More complex issues may need several meetings.

"Be very suspicious," he cautions, "of negotiation which involves only a few people, and go to no more than two [bargaining sessions] without calling a meeting of the whole group."

As Trapp points out, getting officials to agree to negotiate in the first place is often a major task in itself. When Kattie Portis had to negotiate for funding for Women, Inc., in the early days of the program, just to get a meeting scheduled, she had to conduct a phone campaign to Washington.

"Nobody wanted to fund us. People at DDR (Division of Drug Rehabilitation) were treating me like I was a little kid. I mean really, they'd yell at me and say, 'I told you to talk to Joe,' and Joe would say, 'I told you we don't have any money. Why do you keep calling here?'

"One day I was frantic. We were faced with having to close the program. What were we going to do? We had been working for about three or four months with no money, feeding the clients and paying no other bills.

"A staff person walked in and said, 'Kattie, you've been talking about all this networking you've been doing, so now it's time to call it in.'

"The first call I made was to D.C., and one woman in D.C. called somebody in Michigan. They [people from all over the U.S.] bombarded DDR with phone calls. DDR had just yelled at me that morning, but by twelve thirty that day I got a call from someone who said, 'I am the director of DDR, and I understand you want to talk to me.'

"'You said it, brother,' I said. 'I've been trying to get you, and you haven't been able to talk to me.' He said, 'Well, we can meet this afternoon.'

"What happened was one call from Senator Kennedy's office went in to DDR. That scared them so bad, by four o'clock four people in DDR had called me and said that they were willing to sit down and talk.

"Well, those same people who had refused funding for all this time, they tried to get me down there that afternoon, but I was exercising my own power. I started calling the shots from there on in.

"I set up the meeting for the next day. When I got there they were really shaken up. And I told them, 'I bring five thousand women in here with me. You know, I have been working with them and fighting with them.'" Women, Inc. got its funding.

Commenting on Regulations

The thousands of regulations on government books are extremely important statements of public policy. Regulations — set by the executive branch of government — are the rules that spell out exactly how laws get carried out. Advocates know the best law in the land is no good if the regulations that detail its implementation are weak. In order to affect regulations, advocates practice negotiation with administrators by commenting on proposed regulations.

The procedures for making regulations are as formal as those for making laws and issuing court rulings, but the methods and techniques advocates use to impact the implementation of laws are completely different from those they employ in courts and legislatures.

New regulations are promulgated before going into effect. Whenever a new law is passed, the agency or department in the executive branch in charge of implementing the law drafts regulations. Rate-setting for utilities and other regulated industries is also a form of regulation and is handled by administrators.

Existing regulations are modified sometimes. Suggestions for changes in existing regs can come from many sources for a variety of reasons. Some regulations are regularly updated by government; others are ignored for years.

Administrators may propose revising existing regulations if a problem has been identified or if changing conditions make the regs no longer realistic. Administrators may also suggest revisions because the bureaucracy has been silent in the past on issues that need to be addressed.

Sometimes a newly elected executive — a governor or president — wants a law to be reinterpreted and asks agency heads to tighten or loosen corresponding regulations to suit their views. Advocates frequently initiate proposed changes. They meet with administrators informally or write letters stating why regulations need modification. If the agency resists change, lawsuits can force administrators to hold hearings.

Government agencies at all levels are required to notify the public when they issue proposed regulations. Agencies cannot adopt regulations without offering the public a chance to comment. Most libraries carry copies of the federal register and similar state registers that list proposed regulations by agency, commission or department and subject, with a number. Advocates — and any member of the public, for that matter — can inquire at state capitals for booklets that contain proposed regulations. If they know which agency oversees the issue in question, they request that the agency send them proposed regulations to review. Or they ask legislative committees that deal with the law to inform them.

At the top of each regulation proposal are listed directions for submitting written comments. There is usually a two- to three-month comment period, and the agency takes another two to three months to consider the comments and issue the final regulations.

Marlene Sciascia said the moving force in the Mayor's Office for the Handicapped in New York City in the '70s was the Rehabilitation Act of 1973. The compromise bill required cities that receive federal funds to comply with certain directives.

"The scene was that each federal agency had to promulgate regulations that paralleled the federal ones," Sciascia said. "It was a really active time. We were organizing public hearings for comment. We were writing comments on regulations for city agencies. I wrote letters in support of suggestions that the mayor later put his signature to. So we were commenting at the federal level and with the city and state. It was very exciting!"

Advocates hold several measuring devices against all proposed regulations dealing with laws of which they approve. Do they fit the intent of the law? Are they realistic? Are they clear?

When advocates comment on regulations they concentrate on information. Research about the issue and its effects are extremely important to administrators, who need solid information to justify changes. Surveys, studies, charts and statistics come heavily into play when advocates communicate with administrators making regulations.

Sometimes their comments are favorable, but sometimes advocates and groups find flaws and attempt to get a regulation changed or withdrawn. When advocates point out problems with regulations, they also frequently suggest alternatives.

Often staff members of legislators or legislators themselves help administrators design regulations that show an understanding of the spirit of the law.

When the Department of Agriculture was trying to figure out how to distribute WIC money equitably, administrators were stymied about how to allow for urban, rural and suburban populations. Advocates, including Stefan Harvey, said they didn't know either, but pointed out that another agency had devised similar allocation formulas and suggested they follow those.

Testifying in person at an administrative hearing and writing comments have pros and cons. In-person testimony is often limited to three minutes, but written testimony can be any length and is considered equally with statements delivered in person.

Testifying at administration hearings: "We got everyone and their uncles" to hearings about federal regulations about handicapped access. Marlene Sciascia remembered about her city job in New York. "The feds came to each city," she said, "and when they came to New York, they knew we had a community that had to be reckoned with. It was great to be there and demand the time to speak and affect all the regulations we did. I'm very happy we were there."

When the American Indian Center in St. Paul wanted unification of the juvenile court rules, the group wrote letters and attended hearings. "The justices did hear us out," Diane Roach says, "and when the juvenile court rules were redone they did include new rules and they included quite a bit about the Indian Child Welfare Act in their training at the state level. So we thought that was helpful. We sat all day waiting for them to call on us to testify. But our work did have a positive outcome."

"In 1981," according to a CCI statement, Brenda LaBlanc's group "organized over 250 consumers to testify under oath at the Commerce Commission public comment hearing. In the 1982 rate hike hearing for intervenors, the CCI Task Force presented eight witnesses, including the elderly, small business representatives, members of the clergy, the head of a local church-operated soup kitchen and the chairperson of the task force. In the two rate requests that have been decided thus far, refunds have been ordered."

Putting comments in writing: The federal government holds fewer administrative hearings than states and cities, because it is more difficult to get people from around the country to testify. Comments on federal regulations are often made in writing.

This postcard — addressed to William Ruckelshaus, administrator, Environmental Protection Agency — was prepared by CCHW and sent to everyone on its mailing list to sign and mail to Washington.

> Dear Mr. Ruckelshaus:
> OK, I'm willing to stop being emotional about toxic waste if you're willing to act on the facts. According to Princeton, Congressional and other scientific studies, **ALL LANDFILLS LEAK**. It's only a question of how much and how soon. I'm not willing to mortgage our children's futures. Therefore, I urge you to issue an immediate **MORATORIUM** on landfills, pond and lagoon dumping until EPA issues rules consistent with known facts.

Results of comments: Government agencies are required to compile, study and publish comments they receive — at hearings and in writing — when they issue their final decisions about regulations. A summary of comments becomes part of the public record that often includes how many people agreed and disagreed with each regulation.

Administrators have a lot of leeway in what they do with comments. They can withdraw a regulation, revise it or keep it intact. In a set of regulations, they may do different things to each separate regulation.

Taking Legislative Action

"Coalitions exist on the state and local level in virtually every state where legislative action is pending," says the League of Women Voters Campaign Handbook. "The reason is simple—few laws get passed through the action of a single citizens group."

And if advocates need a law or want to prevent one from being enacted, a legislative campaign is the only strategy they can choose. Although lawmaking bodies differ from city to city and state to state, they have a few things in common. Almost all have a committee system, pass laws by majority vote and require the elected head of the executive branch—mayor, governor, president—to sign the resolution or bill into law. Like Congress, most state legislatures have two "houses" that must agree on every law.

Managing Legislative Campaigns

Because legislative campaigns are usually complicated and long-term, close, continuous management by a person or small group representing an advocacy group or a coalition of groups is essential. Paid or unpaid, these advocates—often called "lobbyists"—oversee the process and people involved in carrying out legislated policy change.

Most organizations have one person who oversees the management of a legislative campaign, usually called "legislative coordinator," "legislative action director," or a similar title. Large and national organizations usually manage legislation with ad hoc committees. In addition, state and national branches of groups also have paid staffs that help in the management of legislative campaigns. Groups in coalitions share management responsibilities (see chapters Three and Four for more on these special ad hoc advocacy groups).

The activities of the legislative management group cover a wide range of administrative responsibilities. The management group knows the specific route the legislation will most likely follow and keeps track of that process with a calendar of action the group will likely take. "The first rule of lobbying is to know, really *know*, the legislative process in your state," OWL tells its local chapters.

"How Laws Happen" from NETWORK says, "Knowing the entire process is crucial if we are to exercise fully our right in a democracy to influence public policy and to make our elected officials accountable. . . . Please keep and use this article so that when you receive a targeted Action Alert or a phone call . . . you will understand more fully why *you*, as one member of the NETWORK, are so important."

The League's Campaign Handbook offers a suggested calendar for legislative action. At the start-up, education begins, followed by joining a coalition and or setting up a field organization. The next stages the group identifies are the hearing, the committee vote and report, three months, two months and one month and one week before the floor vote. OWL mentions additional important points, including conference committee and executive signature.

The management group keeps an ongoing head count, identifying important legislators and matching them with constituents. "Nothing is more important to a legislative campaign," says the League, "than an accurate head count of legislators' attitudes. Without this head count, your coordinating committee will have no idea where . . . efforts need to be focused in the field." The League suggests that "the names of all legislators can be entered on 3×5 cards" or on worksheets with information about where each one stands at any time.

In addition to identifying those in favor of the legislation, the group must monitor the opposition. Who are they? What are they going to say? "It is always preferable," according to the League, "to anticipate the opposition and answer their arguments positively before they surface publicly. . . . One cannot always know ahead of time exactly what new techniques and arguments the opposition will think of."

Campaign managers are always on the lookout for other groups and individuals to join the group in coalition or, easier still, go public as "endorsers" of the group's position. The League of Women Voters says that management "will want to enlist endorsements of the legislation from individuals and groups that may not be willing or able to join a coalition. . . . Endorsers should be sought from all interests, but particular emphasis should be put on finding leaders whose opinions matter" to the legislators and the public. "Few of these people will voluntarily and publicly endorse legislation unless they are asked to. . . ."

The management group lets the advocacy group and constituents know about needed actions at appropriate times. The group also educates, coaches, supports and supplies the constituents who carry out the process (see Chapter Nine for specific methods used). It also coordinates the development of materials and expert resource persons to inform and persuade legislators. It puts data and information into legal, fact sheet, letter and testimony forms. The group also keeps accurate, up-to-date records of all activities.

Management has the arduous task of keeping files about and records of every person and event involved. In addition to calendars of events and information about legislators, they keep news clips and copies of all materials used and notes about progress of the campaign.

Persuading the Lawmakers

Lobbying is really nothing more than persuading. Influential leaders, committee members and a majority of members of two legislative bodies must be convinced to vote a particular way. Any advocate who does this is acting as a lobbyist.

"Lobbying is not a dirty word," the League says. "Lobbyists perform an essential function in our democratic process. Lobbying a public official is no more or less than using persuasion to convince a person to vote your way."

Despite the fact that the legislative process is complex, what appeals to individual legislators—in addition to policy itself—is simple and countable: money and votes.

"A lot of lobbyists in Washington are able to back up their information with large numbers of campaign contributions which will make members of Congress more enthusiastic about their ideas. Or they back up their information with a substantial amount of constituency power," says veteran lobbyist Carol Tucker Foreman. "When the National Education Association goes up to Capitol Hill, they automatically get a hearing because there are teachers in every congressional district in the country. And they're very well organized."

Advocacy groups that don't have much money look at upcoming elections as the legislators' bottom-line consideration. Methods advocates employ include having individual legislator's constituents involved at every step. For advocates pursuing a legislative strategy, just like the legislators, it's the number of votes at the end that really matters.

As a NETWORK newsletter points out, "most people never bother to lobby their congresspersons at all, so even a small group . . . lobbying actively can make an impact on a congressperson's local office."

Legislative campaigns have to go through a network of considerations before laws are enacted. At each juncture, advocates work to persuade the lawmakers of their views on the issues using a variety of methods.

Petitions come early in a legislative campaign, if they are used at all. According to the League, "Circulating petitions is a lot of work, so that a final special event should be planned to justify the effort and publicize the petition results. There are two major reasons for using a petition drive: 1) It is a high-intensity, short-term activity that generates publicity about the issue; 2) it demonstrates to the legislature that a large number of people support the desired legislation." In addition, an early drive will identify potential lobbyists for the future. On the other hand, a petition effort requires lots of materials and people in every legislative district to carry it out.

In her autobiography, Elizabeth Cady Stanton wrote about a petition drive in the mid–19th century.

It was agreed that the practical work to be done to secure freedom for the slaves was to circulate petitions through all the Northern States. For months these petitions were circulated diligently everywhere, as the signatures show—some signed on fence posts, plows and anvil, the shoemaker's bench—by women of fashion and in the industries . . . by statesmen, professors in colleges, editors, bishops; by sailors, and soldiers. . . . Petitions, signed by three hundred thousand persons, can now be seen in the national archives in the Capitol in Washington. . . . During these eventful months we received many letters from Senator Sumner, saying, "Send on the petitions as fast as received; they give me opportunities for speech."

Launching the Legislation

When advocates propose legislation they get the policy change goal written up in the form of a bill of law, then find sponsors from the legislature.

OWL and some other organizations have model bills that state and local groups use as a basis to draft proposed laws where they are. Members of the Garden Chapter of OWL in New Jersey decided, after study, to push for passage of a health insurance conversion bill in the state legislature, using a summary of what they had learned and the OWL model bill, according to the group's Organizing Manual.

Sometimes legislators' staffs figure out the actual wording of bills. The Coalition for Basic Human Needs has the Poverty Law Center draft the language of legislation it promotes.

Stefan Harvey recalled that, in 1975, legislation continuing the original WIC law was written by advocates. "Members of an ad hoc advocacy group called the National Childhood Nutrition Coalition, which preceded the anti-hunger coalition in existence today, helped draft legislation. I mean they actually sat down and wrote legislation that was then given to congressional staff people. Staff people did some editing and changing, but not much."

"In your search for the 'right' legislator to carry your bill or to help you draft one, look for one who sits on a committee hearing such legislation—and the better her/his rank on the committee, the better the bill's chances," OWL says. "If possible, it should be someone from chapter members' district. If there is more than one OWL chapter in the state, come to an agreement on the best legislator to approach.

"What you can count on the sponsor's staff to do is to let you know when the bill is to be filed, when it is assigned to a committee, when hearings are scheduled, and which of the committee members need extra lobbying. "Always keep the sponsor of your bill advised of your plan," OWL continues. "Do it in writing if possible and keep a copy for your files."

Janet Diamond says of the clothing allowance bill for welfare recipients in Massachusetts, "We wanted to find a middle-of-the-roader, somebody with some seniority, particularly on the relevant committees, because the first hurdle was to get the bill out of committee. So we got people to call committee people up and visit them. We all did some of the phone work trying to target legislators. I can't remember how many sponsors we got, but it was quite a few."

Lobbying Legislative Committees

"The United States Congress," NETWORK writes, "is a legislature which does the bulk of its work in committees." The same could be said of many state, county and city lawmaking bodies. Thus lobbyists target committee members.

"Because the number of bills for consideration far exceeds the time available for fair treatment," NETWORK writes, ". . .lobbyists play a valuable role at this point. . . . Because each committee member is able to commit resources to only a few bills, she/he may not be well versed on all the bills before the committee."

Bills usually start in an assigned standing committee that determines the bill's fate, with the exception of controversial bills. Sometimes the committee refers it to a subcommittee under its jurisdiction. After consideration, committees report either favorably or unfavorably to the full body.

While the bill is in committee, OWL suggests as soon as it has a number, "letters should be written by all state OWL members to their own representatives and to each of the members of the committee urging support and passage of the bill (by number).

In the "mark up" stage, committee members go through the bill, deleting, adding and amending parts before reporting to the floor. "Mark up," NETWORK says, "is the stage for intensive lobby efforts. It is now that elected officials begin to go public with their positions. . . ."

Amending legislation in committee: When the House Judiciary Committee considered the Immigration and Reform Control Act, NETWORK "objected to language in the bill that would lead to summary exclusion and denial of judicial review to asylum seekers. We lobbied the full committee," a brochure states. "When the bill was reported out of committee, the clauses to which NETWORK objected had been favorably amended. Other interest groups were disturbed by the same clauses, and it was in the interest of the bill's survivability to have those sections revised."

In committee, the Sierra Club, according to Betsy Reifsnider, "stalled a dirty air bill" from getting through Congress several years ago. How? "With a lot of amendments. The good legislators on the committee were able to put on a lot of amendments which would weaken the dirty air bill, and the members were told they would have to go back and back and vote on those amendments.

"The breakthrough came with an amendment that would keep air in national parks cleaner than air on the average. One of the guys in what we call 'the dirty air dozen,' Thomas Morehead of the Pasadena area, voted with the good guys. That brought down the dirty air coalition. The coalition fell apart, and [chairman] Dingle recessed the committee until he could get the coalition back in working order.

"We sent letters to Morehead saying, 'You're such a wonderful person. You made a good vote.' We mobilized all the people who were either swing people or supporters to hang tough and not change. They did hang tough, and Dingle couldn't bring the committee back into session because he knew he didn't have the votes. That was probably the most effective thing the Sierra Club did in the last session of Congress."

Tish Sommers reported that OWL got important legislation through the U.S. Congress by tacking it onto another bill. "There's been discussion for some time about the poor unemployed people who lose their health care insurance. We added on to that: what about the poor dependent women who lost their insurance. "The more you bring it up the more likely it will be attached [to other legislation] sometime. We were pushing for a displaced homemakers bill, and finally it appeared that the best way to get it passed was an amendment to another bill in 1978."

Committee hearings: Hearings are a committee forum where advocates are invited to submit views and where advocates who oppose a bill introduced by others come into the picture. Hearings serve several purposes, according to NETWORK: gathering information, compiling a record of positions, generating public support or opposition and allowing agencies to indicate the kind of support a law might receive from those designated to enforce it, giving publicity to lawmakers.

Advocates, NETWORK goes on, "may request to submit testimony, written or oral. . . . Sometimes the committee solicits testimony. . . ."

NETWORK describes a hearing about the Voting Rights Extension Act to show how important hearings can be. "Representative Henry Hyde (R–Illinois) protested strongly against the bill. . . . During the hearing process, however, the personal stories of discrimination at the polls, given by people of color, deeply moved Hyde. As a result of lobby efforts to bring congressperson and citizen face-to-face in the hearing room, Hyde reversed his position. The cumulative effect of similar efforts passed the Voting Rights Act Extension of 1982."

At state legislative committee hearings, Janet Diamond remembered, "The welfare recipients who testified spent a lot of time trying to explain living circumstances that to us seem obvious, but to legislators [are] not so

obvious. 'This amount of money isn't enough to buy boots for your kids,' a
legislator might say. 'What are you really going to do with the money?'

"Usually people came up with truthful, honest answers: 'I know it's not
enough, but it's a start' or 'You don't shop the sales at discount stores like
I do.' They said the right things. It was consciousness-raising for everybody
in the room."

Sometimes advocates have to lobby just to get a committee hearing. "If
there is a delay in scheduling a hearing," OWL advises, "members of the
OWL chapter should be asked to call on committee members."

"The major goal in testifying . . . ," says the League, "is to demonstrate
to the committee, the media, and through the media to the public that the
proponents of the legislation know their facts, represent a broadbased constituency and can wield political clout."

"In Washington, Senator Proxmire was producing some anti-redlining
legislation based on findings of the home mortgage disclosure act," according to Brenda LaBlanc. "Because of the publicity we'd had in Des Moines
on anti-redlining they asked one of our people to go to Washington to
testify, and one of the people here flew out at government expense to testify
before the Proxmire Committee about redlining in Des Moines."

Kattie Portis of Women, Inc. said testimony is sometimes give before
inattentive legislators, "I learned to wake them up. Very respectfully. I learn
their names beforehand. I know one time I called a representative 'your
honor.' He was impressed, though. He woke up."

Lobbying the Members

The OWL manual says, "If and when a bill is set for a floor vote, that's the
time to bring out the troops. . . . You will need a large number of volunteers."

According to the League of Women Voters, lobbyists must be knowledgeable and businesslike and must hold the legislator accountable later.
The lobbyist should know the organization she represents, know the person
she is trying to influence, and know enough about the issue to present the
general points in her own words. "Unless you are lobbying a member on an
issue before his or her committee," the League warns, "don't assume they
will know any more, if as much as you do, about the subject."

Janet Diamond of the Coalition for Basic Human Needs reported,
"What we learned to do was target" representatives for constituents to contact. Some people are harder to reach than others. Some districts don't believe they have more than two welfare recipients as constituents. Some districts you could do two to three contacts [to get a positive response] and some
30 to 40. It also depended on how many people we could get to call."

The head count kept by the management group is very important at
this stage, because, according to Diamond, "In all cases, you choose your

people to spend time with. On any given issue before the legislature, x people are solidly for you, x number are solidly against you. The question is, how many of the undecideds can you get? And so we concentrate on that middle group.

"We would spend some time with the truly committed to ensure that they were enthusiastic. And we would always spend some time with those members who were totally opposed, for the purpose of trying to reduce their opposition. If you go to a member who has been adamantly opposed to food stamps all along, and he perceives that this will be an important issue in his election, by presenting him data about how food stamps affect the well-being of his district you may persuade him to vote against you but not make a speech against them. That can be important."

Kathleen Sheekey pointed out another measuring stick Common Cause used to decide whom to lobby for a vote against the MX missile: "We select the members we feel are most important, and they would, in some cases, be the more senior members. We'd take a look at regions. For example, there are a number of members in the North Carolina delegation who are important on this next round of votes. We look at who's the most senior member of the delegation and try to make a special effort in that district, because if he reverses his vote, he may well take a couple of other members with him."

Visiting with legislators is one effective lobbying tool. The League of Women Voters says, "There is nothing more satisfying, nothing more fun, than direct person-to-person lobbying for an issue you really believe in." Visits are probably the most effective forum for persuasion, too.

Legislative visits about specific bills are usually in the officials' offices. Visits with legislators are not to be confused with negotiation sessions, because an individual legislator—even a sympathetic or powerful one—cannot change policy except with the help of dozens, even hundreds, of other legislators who vote their agreement.

Nancy Sylvester of NETWORK said people have certain fears and the first thing that hits new lobbyists is the office arrangement. "You can get a sinking stomach when you walk into the office and when you see a huge desk. Everybody's office is a different experience. There are some [legislators] who sit behind a desk and you're about seven feet away and over in this plush little chair and you're sort of looking like a little girl and there's this huge fellow sitting over behind this desk.

"Others will come right next to you, sit right down, immediately put you at ease. Other offices just have like a library table. It's fascinating to watch how different people's offices are arranged. You get a physical sense of power and distance. I tell people they can encounter anything when they walk into those offices. Therefore, they're ready for anything; most of the time they're pleasantly surprised."

The Organization of Chinese American Women uses visits very effectively, according to Lotta Chi. "The government was going to terminate the program that funds educational seminars for immigrants. All the grantees from all over the country went to the Hill to talk to their congressman and say that this funding is very important and 'Please reconsider.' We got the grant reinstated."

OWL suggests to local chapters that they "send a delegation" to talk to elected officials. "No fewer than three and not more than five make an appointment with a representative or senator if it is known they are 'at home.'

"Ask if he/she plans to support it on the floor, and if the answer is 'yes' thank her/him and note that information on your lists, which should be prominently displayed, especially if you sense some wavering. This [wavering] could be countered with pointing out the support already given — few legislators will choose to be odd man out on an issue which concerns older women . . . ."

NETWORK trains constituents in how to visit legislators through materials and seminars in Washington. Nancy Sylvester outlined three different types of visits: introductory (just getting to know each other), investigative (finding out where the representative stands on an issue) and persuasive (trying to convince the representative of an opinion).

When it comes time to talk, Sylvester said, "I tell people to make sure they have a three-minute, a five-minute and a ten-minute spiel ready, because they might get any amount of time with the person." Often, she pointed out, people are talking to aides, some of whom are helpful, some not.

"We didn't mind talking with aides," Janet Diamond said of the Coalition for Basic Human Needs. That's true of most advocacy groups. "Aides are very useful and sometimes an aide can be better because they can give you more time and they can advocate for you with the legislator. Sometimes they're nicer. Sometimes they're more sympathetic. They have time to listen to you and hear the whole story. They're not necessarily thinking about votes right away.

"We have the person [welfare recipient] say in her own words what it would do for her," Diamond says. "That's what the legislator wants to hear — not what will this do for the whole world. And it's not necessary for them to talk about money. That's on the fact sheet. But 'I'm your constituent. I live in your district. I vote in your district. This will help me and my friends, all of whom are registered to vote right now, as we speak. This is how this will help them. We know how you're voting. We will follow your vote. We hope you sponsor the bill. We hope you vote for it. We hope you speak in favor of this bill.' And they say how glad they'll be, how grateful they'll be and how many other people they know. It's a very effective approach, and anybody can do it."

Sometimes a group invites a legislator to visit. "There's a legislative committee on mental health and retardation" in South Carolina, Carol Garvin said. "So if we're having a meeting about some legislation important to us, we might ask Senator Louis Patterson to come and talk to us."

Sometimes face-to-face lobbying is impossible. Letters, postcards, telegrams and faxes to elected representatives are especially necessary when constituents are at a distance from the legislature and cannot meet with officials in person. Advocacy groups encourage members to choose their favorite approach.

A NETWORK newsletter relates this anecdote. "Representative Morris Udall (D–Arizona) advises his constituents, 'Before this year is history, the House Clark will record my vote on more than 450 issues. I need your help in casting these votes. The "ballot box" is not far away. It is painted blue and it reads "U.S. Mail."'"

The OWL manual calls letter-writing "the meat and potatoes of political action" and adds, "The imporant point to remember about letter-writing to elected perons is that someone does read the incoming mail and usually keeps a tally of those letters pertaining to any one specific issue. As bills move toward committee hearings, the files are pulled and the member has an immediate idea of not only how many constituents have expressed an interest in the bill, but who has written. There is a rumor on the Hill that the size and or weight of such files can influence the attention given to a bill.

"At the chapter level, in response to a political action alert from national, as many letters as possible should be sent," OWL's Tish Sommers wrote. "Time within a regular meeting could be given to member writing on specific requests."

"We also did letters," Sandra Kurjiaka said of efforts to stop anti-gay legislation in the Arkansas legislature. "Some people say the legislature doesn't pay attention to form letters, but they do have their impact when one person gets a couple hundred form letters on their desk. They notice that.

"Well, we made up some form letters that we took to the gay bars and we got people to sign them and we took them up to the capitol. Well, we had a victory. The community responded, and that was very important. But, to win! We're all feeling pretty good.

"This year they were going to reintroduce a bill, so we put the network together then, and we dumped letters and postcards and stuff up there like crazy just by telling people this was happening. And then the head of the women's political caucus and I and the NOW people all wrote letters to every member of the House and Senate."

When NETWORK sends alerts to members, it puts core information needed for letters in a box. When writing, the group advises members to be brief and concise, to be encouraging about good votes and to ask a question that requires an original answer. "If the response is noncommittal," they advise writing again.

"Sometimes," Tish Sommers of OWL wrote, "time necessitates telegrams. Personal opinion messages are quick and not too costly." Western Union offers a reduced "public opinion message" rate for a 20-word telegram.

The telephone is another tool lobbyists sometimes use. "When the lead time on action is limited, consider telephoning your legislator's office," NETWORK advises. "Always give your name and mention that you are a member of NETWORK. When calling Washington, ask for the legislative aide that deals with your issue. When calling the local office ask them to relay a message and request a reply. The phone message should be brief."

NETWORK's Nancy Sylvester advised that calls, like letters, have a strong effect. "Twenty calls to a congressman is an incredible lot of calls on one issue. The Hill's just not used to that. If they get one call they think there must be one hundred or two hundred people who think the same thing but don't call. People don't bother to call. So then the power of one person becomes a big voice for them.

"On covert operations, time was such that we couldn't get word to people in the mail. We do it by phone tree then. We then ask the person in turn to call the next person to generate phone calls. If they have time they write to the local office or Washington."

The word "lobbying" comes from people waiting outside legislative chambers (in the lobby) to try to talk to elected officials.

In addition to having people posted in the gallery watching the representatives all the time, the Coalition for Basic Human Needs has used the time-honored approach to lobbying. That is, they stood in a doorway and walked up to legislators to talk to them when they came out.

"Politeness was the key," said Janet Diamond. "You always say, 'Excuse me.' It's manners. You just use them aggressively. You take all those sayings — excuse me, thought you might like to see this fact sheet — and you always have a fact sheet. You always have your hand extended. You shake hands whenever you can. You know, you introduce yourself. 'Hello, my name is blah blah. I live in your district, and it's nice to meet you. I wonder if I could have a moment of your time. I know you're very busy. If you would just read this fact sheet. I'll be sitting up there [in the gallery] if you want anything.' That only takes thirty seconds.

"We were afraid to miss one single day. We wanted them [legislators] to just take for granted that we were there — everywhere they went except home. Even then they couldn't be sure we weren't on their lawns saying, 'Excuse me, but I just thought—'" Diamond laughed.

Common Cause also "does a lot of lobbying off the House floor as members go in and out to vote on other issues," Kathleen Sheekey said. "We spend a few minutes with them talking about the MX. It's hard to buttonhole people, but it's part of the job.

"One member I talked to last week who was leaning to voting for the production money in this next round of votes told me yesterday he's changed his mind. He'd perhaps been influenced by his mail. He wasn't specific. He just said, 'I will be with you this time.'

"Now if I hadn't been standing off the House floor and he hadn't remembered our conversation from the week before, I wouldn't have gotten that information that quickly. So presence is a large part of the lobbying effort."

Getting the Bill Signed into Law

For a bill to become law, it must pass both houses in identical form, so conference committees — composed of members from both bodies — hammer out the final content.

"Lobbying a conference committee is not just a last-ditch effort," NETWORK contends. "The vigilant effort of Representative Clement Zablocki (D–New York) and his aides, as well as intense lobbying of the conferees by opponents, kept chemical weapons out of a conference bill" though the Senate version had them in.

Janet Diamond said getting the governor to sign the clothing allowance bill once it passed the Massachusetts legislature was the last major hurdle. "The governor was Ed King. I think the clothing allowance bill was the only piece of legislation the Coalition for Basic Human Needs got signed during his administration. We had gotten two other bills through before, but he vetoed both of them. And we knew that at the very last minute he could veto this one. It's almost impossible to get a veto override, especially on human services bills.

"We didn't lobby the governor directly," Diamond said. "We let legislators who supported us lobby him. King was completely inaccessible to us. Even if we had just shown him our faces, it woud have given him aggravation." And he signed the bill into law.

Litigation for Change

"Litigation is one way to determine rights and duties under . . . laws and to ensure compliance with them. It is both a practical method for effecting change and a powerful means of working within the system. . . . Any area of concern may be suitable for litigation," according to a League of Women Voters brochure.

Litigation—the strategy that corresponds to the judicial branch of government—is used when laws and regulations are not being followed or are being applied incorrectly. Sometimes litigation is used to test a law. And the strategy is often used as a last resort when negotiation with officials hasn't worked.

Litigation differs from negotiation and legislation because a professional attorney must be used in court, and members and concerned constituents have a somewhat smaller role to play in carrying out the actual case than they do when new laws are made or policy is negotiated.

"I view lawsuits as a tool," said Sandra Kurjiaka, head of the Arkansas Civil Liberties Union and a frequent user of the strategy. "They're something you do to make something else happen—not an end in themselves."

The League points out several ways litigation increases official cooperation in the future. "Lawsuits are often welcomed by officials because court action relieves them of personal responsibility for a decision that is politically unpopular. . . . Bringing suit usually increases the persuasive powers of an organization in future negotiations" and the issue is not brushed aside again, either.

"It is also possible," the League says, "that announcement of plans to sue will cause officials to change course. If this happens, there may be no reason to continue with the lawsuit. The decision to litigate is not irreversible." At most points along the way, the suit can be dropped.

Cases in Point

"It occurred to the Pikes Peak Region LWV, embroiled in a 15-year-old battle to preserve some Colorado Spring parkland, that litigation might provide the ultimate answer to the problem," the League of Women Voters brochure "The Verdict Is In" says. "The League, in concert with a local coalition and six individuals, took the city to court."

"'We had had it,' said the local chapter president. 'Our expenditure of time and money, to say nothing of strength, was not limitless. We decided the court was our last resort and the only way to get permanent protection for our parks.'" The resulting court order proved them right.

Before they went to court, Martha Cotera reported, community groups all over Texas "tried to convince school boards to provide free public schooling for undocumented children of immigrants. We tried here in Houston, in Austin and in San Antonio." When the school boards could not be persuaded, the groups sued.

They were worried about several things, according to Cotera. "If these children were brought here by their parents and their parents were undocumented, then these children could not go to school. And they were kind of roaming the streets. You know they were going to stay here, and chances are they never would go back to Mexico. So you have a lot of children growing up illiterate and providing a virtual slave labor force for people here.

"We were not so worried about them when we did not have integration. These children were going to Chicano schools, and Hispanic principals were not turning them away. But when we got integrated, it was a critical issue because the Anglo principals were not going to do them the same favor.

"So by the time of integration [early '80s] it had been decided in the courts that undocumented children could go to public schools."

People in Des Moines, Iowa, were helped out by a California lawsuit. Both communities were plagued with inspectors saying their houses were unfit with the goal of having them torn down to build new developments. "As a result of that suit," Brenda LaBlanc says, "housing inspectors can't go into your home if you won't allow them.

"I'm sure the only reason they brought in this inspection thing is to be able to condemn property more freely for developers, and they haven't been using it properly to clean up these really bad places that people live in and pay high rent for."

The Black Hills Alliance in South Dakota has "attorneys who have gone to court on the state level and tried to prevent the exploitation of land—not just Indian land, but farmland," Norma Wilson said. "They try to protect the rights of the people from having their water contaminated, because tests drill holes and that sort of thing. I attended a hearing at the state level at which attorneys fought to protect the rights of citizens. The Black Hills Alliance has been instrumental in having lawyers in court fighting for us."

One issue of the Citizens Clearinghouse for Hazardous Wastes "Bulletin" documented 18 cases in states all over the country where companies were forced by courts, after suits by citizens, to stop dumping and or pay fines totaling millions of dollars.

And, according to the "Bulletin," "the owner of Multichem Corp. and Delaware Hospital Services received 25 concurrent one-year jail sentences from a Maryland court for illegal burning and transportation of wastes."

An out-of-court settlement was just what a Detroit group was looking for. In 1983, after 11 years, Focus:HOPE reached settlement of a lawsuit against AAA charging the corporation with racial discrimination against more than 12,000 black job applicants and employees. AAA agreed to pay plantiffs in the class action suit a Michigan record of $4.7 million in damages.

Although it took a long time and the decision didn't come from the court in the end, the organization, of which Eleanor Josaitis is a key staff member, won a major victory for minorities in Detroit. A companion lawsuit charging the company with sex discrimination actually ended in 1980 with the Detroit Federal Court finding AAA guilty of violating the rights of 1,200 women applicants and employees.

Managing a Lawsuit

As with legislation, advocacy groups — sometimes suing as a coalition — use a management group to oversee the mechanics of the long-term process. The management group oversees important budget and fund-raising issues, hiring and supervising the attorney, monitoring the court case as it moves along, publicizing the action and — most important — educating and involving the organization in decision-making throughout the process.

Sally Mead was the head of the group supporting a lawsuit by Dr. Carolyn Brown against Alaska Right to Life. Brown alleged that Right to Life "engaged in slanderous and libelous" speech against her in various publications for performing abortions. The group put out a brochure, "Responsible Freedom — Our Fundamental Choice," with a description of the case inside. They also encouraged people to contribute to costs, contact legislators, write letters to the editor and talk to friends and colleagues about the case.

One of the first ingredients necessary to a group that decides to sue for change is lawyers. Meetings with them serve two purposes: to refine the exact strategy, Stage 3 in the process described in Chapter Eight, and to select an attorney to handle the case. Sometimes the lawyer may be the same, but possibly they will be different.

The committee managing the litigation conducts a search for the right attorney to handle the case. Keeping the fee factor and his expertise in mind, the group looks to institutions and organizations with experience in litigation. Then the group interviews prospective attorneys. As it approaches attorneys, the group makes sure that the organization is clear about its goals and its role in the strategy so that it can communicate well with legal experts.

And representatives generally tell the attorney how far the group may be willing to go to pursue the strategy — the time it will commit, its plans to appeal an adverse ruling and other considerations.

Representatives of the organization also talk about money right away, discussing how much the group can spend and what its resources are. The lawyers are expected to estimate their fees and other costs.

The League advises, "Look for a lawyer with whom you can frankly discuss all the options available and the ramifications of each. . . . Find an attorney with whom you feel comfortable and with whom you can communicate easily." The management group must find an attorney willing to work with the group in decision-making as the case goes on.

Many expenses are involved in litigation for change. In addition to attorney's fees, the advocacy group pressing suit has to come up with expense money and court costs. Because attorney's fees are often too high for an advocacy group to afford, most organizations look for a way to get around paying them. Bar associations and attorneys all over the country do some pro bono work — at reduced rates or without charge — for good causes in the public interest. National organizations like the Civil Liberties Union, the Sierra Club and the National Association for the Advancement of Colored People (NAACP) sometimes take cases they decide are of public concern.

Law schools and legal service programs will also take public policy change cases for a reduced price. With the help of the legal aid society in Des Moines, some tenants took their landlords to court. As a result, according to Brenda LaBlanc, "a really bad landlord just sold all his property and left town."

Some states have special programs to create funding for public interest litigation, and several federal and state laws authorize courts to award attorney's fees in specific public interest cases.

The LWV's "The Verdict Is In" describes how some happy Leagues chose their lawyers: "When the Illinois LWV asked a well-known environmental lawyer for advice on counsel for its suit against the North Shore Sanitary District, he volunteered his services free of charge.

"The Wausau LWV sought out a friendly state legislator to handle its reapportionment litigation. Unable to take the case himself, he recommended the attorney that the League eventually employed.

"And the Rochester Metro Area LWV convinced the New York Civil Liberties Union to handle the prisoner voting rights suit and foot the bill for the court action, too."

The League points out that specific fund-raising drives — "legal defense funds" — on specific issues are easier than fund raising in general. Letters to members, sales of legal briefs, and public solicitations have generally paid for most litigation. One League chapter puts money aside to pay for court cases in the future.

Tell It to the Judge

Members of an organization usually know more about a specific issue than a lawyer, and the lawyer knows more about the legal proceedings and lingo. "The best relationship is one where there is mutual respect for each other's expertise," the LWV says. In addition to being in on decision-making about the process and meetings with the lawyer, the advocacy group may well be called on to do research the attorney needs to support the case.

As well as being the plaintiff in a suit, organizations may get involved in class action suits, in which court action will benefit a large group of people. Advocates may also participate as an amicus curae (friend of the court) with the agreement of both parties or as an intervenor on one side of the suit.

As a member of the Civil Rights Advisory Commission for Texas, Martha Cotera helped with a class action suit. "I was involved with helping people in the Houston/Bowman area, helping them identify expert witnesses and giving them as much information as possible about Austin. We were supportive of the case. As part of the commission we went around and did a lot of research. We pushed them to litigate, you know."

Although the Consumer Federation never filed a suit of its own, Carol Tucker Foreman said that when she was a staff member, she "worked on food issues primarily, not for legislation so much as on legal attacks on how food programs were being administered. We were not leaders of those court fights, but we frequently signed onto suits being filed by other groups."

When the mayor sued the election department in Albany, New York, to prevent the first school board election from being part of the general election, the League of Women Voters there intervened on behalf of the election department. "As intervenors, the League was able to argue the case fully and participate in the appeal," which they won.

Litigation and the Media

"Media attention is extremely helpful in maximizing the public interest purpose" of a lawsuit, according to the League, but careful planning is required. Accuracy and completeness of information are necessary so the other side and the public don't get confused. Also, the attorney is consulted about the content of media communications and the timing.

Although Sally Mead and others working with Dr. Carolyn Brown in her pro-choice lawsuit sat at tables at fairs and passed out position papers, Mead said, "There's also concern that we don't want to publicize it too much. One reason is if people are selected for a jury and there's been an awful lot of information out about the subject, sometimes that can prejudice a jury. They might need to move the trial, for instance, to another place." (See Afterword to find out what happened in this case.)

Generally, litigation enhances an organization's reputation. When the League won in Albany, "the group loomed large as an organization with political clout," a brochure states. "Our membership blossomed, and the next finance drive was very successful. As for subsequent media coverage, the League finally got off the women's page in the two daily newspapers."

Part Four

PERSPECTIVES ON ADVOCACY

Chapter Eleven

Finding Their Place:
Advocates Search for Identity

*That's what keeps good people going forever — the energy, the
emotion, the love you put into it.*
— Martha Cotera

"Who are you?" the caterpillar asked Alice as she wandered through
Wonderland. For many advocates and those around them, the question is
as befuddling as it was to fictional Alice.

"What do you do?" forthright people ask. Others form an image when
they hear the word "advocate" that may or may not be on the mark.

"Sometimes I do have a sense of isolation from my friends," Carol Garvin said, "because I don't think they understand what I'm doing. I find I
don't mind people not understanding so much as *mis*understanding."

Advocates frequently talk about isolation and misunderstanding because their jobs are not commonly understood by the general public. As advocates go about their business, some of their problems — both personal and
professional — stem from the fact that no one else really knows what their
"business" is. Worse yet, some people have developed limited or sterotyped
images of the job. Because, as of yet, advocacy has no official status in the
academic or professional realms, advocates themselves have trouble defining exactly who they are and what they are doing.

Answering the Caterpillar's Question

In addition to educating the public about the issues, advocates also
have to explain who they are, what they are doing and why.

Whether one is a volunteer, a member of a committee, an officer, a

203

staff member of an organization, a freelancer or a government official, what is important is to be absolutely straightforward with everyone about who one is and what one does. No specific role is any better (or worse) than any other. Being a volunteer does not equal sainthood. And being a paid staff member does not equal professionalism.

People who work for public policy not only identify themselves as advocates, but also tell their specific title and briefly state the issue or issues they are working on. Example: "My name is Joan Jones. I am a member (president, staff member, expert consultant, etc.) of the Environmental Action Group. I am concerned about enforcement of the Clean Air Act."

If possible, the person goes on to say what he or she and the group, if applicable, are doing. "I plan to write letters, testify and help set goals for a campaign we have going to get the EPA to look at several cities' performance."

By being open, honest and specific — though brief — about who they are and what they are doing, individual advocates show their pride in and understanding of their work and thereby ask for recognition and respect from others.

Some advocates make the mistake of talking in detail about their organizations. That's only necessary if the group is unknown or if the advocate is the sole spokesperson for the group in a very official setting. Otherwise, mentioning the group's name and its support for the issue is usually sufficient. People are more interested in who they see and the issues, not in an explanation of the purposes, processes and membership of an advocacy organization.

Authorized Voices

Many people identify themselves as advocates when they speak about public policy change. Anyone with a point of view about a policy can honestly state that he or she is an advocate.

But advocates can claim to *represent* other people only if they have their permission and participation in the decision-making process that led to the policy stand. Membership organizations have the least difficulty identifying who represents the group.

Unfortunately, some government officials and people who work with service delivery agencies and professional organizations have been known to say that they represent groups of people — especially service recipients — when they have not been authorized by those people to do so.

Advocates affiliated with agencies can always legitimately say they speak for those agencies, especially when they advocate for agency needs, like additional funding and programs. But agency people—public and private—cannot properly take the giant leap to say they are representing a group of people unless those people have participated in the decision-making process that is part of the five-step policy change campaign.

By the same token, government agencies may say they *serve* certain constituencies, but they do not represent them in policy matters. Even non-profit service providers cannot say they represent clients unless they can show how those clients had input into and support the policy stand.

An advocate might correctly say, "I represent the State Department of Elderly Services." Or, "I work for the Springfield Senior Lunch Program. We need *xx* dollars to continue feeding 100 people a day." Or, "The 100 seniors who eat in at the Springfield Senior Lunch Program have said their biggest problem is health care and have endorsed the following: . . . I am here to speak for them."

But it is incorrect to say, "I work for the State Department of Elderly Services. We/I represent the elderly people in this state." Or, "We are advocates for senior citizens in this state." Or, "I represent the 100 people who eat at the Springfield Senior Lunch Program. They need increased health care services."

Advocates who claim to represent people abuse a public trust if they have not gotten those people's consent and input before hand.

When someone claims to speak for a group of people, it is completely proper, and even wise, for other advocates to ask what say-so the people had in the policy position. If the people "represented" did not participate, the "advocate" needs to be stopped and corrected. Well-prepared advocates, on the other hand, state briefly how the people they represent showed their support of the policy stand.

Making sure that advocates are really representing whom they say they are is very important for reasons of clarity and ethics. Everyone needs to be aware of the very special conditions under which people can legitimately say they "speak for" others. Unchecked, anyone could claim to represent any group—leading to widespread abuse of public participation in advocacy.

Advocacy Specialization

Successful advocacy includes such an amazing spectrum of activities it's a wonder any advocates exist at all and remain sane. They do, but some of the work often gets neglected.

More and more advocates are beginning to specialize. Skills and interests steer some individuals toward some activities and away from others. The problem is that an entire range of actions needs to be taken to succeed at policy change.

Some groups divide advocacy tasks consciously among various people. Example: One person oversees group management. Another oversees recruitment efforts. A third coordinates policy change campaigns. Others might specialize in specific strategies and methods, such as media or newsletters. In this way, the group makes sure that no important area of activity gets neglected. The difficult part is keeping in constant communication and weaving the activities together. What is important about shared advocacy roles is that all the tasks be considered before the advocacy pie is divided.

Same Purpose — Different Roles

The fact that an advocate may be employed by an organization, be a member/volunteer with an organization, work freelance as a public policy consultant or actually work for government certainly adds to everyone's confusion. Advocates' activities in each of these four roles are practically identical, yet the conditions of their work are very different. Many advocates end up taking a variety of roles as they go along.

Advocates often work on issues while they hold down other jobs or in conjunction with other jobs. Stefan Harvey looks at her lifetime of advocacy and says, "I don't think of advocacy as a career as much as I do as a cause. I think you can advocate for social change by having a variety of careers or several careers."

Volunteer leaders: Norma Wilson, Dorothy Ridings and Sally Mead — and probably the majority of advocates today — have many hats to hang up neatly and separately. They are wives, mothers, hold down important, vaguely related jobs — and they are volunteer public policy advocates. They give their time freely to work for causes they believe in. When much of society is just getting accustomed to the idea of women working outside the home, these women are going one step further as they devote more time to the world through their advocacy work. It's a startling occurrence.

Some volunteer leaders, like Martha Cotera and Carol Garvin, admit they are sacrificing full-time paying jobs, with the help of their husbands and families, to be able to work for their issues.

Being a volunteer is "a little bit of a tricky issue," said Garvin, then president of the Mental Health Association of South Carolina, "because it suits me personally. My husband and I feel it's very satisfying for me not to have a paid job. And yet I do feel very strongly that women should work if they want to for pay. For me it has worked out just right."

"Other people will sometimes become apologetic in terms of the time I put in versus what they feel they put in. And I have a little discomfort with that. I want the association to be seen as a place where you can be a successful volunteer part-time."

Many people—both men and women—are keeping homes together while they also work 40 or more hours a week. At the same time, people are being encouraged to donate time and money to "good causes," mostly through service delivery.

Although promotional materials and television ads emphasize service delivery volunteerism, advocacy groups can build on the spirit of individual contributions to society's betterment by soliciting people to work on some of the root causes of people's needs in the first place.

Organization staff: Paid staff people who do advocacy, like Betsy Reifsnider, Nancy Sylvester, Kathleen Sheekey and Diane Roach, are confused with volunteers more often than the other way around. Paying staff to work for public policy change is a relatively new phenomenon to many non-profit groups. Although paid organization staffers don't have to worry how they will put food on the table while they do their public policy work, they do have other problems.

For example, it is often assumed that directors do policy advocacy as part of the job description. In other groups, who leads advocacy efforts in a particular year depends on personalities and interests of staff members, not clear-cut job descriptions. Another challenge for staff advocates is to keep in touch with constituents and not become isolated in the office or hearing room.

Advocacy groups that know what they're doing decide how much and what kind of policy work they need to do, then assign a staff person to oversee and support it.

Employed advocates have fewer identity problems than volunteers. Betsy Reifsnider said, "I really like it when somebody asks me, 'Betsy, What are you doing now?' I say, 'I'm working for the Sierra Club.' Oh, that's a good feeling!"

Many membership organizations employ people to oversee or perform advocacy work. Their roles often have clearer definition. These staffers—called "public affairs coordinator," "legislative liaison," "lobbyist," "action coordinator" and similar titles—oversee and help manage the full range of activities in action strategies. The danger organizations face when they have advocacy staffers is the same they encounter when they hire lawyers: members may think that "everything is taken care of" and reduce their own participation so much as to let the staff person decide alone what the issues are. One paid staffer cannot replace, but can only support and guide, members setting up and carrying out public policy campaigns.

Public policy consultants: Some public policy consultants who work for non-profit advocacy groups provide a positive alternative to the fat-cat corporate lobbyist corps. Former affiliates of non-profits open offices in capital cities to make themselves available to groups with good causes. Advocates who have built good reputations working for organizations go on to work for themselves or a firm as a freelance consultant, as Carol Tucker Foreman has done.

Good public policy consultants — unlike typical lobbyists — do not hog issues, work behind closed doors or deal heavily in favors. They work just like advocates affiliated with specific non-profit groups.

Although the number of consultants who help groups with legislative strategies is growing, there is a lack of freelance expert help tailored for groups that decide to use litigation or negotiation strategies. Advocacy groups and people with legal and negotiation expertise could both gain by working more closely on issues.

It's also possible some consultants will begin to hire themselves out to organizations to start policy campaigns at Step 1, then guide the group through the complete five steps. It's a good idea, especially for groups with less experience in managing policy change from beginning to end.

Lois Gibbs advises groups fighting hazardous waste. "I don't necessarily define things for them," she explained. "I just ask questions. They [members of the local group] define things themselves."

Citizens Clearinghouse for Hazardous Wastes is basically a consulting group that helps communities around the country deal with specific local problems under Gibbs's leadership. CCHW provides a range of invaluable expertise and services to client communities confronting mammoth problems. One of CCHW's best qualities is its emphasis on listening to people in each community and working with residents as they plan and make their own decisions in the change process. CCHW also helps communities find out what others are going through, get technical information and learn what has worked for others.

Having more national advocacy consulting groups like CCHW would benefit advocacy for all types of problems. If the same type of national advocacy consulting group existed for localized welfare issues, education, housing, health and other issues, changes would occur much more quickly and people would feel better dealing with their problems.

In addition, the services of lawyers and expert negotiators as consultants are much needed by organizations that want to expand their advocacy skills and learn how to conduct campaigns (see Chapter Twelve).

Government-affiliated advocates: Advocates who are elected, appointed or employed by government have the most difficult of all four roles. They are always under suspicion as having been co-opted, and government is a very unstable group.

Some advocates do get co-opted. Everyone knows at least one story of a grassroots advocate who got a government job or appointment, vowed to advocate "on the inside" and was never heard from or seen again — or worse, turned up to testify against the group's next policy proposal. But sell-outs seem to be the exception, not the rule. Many advocates affiliated with

government continue their work for people and issues even after years on
the inside.

Government-employed advocates work at the whim of political ma-
neuverings and changes. Marlene Sciascia said she had to quit her position
in the New York City Office for the Handicapped when politics interfered
with the advocacy. "We were falling out of grace with the mayor because
we were doing what we were supposed to do. There was this issue with the
city council that the mayor wanted to push one way and the community the
other."

Many insider advocates feel they have to battle superiors constantly on
behalf of constituents. Sciascia believed she acted as a bridge between the
blind community and the city administration until her role became complicated by her co-workers and the mayor.

Sciascia remembered, "There was a lot of politics involved in the existence of the office. The continuance of our existence depended on politics
to a certain extent. Everyone had to pay attention to politics to stay in good
graces."

Sometimes advocates are never fully accepted by the government
agencies they end up working for. Carol Tucker Foreman said that during
her tenure as assistant secretary of agriculture under Jimmy Carter, "Most
of the negative response to me didn't have to do with food stamps [for which
she had advocated before her appointment]. It had to do with the fact that
rural members of Congress were appalled at having a former consumer advocate in *their* Department of Agriculture. The farmers were very upset.
They were sure that if they let me get in the Department of Agriculture the
walls would come tumbling down.

"The farmers were very honest and straightforward about it: 'It's our
department. You shouldn't have anything to say about what goes on there.'
When I met with them it was always, 'Why should a consumer advocate be
in our department?'"

Barbara Reed also knows what it's like to be an advocate in and out of
government. As an administrator, "You're afraid that your funding will be
cut or that you'll be monitored," she said. She pointed out another contrast.
Advocates employed by government have a chain of command to observe
while other advocates "do not have to go through the hierarchy."

For advocates who work with groups, "There is nothing to keep you
from contacting the governor's office, for example, if you work on the state
level. There's no going to your boss who goes to his boss. . . . You have more
freedom as an [independent] advocate," Reed said.

"We had more accurate, quicker information," she said of her days as
a WIC advocate outside government. We found that we had regional office
people who had control of the program calling us and asking us for legislative information that had not come down the chain of command."

It would be easy to recommend that advocates never try to get elected, employed or appointed by government. That would eliminate many of the dilemmas involved. But the fact is, the public needs committed advocates working inside government.

Taking Action for People and Policy

Which is more important to advocates, people or policy? Neither. They are both equally important to advocacy success. Without people power and participation, lasting policy change doesn't happen. Conversely, if advocates just educated and put together groups—constituents, advocacy, government, etc.—and never tried to change anything in reality, there would be no purpose in putting the groups together, except perhaps for moral support.

It's a lot easier, however, to *say* that both people and policy work are equally important than it is to *behave* that way in real advocacy situations. Here are examples of problems advocates encounter in seeking balance:

1. The public or the advocacy group itself doesn't understand the importance of both. They are "into" recruiting members only. Or they like to meet with government officials but don't think members have to be consulted before they formulate and work for a policy goal.

2. The people aspect takes over when groups feel insecure, new, young. These groups set policy goals based on one criteria—what will expand the group's stature with the public, expand membership, win publicity, etc. Some groups believe they need a win, any win, to encourage esprit de corps. Their motives are more anti-authoritarian than pro-policy.

3. The policy aspect tends to take over when leadership does not consult and make use of constituents or follow a group decision-making process with such excuses as speed or ease (education and communication take time and energy); or when advocates get isolated from constituents, geographically or otherwise; or when media attention and other "public education" is considered sufficient outreach. The result is that there is no room for input from constituents.

A balanced approach to cultivate both people and policy is required for long-term success of groups and issues. Values, as well as skills, must be very holistic to actually make the policy and make it stick.

No wonder advocacy is hard. Although advocates must consider their people and policy work equally important, they must also differentiate between the two when they carry out specific activities. When cause and effect are confused, methods get confused and change is unlikely to occur.

To say, "We are trying to get this regulation passed in order to attract new members to the group," is absurd. Yet advocates easily get confused about goals and have been heard to make such statements. Correctly, the group is trying to get the regulation passed to change a policy. That is the first goal, and all efforts should focus on it. Perhaps new members will be attracted to the group. And advocates will make joining easy as they bump into interested constituents. But membership recruitment cannot be the primary goal of policy change activity.

An opposite example would be, "We are doorknocking to get a federal law changed." An alarm sounds immediately. Doorknocking is a great technique for recruiting constituents for local issues and, possibly, for gathering information. It is not a method for changing policy.

Advocates are becoming more aware of which methods to use for which goals. When performing activities that have various goals, advocates have to prioritize those goals at the outset. It is always important to keep in mind the two major purposes—people and policy. Although advocates are always interested in both, the major goal of each individual activity is one or the other—people or policy. Otherwise the activities and the people carrying them out become confused and lose focus.

Sometimes activities and goals are clouded because of different people's interests: "I am a membership person," or "I'm on the legislative committee." Although both of those functions may be important, one sometimes take a back seat to the other, depending on the purpose. If an advocate notices the entire group seldom has an activity with a goal in one area, then it's time to worry—and start planning one. But every single activity cannot highlight every area of advocacy concern. There are too many, and specific activities just become diluted and ineffective unless goals are prioritized and articulated.

Dozens of methods are used to put together various groups of people and to process different public policy change strategies. Knowing their tools and being able to use them is as important to advocates as it is to surgeons and carpenters.

No matter how big an organization or its goals or how large this country is, the personal approach is always the best when working with people and policy. When given a choice, wise advocates choose to have personal acquaintances of targeted individuals contact them. Second best is to use people who have something obvious, such as a home state, in common with the targeted persons. When the element of trust is already built in, persuasion becomes much easier.

In the same light, calling people to get them interested is usually chosen over writing, visiting over calling. Likewise a conference is perferable to a media campaign. Direct, person-to-person methods are always best. This gives the other person the ability to see, possibly touch, have a full conversation with the advocate and make a commitment to the group and or the campaign on the spot.

Many times, in-person advocacy is impossible because of distance or time constraints. When more distant methods must be used, advocates should keep in mind that the goal is the feeling of the personal touch—one of mutual trust and exchange of ideas and information.

Whether advocates are trying to get constituents to join, get involved or take policy action, they have to use hooks—action requests—and they have to use them consciously. It is useless to go on and on about an issue in speech or writing and not offer the listener or reader an action or a choice of actions to take in response.

Advocacy: New Training

Part of advocates' identity crisis comes from the variety of skills they need and the way they have to get them on-the-job.

Most advocates have learned advocacy in a very haphazard way. They use phrases like "seat-of-the-pants" and "trial and error" to describe how they learned their jobs. Most of them say they have learned "by doing" and "from informally observing others" when they had a chance (see Chapter Two).

Except for attending some specific group workshops, most advocates have developed their skills through the very natural observe-and-practice learning process. It's amazing what advocates have accomplished on behalf of issues, considering the painful learning process most of them have gone through.

Most advocates have strong communication skills. They have talent and, most important, determination to fix policy that is wrong or inadequate. But in a society that offers full training and education programs in every other professional field, advocacy and the issues suffer for lack of more structured education.

Talent and determination are not enough. Most advocates, paid and unpaid, are in some way crippled by lack of training. Despite the fact that advocacy is as old as this country, someone still has to reinvent the advocacy wheel each time a public problem surfaces.

More Structured Education

Chemists, day care workers, architects, lifeguards, clergy—almost every skilled occupation imaginable—have education programs. Practitioners may have personal talents and drive in those special areas and be very capable of learning from on-the-job-training. But neither the job-holders, their co-workers, their employers nor society in general would tolerate their workers having no formal training.

Just because they take courses, chemists, teachers, lifeguards and members of the clergy are no less interested, devoted, committed or talented in their professions. Training in advocacy would in no way harm the "purity" of the profession. In fact, with more knowledge would come higher standards of performance and ethics.

Today's advocates should not be faulted for not taking courses in advocacy. There aren't any. How to put together groups and keep them together and how to attain policy change go virtually untaught in educational institutions today. Advocates and the issues they work for are forced to undergo the frequent failures naturally associated with trial and error professional practice.

There are very limited resources for ordinary people who want to learn about advocacy. There are "organizing manuals" and workshops, dealing almost exclusively with setting up local issues groups. Courses analyzing policy itself and the history of policy, mostly national policy, abound in university political science departments. High schools usually offer a civics course, mostly about government and how it works. Advocacy groups themselves publish materials and hold occasional workshops about how to do specific activities. For the most part, only advocacy group members know about or have access to that education.

To make advocacy education more widely available, high schools could include advocacy as a part of civics courses, and some might offer complete courses in how citizens work on policy problems. Colleges and universities could offer advocacy overview courses to undergraduates. Political science departments might even include courses in advocacy as a major requirement, thus reflection the position of citizen advocacy as the strongest force in public policy in this country.

In addition, graduate programs in public policy advocacy and special training programs would benefit people who want to make advocacy a career. Such a sophisticated profession needs an entire program to fully prepare a someone for the complex world of advocacy.

Advocacy education programs would, of course, include lots of practice and observation as part of the education process. But those activities would be guided, supported and formally evaluated by peers and advocacy staff. People committed to policy change would get an overview and training in specific tools and methods for doing the various activities advocates are called on to carry out. Advocacy students could also take content courses in specific policies and issues.

The Law Degree Myth

There is today a trend in the advocacy world to assume that lawyers have been trained to be public policy advocates. The fact that "advocate" and "attorney" are synonymous in some contexts adds to the confusion.

A recently published ad for a public policy coordinator that appeared in a national magazine said applicants for the job of director of an advocacy group must have a law degree in addition to advocacy experience. A woman introduced herself at a public meeting not long ago by saying she was studying to become a lawyer because that was the only way she could change public policy regarding minorities. Organizations that are still unsure what advocates actually do can be fooled into thinking they have to hire lawyers to be policy change advocates.

A law degree is usually necessary to argue a case in court. Legal training prepares people to try cases and draw up legal documents, etc. Occasionally advocates need to work with a person who has those skills.

But law schools do not teach how to run a policy change campaign, how to work with and lobby a legislative body or how to recruit constituents, manage advocacy groups or work with a variety of government agencies and groups. Lawyers know no more and no less than anyone else about the methods and tools involved in working with people and issues to create better public policy.

Ron Simon, special counsel to CCHW, disputes the law degree trend. He writes in *Everybody's Backyard* addressing member organizations, "You should remember that a law license is not a diploma in politics or community organizing."

Toward a New Vocabulary

Advocacy has been limping along without a terminology of its own for a while. Communication—so critical to the field—has been thwarted and muddied by the lack of precise ways of talking about who advocates are and what they do. Just as the word "advocate" has come into more use lately, so a new vocabulary to describe advocacy activities is emerging.

Many words now in use were borrowed—first from the labor movement and then from "community organizing." Although those efforts and the vocabulary that they spawned served advocates well for decades, advocacy has reached the stage where the terminology needs to be expanded. The word "organize" has been burdened with meaning too much for too long.

This book has used specific terms for specific advocacy activities. In order for advocacy to be understood and practiced by more citizens, it is necessary for advocates to adopt and promote a new, more specific lingo.

At a recent workshop sponsored by a national professional organization, an expert was brought in to run a training session on "organizing." Although the hands-on three-hour workshop helped members focus on improving a range of specific activities, participants and trainers got confused when each exercise was discussed. The problem was the word "organize."

After participants wrote lists of activities members attended that year and why, someone said something about attracting new members. The workshop leader tried to clarify the discussion when he said, "Now we are focusing on organizing." "That's what I mean," said a participant, "organizing new members." "No, no. Now we're talking about *internal* organizing," the leader replied. Everyone was completely confused about which activities were for which goal throughout the session.

If people who actually do it don't understand each other, the public certainly conjures up more myth than reality when they hear words like "organizing." For people trying to inform and persuade, it's not good at all that the terminology they use to describe themselves and their activities carries so little meaning.

Recruiting constituents and educating the public are some specific activities that might fall into the category called "community organizing." "Internal organizing" is much easier to understand when it is called "involving members."

The "organizing" words should be honored and retired. More specific nomenclature for the variety of activities advocates engage in will help advocates, the public and the causes they work for.

Organizations for Advocates

Diane Roach spoke about the need for getting together with co-workers. "We already have Indian child welfare components on each reservation. I network with all the Indian child welfare workers in the state. We have a bi-annual meeting where we all get together somewhere in Minnesota. And then all the Indian Child Welfare Act workers meet there. We don't do much business. We exchange ideas and kind of socialize and get to know each other. So it's just a networking meeting. But they are real valuable because sometimes I need to know who these people are to talk to them. We have to have some credibility amongst ourselves."

Ironically, advocates have put together every kind of group except organizations for advocates. Organizations for advocates—like other professional organizations—would bring together people who work with people of all kinds for public policy changes of all kinds. All roles would be welcome—volunteers, staff, consultants and service deliverers—as long as they saw themselves as advocates. These organizations could be formal or informal, local, state and or national. They could be made up of all women, or men and women.

Some issues a professional organization for advocates might deal with are advocacy laws and regulations that govern them and non-profit groups; advocacy education; and ethics. In addition, an advocates' group could see that everyone—members, government and the general public—became more familiar with who they are, what they do and how that benefits the public.

A professional organization could sponsor workshops or courses on the various aspects of advocacy, providing new skills to members and or the public. In addition, discussion of subtle advocacy issues and problems could be fostered this way.

In addition, members could pursue the problem so many advocates face—the general lack of funding for issues campaigns. The advocates who speak in this book illustrate very well that, despite differences of age, ethnic background, geography and issues, their activities, motives, professional issues and goals are very similar.

For groups of advocates to sit down and talk together would be a real boon to the field and to policy change activities, too. Today, advocates say they feel isolated, worried about not being taken seriously and concerned that few people know what they do. Together, advocates could begin to cure some of their individual woes while they work to improve the atmosphere for advocacy in general.

The Critical Matter of Conduct

Style and conduct are controversial subjects advocates discuss informally. Another symptom of the advocacy identity struggle is that there are very few commonly accepted standards of practice for advocates.

Yet, for everyone, questions about how to look and—more important—how to behave come up often.

Keeping Up Appearances

"We had a dress code among other things," Janet Diamond said of a campaign for welfare increases. "Welfare mothers are lobbying for themselves. You have to be very careful about the kind of impression you create. Something that won't offend. You don't want to offend them anyway because it's their ball game. It's their vote. It's not your ego. It's too important [not] to worry about whether pants or skirts are better. We wore skirts.

We were representing symbolically a whole class of people, and the potential benefits that came from wearing a skirt were such that you put on the damn skirt.

"I would not wear these earrings [the ones she wore during the interview] because they do not identify me as a welfare mother. They are too flashy. But on the other hand, you can't dress too sloppy. You have to dress by this code. It was the same when we put people on TV. Cotton blouses. Denim skirts. That's our uniform. It's designed to be non-threatening.

Diamond described her group's behavior. "We are supplicating. Smile. Smile. Smile. Be sweet. We don't take it too seriously, and that is how we save our integrity. We can go home and laugh about it later."

Betsy Reifsnider, legislative coordinator for the Sierra Club in Los Angeles, said, "I never dress in jeans. I always try to dress as a professional—maybe like a lawyer. Often with a group like the Sierra Club, they think we are going to show up in hiking boots and jeans."

Sandra Kurjiaka said in Arkansas dress is "something I've talked about as an ethics question with a lot of the women here. And mostly we've decided we really want to win. And if pantyhose and makeup and high heels are part of that, we'll do that.

"But there's a little piece of me that says there's something wrong in this. You know, it's like acting, I guess. I don't know what it's like. The first time I dressed up, and we were successful, I felt a sense of having prostituted myself. And yet intellectually, I know perfectly well if I go up there in my blue jeans and T-shirt they are not going to hear me. So it's doing what we call 'dressing like them.'"

"I'm consistent, especially in my dress," Washington, D.C., advocate Stefan Harvey said. "I wear not so much what I think I should wear but what I feel comfortable in. If I'm going to Capitol Hill I feel much more comfortable in a suit than just about anything else."

Brenda LaBlanc in Des Moines told about a "fun meeting" her group had with representatives of a local savings and loan. "We all decided to dress very smartly in suits, etc., and be very official. We had an agenda and we behaved in very businesslike way. They were rather startled. They expected a bunch of people dressed in jeans at their door." The group basically "ran the meeting" and got the bank officials to agree to all its requests.

Diplomats—Not Warriors or Wimps

Most advocates behave in a non-confrontational, professional manner. They're tough, but they're fair. They use information and experience as their tools, always walking the wide middle road between being antagonistic and weak-willed.

Most advocates agree. The ideal advocate is diplomatic, informed, willing to listen to and share information, and all-inclusive in her approach to people and issues. But everyone has bumped into advocates and groups that do not take such a positive, moderate approach to problem-solving.

A combative, militaristic, us-versus-them philosophy can still be found in the public policy realm. Individual personalities and traditional "organizing" sometimes promote anger and antagonism as policy-making tools. These advocate-warriors stand in strong contrast to most of the more successful advocates today.

Enemies, targets (people), weapons in an arsenal, wars, battles, score a hit, put in the kill, confrontation, army, power to attack. . . . These violent words are taken directly from books, manuals, speeches and workshops about how to do advocacy. Some advocacy education language sounds more like Marine boot camp training propaganda than public policy talk. None of the advocates interviewed for this book regularly uses war terminology to describe what she does, but some very established groups and individuals employ the language of violence.

The following excerpt from a manual is not only confrontational, but also sexist in its treatment of the non-aggressive advocate:

"Your research should set up a 'good guys, bad guys' situation. It is not objective. You are trying to prove a point and make it obvious that we are the good guys. If your researcher loses direct contact with the anger of the issue, he will begin to see the gray areas of the issue. He will start to become 'objective' and see the opposition's point of view. It is essential to keep the researcher part of the issue, if he becomes isolated then you have a eunuch on your hands."

This paragraph is not only offensive but tactically wrong as well. As successful advocates point out again and again, researchers should always try to find out the other side's point of view so they know how to argue against it.

TRAIN Institute, for example, sees what it calls "research for organizing" as a way to "dig up dirt" about corporate and political "opponents" in order to "harass and hassle" them. The cover of one of their booklets says all over it, "Research is not a tool; it is a weapon in the organization's arsenal and should be used as such."

A good book that came out in 1987 about public policy campaigns and advocates in Washington was blemished by the unfortunate title *The Giant-killers.*

Betsy Reifsnider said she has "seen the effects of one bad style—the combative one. We had a volunteer in a strong leadership role," Reifsnider reported. "She went into a legislator's office and said, 'You know we're getting very involved in politics, and we'll see that you get defeated next time.' The legislator said, 'Are you threatening me?'

"Obviously, this was horrible. She was very combative and had a very antagonistic point of view. When I went in, I said, 'It's such a pleasure to meet you.' We talked about the Clean Air Act." And Reifsnider mentioned reading articles about the legislator when she was on the school board. "Again, she [the legislator] would say she disagreed with this or that, but I told her about some interesting studies. She left all smiles, shaking hands. She'll have a better view of the Sierra Club now than from the other woman who just went in and antagonized her.

"Even though advocacy has been compared to war," Reifsnider said. "I don't treat it antagonistically. . . . In actual practice we are dealing with people and trying to convince them on a very peaceful level."

Good advocates aren't wimps either. Sometimes advocates anger officials even when they are not antagonistic. Ridings described the time the League took out an ad asking constituents of a congressman from Cincinnati to tell him how they felt about the Clean Air Act when he opposed it. "There was a tremendous response," Ridings said. "He was very annoyed with us. So maybe I should say in a traditional sense we're not confrontational. We didn't set out to make him mad.

"It was an unusual method for us. We are normally a bit lower key. We work behind the scenes because that's where those things are done. But when it comes time to go public, we never hesitate. It's illustrated by the Cincinnati example, but also by some of the strong statements we make."

Martha Cotera said, "I've watched men [in meetings with officials]. We women, I think, are a little bit more aggressive. The guys just sit around and bullshit together for a long time. And they say they want to think about it some more. We walk in and bonk, we say we want you to do this. I think we're very direct. They seem to be more hesitant, more roundabout."

Most advocates try to avoid groups and people that are total wimps or total warriors. Wimps will do anything to please and forget all about issues and constituents while they bend over backward to please anyone with status, money or power.

Warriors just have some old anger they are working on, and will often commit campaign "suicide" if it looks like they are about to resolve an issue satisfactorily. Just as wimps aim to please, warriors aim to displease. Since neither really aims to get people involved in policy change, they're pretty worthless to advocacy.

"Now if you were Gandhi," Sally Mead wondered aloud about the abortion rights lawsuit she was working on, "how would you try and solve this problem? Would you take it to court? Will that solve anything? Will this change anybody's point of view? That's a real large question. Or does it make them even more rabid in their opinion? And if you win the case maybe they would be more careful about how they presented their material? But would you really change their minds? No, I don't think you would. But, you know, how many of us are Gandhis and can find a way—a nonviolent way to do it?"

Carol Garvin reflected, "I think that the more successful advocates are people who work well with people. And they are very careful about choosing the time when they are adversarial. I think there's a time to express anger and indignation over injustices to whomever you're concerned about. But I think there are a lot of times when keeping the door open, keeping conversation going, keeping the relationship intact probably does more for your cause than a lot of red-hot indignation."

Stefan Harvey is concerned with other people's comfort as part of her successful advocacy style. "The objective of lobbying is to convince someone of your particular point of view. You can best convince them when they are the most comfortable. If Congressman Moakley is most comfortable talking about your kids, you'd be a nut to put him off of that issue with which he appears to be comfortable onto issues which may not interest him at all. A good lobbyist is someone who is articulate, is persistent, without being arrogant or rude, is convincing and someone who listens."

Betsy Reifsnider said she heard "from different sources" that the Sierra Club is considered to be "reasonable. Usually when we go before [government] groups that we think might not agree with us, we try to be very reasonable.

"We say, 'We understand.' Then they compromise and say, 'We can live with this, but we can't live with this.' So they know we're not wild-eyed fanatics. We do have measured programs. So if a person [who] goes before a commission appears to be reasonable, it helps.

"When I go in to talk to someone I try to imagine where that person is coming from," Reifsnider said. "Then I can see more of a soulmate and I can better get my point of view across. Joking and humor are very good, too. I don't get angry when someone is clearly opposed. I say, 'Well, that's an interesting point. I can understand your view. But you should also consider this.'

"In private, when I see strip mining in the wilderness areas, I clench my fists and scream! I go next door and say to the other Sierra Club person, 'Did you hear what's going on!'"

Lois Gibbs discussed the language to use when expressing goals to officials. "Some groups are tough and call these goals 'demands.' Others feel that this is too strong a way to put it and call their goals 'the needs of the community.' You shouldn't be wishy-washy," Gibbs wrote in the CCHW handbook, but you should be careful about turning off people with language that is too strong. Public officials tend to go crazy when they are confronted with 'demands' . . . you may want to use 'needs of the community' instead. Who can argue with 'needs?'"

Dorothy Ridings agreed. "If I had to characterize the League of

Women Voters' style, I would say it's basically non-confrontational. That doesn't mean we do not confront our opponents at all. But I think most people think of confrontational as being antagonistic."

Leaders—Not Stars or Heroes

Carol Garvin commented, "I think in a sense [advocates] are kind of a motivator, particularly with a volunteer group. If volunteers aren't getting paid, what else have you except that they care a lot, so you're trying to firm up their caring and their commitment?"

Betsy Reifsnider added that patience, humility and some toughness are the qualities she finds important to advocacy. "Our issues aren't the kind that are won or lost in one legislative battle. . . . I think in my personal dealings, I try to be humble. And I'm not impolite, but I let them see enough toughness that they know we are not going to back down on an issue just because they say we should. Having the Sierra Club behind me helps. I'm tough in a nice way.

"Persistence is important, too," Reifsnider added. "We can't rely on money, so we have to go back to public officials time and time again to let them know we are there."

Most advocates believe and behave as true leaders. Unfortunately, as in every other profession, advocacy has a few people practicing it who are really just in it for themselves. Since there's not a lot of money to be made, advocacy "stars" are unconsciously after personal acclaim. They want to be quoted. They want to get their pictures in the paper.

Stars and heroes are to be avoided. The people who are "in it for number one" are easy to recognize because they don't care much about constituents or groups or change and usually seek a lot of media attention for themselves. They say "my goal," "my issue," "my group" a lot. Sometimes they try for a sort of martyr or savior image, too.

The media and the public love heroes and stars; they are so much easier to talk about than complex issues and groups. Individual advocates may end up getting a lot of attention they don't seek. If the person tries to credit others, works with groups and listens to people, he or she is doing OK. But all advocates have to watch out that a lot of attention doesn't go to their heads and make them act like stars.

Why not? Because one person is much easier to discredit and isolate than an entire group. The forces that oppose change prefer that a single person is identified with an issue. It makes it easier to knock down that issue.

Although true leaders may also get in the paper and invited to lunch with bigwigs, they have constituents and policy in mind at all times. They are secure enough to see themselves as representatives, conduits, coordinators—facilitators of the show—but not the show itself. Heroes, stars and those who want to make themselves into powerful figures have no useful place in the advocacy realm.

Educators—Not Truthgivers or Truth Twisters

Stefan Harvey described her style, "In terms of my approach to people I think I am more professional than anything else. It's not so much that I want to be taken seriously as it is a certain shyness on my part. It is easier for me to be Stefan Harvey, the WIC advocate, because that is a very knowing person, and that is a person I am very comfortable with."

A good advocate, Harvey added, is "articulate, persistent without being arrogant or rude and is someone who listens. You have to be able to listen because you have to be able to understand what kind of reaction you're getting so you can respond to that."

Although Carol Garvin fights the notion that she is some kind of mental health professional as she works as a volunteer with the Mental Health Association, she admitted she is "professional in the sense of knowing how to use other people's time and to be sure I know what I'm talking about."

Betsy Reifsnider said, "It's important to listen a lot to what people say. I try to explain our positions in terms that legislators can appreciate. For example, when an urban legislator talks about problems with the environment, I let them know about our inner city program. Then we get a nice friendly talk going, even if it's not about the particular issue" she approached them about.

She added, "It's important to make points cogently and effectively rather than rambling on and on. Knowing when to stop, when to call in the chips, when to call in all the volunteers . . . and knowing when not to put in a great deal of effort so as not to dilute the effort later on" are all important to Reifsnider.

Three kinds of advocates to beware of use information only for their own gains. The "truthgiver" or preacher only pretends to share it. This type of advocate, unlike Ridings and others, likes to give analytical speeches, uninterrupted by questions and comments. Although there are not many of them, "truthgiver" advocates can be easily spotted because they describe the way things are (in their opinion, of course) in absolutes and use the imperative, command form to tell others what to do.

Truthgivers should never be confused with people who tell the truth. Being honest and forthright is a bottom line rule for advocates. Those who don't tell the truth or who deliberately omit information are to be completely avoided. Very soon everyone knows who these people are, anyway.

The "gatekeeper" is another form of the same animal. As soon as this person gets information, he or she guards it carefully from others in order to have power. Gatekeepers are smart in that they recognize the power of information, but they make poor advocates because they keep it to themselves or part with it very selectively so they can seem "in the know."

The "truth twister" never tells the whole story to those he or she deals with. Government officials are usually the first to recognize these people, because they are the first victims. Usually others can, too, because these "advocates" almost always end up twisting the information for constituents, too.

According to Dorothy Ridings, a person who is seeking to influence legislation should have an informational approach. "A lobbyist knows more about that subject. Of course they have a point of view. But a good lobbyist is going to make sure that that candidate, that political figure or his or her staff (where the relationship is really functional) has the information. They'll find out quickly if you can be relied upon.

"They want to know the down side of your issue too," Ridings explained. "So if I'm a tobacco lobbyist and I totally deny that there's any statistics or evidence to prove tobacco has anything to do with health, they are going to write me off. They'll never listen to me again."

The Price Is Never Right

Bribery can take many forms, and the approach is usually subtle. The offer may be money, a job, an appointment or just prestige. Most advocates have thought over how to deal with such offers.

"It's having drinks with people as opposed to just walking over and saying: 'Hi, this is what I want to talk to you about.' Where do the lines [between proper and improper behavior] go?" mused Sandra Kurjiaka. "We talk about it a lot here, so we win without doing anything over the line. Accepting anything from them would be over the line," is her group's standard.

Someone tried to bribe her. "I had a third person come to me on behalf of someone to let me know that I could be a rich woman. And I was thinking 'Oh, this is how they do it . . . through someone else. Then they haven't been turned down or insulted. There's no issue between you. [They can say] It never happened.'

"Or if you sit and drink scotch with them until two a.m. and they yank the bill you don't want the next morning at nine a.m., I mean you know it wasn't because of anything in that bill or anything that you said."

Advocates who are antagonistic in style or unduly interested in personal power should be ignored by other advocates as much as possible. It's not just because there's "good" conduct and "bad." It's because negative conduct harms people and issues, and advocates who conduct themselves well should not be burdened with the ones who don't. All they can do is try to educate the stars, truthgivers, wimps and warriors, and—if that doesn't work—refuse, whenever possible, to work with them.

Support and Rewards

Families, friends and co-workers often give advocates the support they need in their difficult jobs.

"A lot of women face this challenge to keep various parts of your life in balance," Carol Garvin said, "to get dinner on the table and not to abuse my family." Garvin said her husband is very supportive. "Oh, he's wonderful. And my children. Very supportive. My family's been great."

Martha Cotera said her husband is also supportive. "If he required that I make a living like he does, I'd never make it. I take a lot of time, and he's never asked me to make more money. I go to lots of meetings. It's voluntary; it's not part of a job."

According to Marlene Sciascia, personal support is critical. "The joke was, if we saw one of the three of us going into the bathroom it meant we were going to have a good cry and the other ones would go rush in to hold hands. It was just having someone help validate me to draw my strength, because you can't do it in a vacuum. You need someone to mirror it for you. You can function a lot better when there are people you know rooting for you."

Janet Diamond said, "I have a support network. I think that makes a difference." When she was on welfare she was on a board as the representative of welfare recipients and feeling pretty insecure. "I went to a friend who is also a welfare mother and spoke to her," Diamond recalled. "I said, 'I'm stupid. I can't ask them [people on the board] what all these things mean. They keep using initials for everything. What do I do?'

"She told me a story about the first board she had ever been on as a member of the Coalition for Basic Human Needs. She went to this big meeting with all the lawyers and they kept saying CBHN this and CBHN that.

"She said, 'Excuse me, but what does CBHN stand for?' They said, 'Dear, that's the name of your organization.' She was mortified. She was humiliated. She felt like she could never go back.

"But she was able to tell me her story, and we were able to laugh about it. I thought, well, nobody could ever be a bigger fool than that. It's a support system."

Later, when Diamond was one of the leaders of the legislative campaign for a clothing allowance, she found the intense lobbying "was a real family affair. It was a lot of fun, and people got very, very close."

Advocates who are in it for the long haul have a unique perspective. Martha Cotera continued, "Sometimes I think I just want to go home and I just don't want to worry about the next thing or write my books. I don't know. I think it's because you get on a treadmill. You know, you've been working at it so long—the bilingual issue—that it's the last thing you want to hear. I thought it was a dead issue, I thought we had everything in order ten years ago, and it still drives me nuts. On the other hand it's like a good marriage, you're lucky to have one.

"And so it looks like we're going over and over it [bilingual education] again but actually it's only an hour or so, versus nineteen sixty-seven when it kept us busy for two solid years.

"But you just want to take these issues and put them to bed once and for all," Cotera said. "When I look around at the issues they're very similar. You know, there are some issues that you never put to bed. But you need to keep on refining them so they can be worked out.

"Well, I've got five years, let's go on to the next five and then you go on to the next five. Then you say, 'Well, I've got ten years in and I can't give up now.' There's just too much time and energy invested. And you can't let it go back down the drain."

She described another neverending committee, "We worked good and we worked fast and here we are again. We got good recommendations and stuff so I thought, 'Not again. I don't want to serve on another committee.' And I look around and I say who has got the background and who is committed to the school money-wise. We got a good group together. I didn't do it all. We had twenty people. There I was looking at twenty hours a week for something like a year. And now they say, 'Well, you can't drop the ball.' I guess you can never drop the ball. You can't take your finger out of the dike."

Despite difficulties, most advocates agree with Cotera: "I can't give up. There's just too much time and energy invested. That's what keeps good people going on the issues forever—the energy, the emotion, the love you put into it."

Garvin said she gets satisfaction from "the awfully nice people all over the state of South Carolina" that she meets. "I've had the pleasure of working with some really good people. And so there's been a lot of personal satisfaction in the relationships I've developed."

Barbara Reed said, "The neat thing about our local housing relocation project was how good people felt about themselves. The director of this project is a bastard, OK. You know that he does everything the way it's not supposed to be done. 'That I have power—that I may be a welfare mom but, by God, we got this guy out of a job.'

"They felt, 'I have some power, some control. Now I can have some impact over the circumstances that affect my life.'

"And I guess that's the thing that keeps you going in terms of an effort. It's worthwhile to come to these stupid meetings knowing that in fact I have some role."

Stefan Harvey described some of the highs of her advocacy career. "I think the thing that has been the most fun has been working with people all over the country. We come together in a very real sense and know that we have succeeded at something.

"It would be crazy of me to sit here and say it was not fun when we overrode President Ford's veto of the child nutrition bill. I mean that was damn good fun. What Congress told him was what he had done was outrageous. It was.

"It was also fun to hear that the White House got so much mail when Carter wanted to veto the child nutrition bill. The only two other issues that he got more mail on were the Panama Canal and gun control. That was great fun!"

Chapter Twelve

In This Together: Harnessing People Power

I know it's possible that working together we can achieve change.
We can have success.

— Nancy Sylvester

The list of people advocates work with includes almost everyone — advocacy groups, constituents, government, experts.... Even though advocates may prefer working with some groups over others, unless everyone agrees she is a specialist of some kind, she must absolutely work with *all* groups to get anywhere.

Advocates focus on empowering average people; empowerment is both the cause and the effect of good advocacy. Although people cannot vote on issues directly, they can still affect their outcome.

Advocacy groups have become more powerful over the past decade. Some environmental groups, for example, rank among the top five in funds used to do lobbying in Washington. Legal and scientific experts, academia and business have been empowered in new ways by applying their skills and resources to effecting needed change. Government gets empowered through advocacy, too. Although government officials may seem powerful, their jobs are often insecure and difficult. By dealing correctly with issues, responsible government officials and bodies — elected, appointed, or employed — feel the same sense of positive power as other groups when they see enacted policy change that benefits the people they serve.

The Powers of Different Groups

Advocacy groups come in as many shapes and sizes and personalities as individuals. Many of them sprang into being without a lot of conscious thought, then went on to get more formally organized. They suffer from the same confusion about roles that individual advocates face. The different types of groups that do policy advocacy today—informal, membership, professional, service delivery and combinations—have different primary focuses. The tax law treats each type differently, too. (See chapters Four and Thirteen for more information about the structure of advocacy groups).

This confusion does not help advocacy. It can keep constituents away and separate groups that might communicate and work together. Those who don't like change love a confused advocacy community.

Informal groups, especially those that work on specific local crises and in political campaigns, can be very effective because their activities are not hampered by the tax code. They have to take care that they do have an understanding about goals, structure, support and decision-making or they have trouble holding the group together.

Before a group plans to become more "official" by incorporating as a non-profit organization, members should decide if a new group is needed. It is foolish to form one if there's already one in existence with a similar purpose. If it's open, others can get needed attention for particular issues without going through the trouble of forming a new group. It's wise for those who discover a set of issues to do some research before creating another advocacy group.

The CCHW Leadership handbook says raising money and protection for leaders is not necessarily helped by incorporation. But being a 501(c)(3) does allow tax deductions for donations. And some people believe that incorporation adds to credibility and perceived legitimacy.

Each type of group—in legal and other terms—has advantages and disadvantages. In any case, it's a good idea to explore all the options of non-profit status before deciding which identity to assume. And that cannot be done correctly unless everyone agrees on a basic agenda of goals.

Membership organizations emphasize their public policy change purpose. They tend to spell out their advocacy activities to members and the public clearly and consciously. Membership groups are likely to employ staff members who devote their energy to overseeing policy change activities. Members are likely to be aware of and want to take part in advocacy efforts.

Professional organizations, unlike other types of advocacy groups, have members who benefit personally from advocacy work while serving public. It can be arued that, of all the groups, professional ones have the easiest time in terms of raising money, attracting and keeping constituents, working with government and getting policy passed. Potential members in professional organizations are easy to identify and communicate with, and they remain relatively stable over time. They are very aware and interested in working on policy change that will benefit them and the public. It's all part of their jobs.

Service providers, on the other hand, sometimes do policy advocacy as they react to specific problems their organization or its service recipients experience. Volunteer and direct service groups run the spectrum of consciousness and perspective about their advocacy activities, depending largely on the leaders' focus. Some are much more aware of policy change needs than others.

Providers vary widely in the extent of the advocacy they do, too. For example, some are content to testify for their own agency's funding if needed, while others advocate for policies to serve all.

Having several types of groups under one roof can make sense if the group has a variety of goals and wants freedom and resources to pursue all of them (see Chapter Thirteen).

Staying in Harmony

Communication and decision-making are the biggest challenges national advocacy groups face. They have national, state and sometimes local boards and members. Most of them, like the Sierra Club, the Mental Health Association, the Civil Liberties Union and the League of Women Voters, very consciously divide up decision-making and communication responsibilities. But it's not easy, and the flow of information must be maintained constantly.

Many groups are good at recruiting members and supporters, but have trouble figuring out how to hold on to them. Just as much work is needed to keep constituents involved as to grab them in the first place. Giving and getting are the keys. Individuals have to be provided routes to both. Services and education are the two things they often get. Constituents also should be given ways to contribute to services and activities, if they are going to stay.

Infighting is a big problem all advocacy groups come up against at one time or another. It happens when a group does not resolve—or has no structure to resolve—differences among members.

"Poor planning and lack of focus are common structural causes of infighting," says columnist Will Collette in CCHW's *Everybody's Backyard.* "If your goals are not clear or are not shared in common by the members, there will almost always be infighting of the worst kind over the purposes of the organization and how it should carry on its work.

"Or when the group is not actively dealing with the issue, or has suffered some setbacks, members may find it easier to start attacking each other," Collette adds.

Sometimes infighting will occur after a victory as well, when group members deal with the transition from Step 5 back to Step 1 and a new issue.

"Turn the energy that could be used for infighting to dealing with the issues at hand. Find a niche for each person [or group] to accomplish something within the group that furthers the cause," Collette advises.

"You can try to ignore infighting, especially when it's minor," he suggests. Or, when problems are spotted early, "internal disputes can be subjects of group discussion."

> Have clear rules of operation in order to deal with infighting. If your group normally conducts meetings with a set agenda and a stated purpose, you as a leader could gently but firmly get things back on track by reminding the infighters that "the purpose of this meeting is to plan for next week's public hearing."
>
> The best response to a splinter group is to try to make a peace with them that acknowledges your differences. If you try to fight them, or denounce them publicly, you serve no one's interests except your opposition. "Agree to disagree," if you can. It doesn't hurt to work together on things where you still share a common interest.

When infighting occurs it's obvious why advocacy groups have to be well-managed.

The Challenge of Cooperation

Advocacy groups for similar issues but with different focuses need to communicate to see what they have in common. A direct service organization like Women, Inc., and a membership one like NOW might have more similarities that are apparent on the surface. A group that concentrates on education might do well to work together with a non-profit lobbying group or hire a lobbyist from time to time. Simple sharing of materials and experiences among groups could revolutionize and greatly speed the betterment of public policy.

Relationships among groups concerned with similar issues run the gamut from close cooperation to outright turf wars. Barriers between groups have to be broken down in order to facilitate cooperation.

Turf wars arise when groups are unable or unwilling to see similarities and appreciate differences between themselves and other groups. This was the problem that divided the handicapped people and senior citizens Marlene Sciascia encountered in New York.

"Access!" exclaimed Marlene Sciascia. "Making things accessible for people with wheelchairs and what-have-you would make things a lot nicer for the rest of us. Older people have such a hard time. But that was one of our problems. We couldn't ally ourselves with the aged who wouldn't ally themselves with the disabled, because 'those are sick people.' We had trouble building coalitions."

Even though family groups and the Mental Health Association have slightly different memberships and focuses, Carol Garvin spoke about a positive working relationship between the two that overcame superficial differences.

Garvin said, "Family groups tend to be a little more militant than we are. I got a letter from this woman about the funding for a facility they run for people to stay in after they come out of the hospital. And they want some funding through the department of mental health. She had talked to someone in the department and she wasn't satisfied with the response she got and so she wrote me and said, 'You know I don't know what they're trying to communicate.'

"So I talked to this fellow [in the department of mental health] and he was kind of irritated. He tried to indicate what he meant. So I wrote her back and said, 'You know, I've talked to this fellow. This is what he said. This is what I think he's trying to do. I'm going to send him a copy of this. But I don't think he was playing games with you.'

"That's another way in which you try to keep people talking back and forth with each other. Hopefully you don't waste a lot of energy on antagonisms that just don't get anything done."

Communication that comes too little, too late can end up pitting groups against each other. When one group publicly advocates a 10 percent cost of living increase and another wants 15 percent, that usually means they didn't do a thorough job at the research stage. That's the time groups sniff around to see what other advocates are thinking of doing, so they don't end up in a public conflict that damages the entire issue.

One of the most effective types of groups doing advocacy today is the ad hoc coalition. Coalitions can share resources to conduct campaigns too big for only one group to tackle. And they can share skills. Coalitions offer advocates and groups a chance to specialize at what they know best.

It sounds easy and wonderful. But if working with one advocacy group is hard, working with several in unison is very difficult. Groups should get to know one another well enough to help each other out, filling gaps for each other.

Coalitions that are set up to provide quid pro quo on a range of unrelated issues do not work very well.

NOW, according to Janet Ferone, learned this through experience. "In the early years of the movement NOW felt taken advantage of, that people just wanted us in coalitions because of our numbers. When it came down to the meat of the matter, they would not come out for causes. There was a lot of lip service by many groups for the ERA, but we were burned many times in many states when the groups suddenly switched around their priorities and their support for the ERA vanished after we had given them support for their issues.

"Since then, NOW has developed strict guidelines for joining coalitions," Ferone said. "The groups that we are in are fairly feminist groups, and the issue is reproductive freedom."

Coalitions can be very powerful at changing policy, but, because they are complex combinations of groups, forming them can be difficult. Groups that plan to work in coalition have to find common ground and respect differences before they can cooperate.

First, people have to find similarities among themselves. Once group members can identify with each other, they have to agree on problems and goals for solving them before they can work together.

Then, the more approaches the better. "It's like family," said Betsy Reifsnider. "You have your more outlandish family members who can get into different areas. For example, the Alliance for Survival on nuclear issues is a very good organization, but we can approach constituencies they can't, and they approach people the Sierra Club could not."

Occasionally groups with similar goals choose not to work together. However, if they are concerned about the issue they are careful to see that their goals and efforts are not in direct conflict with each other. If there is outward disagreement, failure of any policy change campaign is nearly guaranteed.

Most damaging can be the notion that coalitions are permanent. The League of Women Voters handbook "Making an Issue of It" says, "Necessary as a coalition may be, it's important to remember, it is not a marriage for life. It is really an ad hoc sometime thing."

Delivering Services vs. Changing Policy

Which is better, providing direct services to people who need them or working to change public policies that make those services necessary?

In some advocacy circles this is a raging controversy complete with name-calling and moralizing on both sides. It is a debate that is never resolved, but it does leave everyone in both camps with hard feelings. Groups that actually have much in common feel isolated instead of empowered whenever they get involved in this fight. The question has no real answer. Be the issue food, housing, the environment or any other, both practical action and policy change are worthy and compatible enterprises.

For service providers and policy advocates to argue about their relative worth is like employees of an automobile manufacturer fighting over who is more important—the auto designers or the assembly workers. Both are needed to make cars. An extended debate on who's better will slow down—and may even halt—production.

Advocates and groups tempted to get involved in one side or the other in the services versus policy argument should note that the only winners will be the forces that oppose both. Once a distracting debate gets going, the groups are split into two weaker ones. Their activities are then much less effective than if both types of organizations respected the other's activities and supported them however they could.

If such a debate starts—in the anti-hunger community, for example—advocates should watch out for a "star" or a "warrior" at the helm of one or more of the organizations (see Chapter Eleven). When leading a group is not enough, people involved in advocacy, because of a need to feel personally powerful, may feel a need to compete with other groups using any reason they can find. Such impulses harm both of the advocacy groups.

Coping with Strange Bedfellows

Although the majority of people who work with groups on issues are extremely helpful, every group, at one time or another, has to deal with constituents—and sometimes entire groups—that don't help the cause.

At the root of many internal conflicts in and between advocacy organizations are chronically troublesome groups and group members—anti-authoritarians, socializers, scaredy-cats, road hogs and occasionally, in international issues groups, infiltrators—none of whom have any interest in carrying out activities to change policy. These group members are cousins of the warriors, wimps, truthgivers, truth twisters and others described earlier.

People who are not fundamentally motivated to change policy join groups working for policy change for personal reasons. Members, like leaders, who put personal agendas before public ones can cause dissension and failure—often before any action can be taken.

Advocates with experience learn to spot troublesome constituents and groups fairly early. The following descriptions can be applied to organizations as well as individuals that hold back progress from the inside. Although almost everyone has some of the tendencies described below, extremists are the ones who will spoil things.

Anti-authoritarians: Some people get involved in advocacy not because of a commitment to a cause or issue, but because they simply detest authority. When a group comes along that provides an easy vehicle for their expression of anger, they join up.

The psychological reasons for anti-authority types being so hateful of anyone with "power" are not really important to advocates. What is important is that those people love to talk about problems and point fingers at who caused them. But they put forth very little effort to help solve them.

When it comes time for the group to take action or actually deal with the authorities, these people are not to be found. When it comes time for the next meeting to talk about an issue, usually during the research stage or earlier, they reappear, once again ranting on and on—sometimes with knowledge and persuasiveness—about those awful "powers-that-be." Antiauthority folks can be great at getting others excited about problems, but advocates don't count on them to do anything else.

Socializers: Some people just want company and support, and those are legitimate benefits of belonging to an advocacy group. But if socializing is all they want, they've joined the wrong group. The people who join for personal support generally cause no damage except static cling. Unfortunately, socializers can easily slip into the next category.

Scaredy-cats: When push comes to shove (i.e., it's time to take action), scaredy-cats head for the door. Or, worse yet, the scaredy cat tries to convince everyone else not to go ahead. If a person questions ideas in planning meetings, but is willing to go along with a consensus, that's one thing. But a person who opposes all actions is probably just scared. In a common scenario, the advocacy "chicken" is not around at all when decisions are made about organizational activities. They call in afterward to criticize what was just done.

Scaredy-cats almost always have "reasons" for objecting: it's the wrong time, the wrong strategy, the goal isn't expressed exactly right, it's too much, it will never work, etc. Their real problem is fear of doing anything.

Once again, it takes a little experience to spot the habitual naysayer. Reasonable people ask questions every once in a while. But if one person refuses to go along with the group's decision for almost every issue and at each step, it's pretty easy to realize the person is really afraid to take a risk to try to change anything.

A member of the board of the Arkansas Civil Liberties Union pulled a "scaredy-cat" stunt on Director Sandra Kurjiaka after she made a speech. "I have a board member," she said, "who felt I went too far in my speech to the Gay Pride rally—that I went further than ACLU policy and didn't use good judgment. And I said, if we can't say it nobody can say it. And the board member replied that I didn't use good judgment.

"He wrote a public letter calling for my resignation because of a side comment I'd made. I said that everybody in the community, including butchy dikes and drag queens, should be allowed to lobby. That was what everybody was objecting to, and the reaction of the crowd was to roar with laughter.

"Well, foolishly, instead of just skipping it, I wrote to him and sent him copies of our policy on the issue. I also wrote him a rather lengthy letter explaining to him about the problems that gay people had in Arkansas. Even though he was an ACLU member I was not communicating with a reasonable person. He wrote a ferocious letter to the board saying they should take action against me. In the end the board decided that I had done what I was charged to do. But that's part of what you have to put up with."

Road hogs: Almost every advocacy group has either had a member who was a road hog or has had to deal with another group that had the same problem. Road hogs are looking for power and not much else. The person or group talks on and on, not giving others a chance. Road hogs demand a lot of credit and reward for doing the slightest thing. They constantly distract the group onto their personal agendas.

Unfortunately, the road hog person or group often volunteers to be on every committee, too, just to get more air time. Poor folks. No one else pays them enough attention, they think, so this group of volunteers will have to. It's not hard to recognize road hogs. They ask for recognition immediately and articulately.

Will Collette of CCHW suggests establishing clear rules that would allow group leaders "to enforce proper rules of behavior."

Infiltrators: It is possible for advocacy groups to have members, even founding members, who are government infiltrators. It is likely that groups that deal with international issues such as disarmament and Central America get infiltrated more than others. In 1983, President Reagan issued an executive order that for the first time in history gave the CIA permission—in contradiction to its own charter—to infiltrate domestic organizations. Break-ins where only papers were taken—not money or expensive equipment—occurred in offices of groups working on Central American issues several times.

It is nearly impossible to prove someone is a government infiltrator. But infiltrators behave in certain ways that are intolerable to advocacy groups and fairly easy to spot. First, they mess up everything they touch. They may "lose" significant amounts of the group's money. Or they may repeatedly put themselves in charge of all the papers and the refreshments for an event and then "forget" them. They antagonize friends and insult pals who agree with them on the issues.

Some infiltrators commit or advocate violent and or illegal activities. They may try to get others in the group to carry out illegal activities, too. If those activities are done in secret, the group has been blackmailed.

Infiltrators try to keep their names off everything. If they are also in leadership roles of groups they create, they may obscure names and addresses of the group on materials and operate without an oversight committee or board.

An infiltrator and any groups he or she creates may also have plenty of money to perform fairly expensive activities, sometimes using expensive equipment. On thinking it over, other advocates for similar issues struggling to raise funds realize they have no idea where the well-off advocate got the money. And, of course, the infiltrator doesn't want to say, or says he got it going door to door or from anonymous donors.

Dealing with Troublesome People and Groups

As with infighting, the first and best defense against the negative effects problem people cause is a strong, well-managed group. In meetings and in making all decisions, a democratically led advocacy group has several avenues it can pursue to cut down the impact of troublemakers.

First, the group can use the limits and rules and processes it has to restrict the time and energy people take up with their personal agendas. Any methods that work to ignore the person are good ones. The less time, space and energy the anti-authoritarian, scaredy-cat, road hog or infiltrator uses, the better for the group and its goals.

Second, if those limits don't work, the group doesn't have to protest if the person decides to drop out. But it has to be strong and confident enough to withstand the temporary "badmouthing" it might have to listen to if the person goes.

Lois Gibbs said that in at least four communities, some scaredy-cats tried to dissuade the majority of people from adopting strong stands like "no landfill." In each community, she reported, the scaredy-cats "left the group because they felt the goal was too strong. It didn't hurt the groups because these people were so wishy-washy they wouldn't have been much help even if they stayed. Their departure made the groups much stronger." In all four communities, the industries gave up, and the groups won their "no-landfill" goals.

Sometimes it's harder to get rid of disruptive people. Affiliations of individuals with unions and professional organizations are much tighter than others, and members are much less likely to just walk away from the group when things don't please them. Those groups have to use rules and procedures to limit the effects of troublesome members as much as possible.

Infiltrators are also unlikely to stop participating. After all, they're being paid to stay and interfere. In addition to enforcing rules and processes, it's a good idea for groups to give people who constantly mess up *absolutely nothing to do*. It is impossible to prove that a person is an infiltrator; infiltrators' identities are official national secrets. Any group looking for proof will not find it. It doesn't matter. Handle all who habitually mess up by giving them no responsibilities.

And, of course, no advocacy group worth a mention would ever sanction or conduct any activity, no matter who suggests it (likely an infiltrator), that is both illegal and covert. Any group that goes along is virtually owned by the instigator afterwards.

Although infiltrators' behavior is pretty easy to spot once people know what they are looking for, confronting the fact that a group member or leader seems to be systematically working against the cause can be extremely upsetting to people.

Whole groups, especially small ones, can be set up by infiltrators. They share the same characteristics as the individuals who practice this deceptive occupation.

Expanding Views of Constituents

Sandra Kurjiaka said her "most important advocacy issue is building grassroots networks. . . ." Although constituent recruiting is one of the most heavily emphasized areas of advocacy, more sophisticated, more inclusive methods for recruiting and keeping constituents involved are needed. Most outreach has been based too much on the advocacy group and too little on the interests of constituents.

Recognizing that there are four types of constituents to recruit— depending on the issues—and developing more methods for reaching out to them could revolutionize advocacy.

The groups are people with a local crisis; people born with a special condition, such as race, gender or nationality; people who have a particular life situation, such as illness or poverty or a particular job; and members of the public who are aware of and concerned about public issues in general.

The vast majority of material written and taught about recruiting supporters has assumed that constituents all share a local problem. Reaching out personally for supporters in one's own neighborhood is relatively easy. Not enough has been said or done about recruiting people from the other three groups, people who may or may not live in the same area.

Constituents for issues who are service recipients are not as prepared from the start, nor do they have as many resources to support advocacy activities, as members of other types of organizations.

"If you want to organize a group [of recipients] it's a slow process," Barbara Reed said. "You might not end up with the same kinds of gains for the people you are working with. Life is such a survival kind of thing for a lot of people. It's a lot to ask them to put a lot of energy into bringing about that change. It's such a major sacrifice. Although I'm still convinced that any long-lasting change has to give people some sense of power."

Resources available from one of the four groups—people with concern about issues—have gone largely untapped. Some groups that have focused only on recruiting constituents directly affected by problems have ignored other potential supporters. If all advocacy groups—including those that gear activities toward getting better treatment for service recipients—could develop outreach efforts to and include members of the general public who sympathize with, but aren't necessarily personally affected by, the issues, the service groups could be strengthened considerably.

There is no reason that the Coalition for Basic Human Needs and similar "recipient groups" could not have individual memberships and built-in participation mechanisms for people with general concerns about issues. Then people generally concerned about families and poverty could join CBHN, too. In that way, those directly affected by policy decisions and concerned others could work together for needed change to strengthen the effort a great deal.

The Mental Health Association is an example of an advocacy group whose membership comes from both people who are directly affected by mental health issues and members of the public who are generally concerned.

Barbara Reed said of Interfaith, Inc., "Our constituency is in part the people who live in the housing Interfaith, Inc., developed. But it is also, in part, the middle and upper middle class folks. The combination of these two groups coming at the same issue in the same way in the name of the same organization is pretty effective."

One of the worst recruiting tools is the four-page single-spaced letter—looking for people with concern—that screams about a problem and asks the stranger who receives it to join the group and or contribute money. Where this recruiting device came from and who reads these "cold mail" diatribes is unknown.

Government: Mixed Feelings and Actions

Some advocates are strongly and openly involved in getting people elected, hired and appointed to government office. Others strictly adhere to a hands-off policy when it comes to this side of politics.

But many advocates are overcoming the problem of attitude extremes as they realize that, like everyone else, each government official and body has to be analyzed according to its own behavior and dealt with accordingly.

Though they are seen as the embodiment of power, most government officials are in very temporary positions. Advocates often outlast officials, who rise and fall with the most recent election or the latest poll. In that way, advocates, who don't rely as much on favorable politics to keep them going, have more power than the officials.

Advocates who take their roles seriously and really want to see change instituted might consider accepting more out-front roles in the political arena. Martha Cotera, Lotta Chi and Juanita Kennedy Morgan—all of whom work for minority rights—make no bones about the fact that they and their colleagues work to get people on their side inside government.

Juanita Kennedy Morgan said, "We feel that many black women do not recognize that politics is the answer to many of their problems. They feel they should get away from politics, that politics is a dirty word. We try to train them. We say, 'You better become involved. You can make it a clean word.'

"We also tell them that unless they become involved in politics, they're going to be at the bottom of the heap. Because politics is the education of your child. Politics is the house you buy, the interest rate you pay. Politics is the very air you breathe and the water you drink. Without these things, you really can't survive. And all of these years—the last 100 years—black people and black women especially have not become of a part" of politics.

Chi pointed out that her non-profit organization itself does not get directly involved because the out-front help to candidates would put the group's non-profit status in jeopardy. Instead, Chinese American women work as individuals to support politicians on their side.

Martha Cotera also belongs to informal groups that "work on three to five political campaigns every year and thus enhance Mexican American women's clout. I find this strategy pretty effective. Once our candidate wins, she explains, "we can lobby for appointments, contracts for minority businesses and affirmative action policies."

In addition to the informal work advocates do, some groups form special connected PACs that come right with working endorsements— offering money and work to candidates that support them on issues. More and more professional organizations have special PACs through which their members donate money to campaigns. And some membership organizations, like NOW, have PACs too. The national disarmament group SANE, of which Norma Wilson is a member, was involved in nearly 100 U.S. House and Senate races in 1984 through its PAC. Obviously, those groups endorse and work for candidates. Unions typically endorse and work for candidates very openly. And the law does not limit that.

PACs are controversial. Although they were invented with the intention of giving non-wealthy citizens the chance to run for office, many groups, such as Common Cause, see them as institutionalized graft, through which incumbents, mostly, get swamped with contributions from special interest groups, many of them corporate, that want favors in return.

On the other side of the political involvement question is the League of Women Voters. The membership organization repeatedly emphasizes this contrast although the group supports certain policies and does "voter education," or is nonpartisan and never endorses, works for or shows any favoritism to particular candidates for office. The handbook "Making a Difference" makes this demand of League representatives: "never support or oppose a party, a faction of a party or any candidate—whether in . . . elections or in the day-to-day work of government."

The LWV goes so far as to say, "Program/action and Voters Service/ Citizen Information must be handled separately and by different board members" to prevent misunderstanding.

The line the League draws between doing "voter education" and taking stands on issues must be extremely fine. An LWV workbook spells out the contrast: "Voters Service/Citizen Information is designed to give citizens facts on issues, as a foundation for reaching decisions, without recommending a course of action. In contrast, League program, based on member study and agreement on selected issues, involves action in support of or opposition to specific measures."

Conflicts can nevertheless arise. The handbook warns, "When your League is asked to speak on a ballot issue, be sure to determine whether the request is for a straight presentation of information or for a presentation of the League position. Don't mix the two in one meeting."

Although extreme attitudes are leveling out, some advocates and groups deal with government on uneasy terms. Many groups shy away from issues and candidates. And candidates have not used groups and their thousands of members nearly enough. Although many non-profit groups are afraid of repercussions from political activity, no one can stop the same people from forming other informal groups that work for candidates who favor their issues.

"Work" is an important word here. General "here's how the candidates stand" statements aren't much. Neither are endorsements, by themselves. Good politicians need to have real support from advocacy organizations. There's money from groups that can legally give it. But there are also leaflet drops, poll workers, parties and other contributions that make a big difference.

OWL and CCHW, for example, emphasize telling the public where candidates stand on issues and letting members decide what to do based thereon. This approach may help members decide whom to vote for and keep the groups within the tax laws, but it doesn't provide anything close to working support for candidates on their side of the issue. In fact, in a decade when people are having a hard time connecting candidates and the issues they are interested in, an analysis of candidates' stands buried in a newsletter somewhere may have little or no impact on members.

"Working in the political process has to be a little bit disillusioning at times," Carol Garvin reflected, "although I don't know what the illusion was in the first place. It's the sense that you're giving people this wonderful cause that has to do with people's needs and they're responding to other things, some of which are not so terribly noble as you perceive yours to be. I suppose that's disillusioning. But on the whole I don't think that working in the process is that disillusioning. It's more momentary than permanent. The next morning it doesn't seem so important."

Special Handling

Special groups in society—including churches, hospitals, universities, businesses, experts and institutions—are very important to advocacy, too. Few groups or issues can get along without the knowledge and support of at least one of these groups. Both advocates and their special friends could probably do a better job of educating one another about what they do and what they have to offer each other.

Experts and institutions make necessary, but sometimes difficult, advocacy partners. There is always the threat that these "outsiders" will take over the group or its efforts. They can only do that, however, when groups let them.

Specialists take over when advocates indicate they are helpless without them or when the group changes its identity and methodology because specialists tell them to. It is the job of any advocacy group to make lawyers and other experts serve the group, not the other way around. Specialists who do not see themselves as servants of the group and the cause should be replaced.

Another problem with legal and scientific experts is that they are used to being paid for their knowledge and training. Advocates must either raise the money to pay their fees or make other arrangements with them for inexpensive or free services.

Institutions are in danger of taking over when they give money, goods or services. Once again, advocates have to bite the bullet and let businesses, universities and foundations they work with know that the group's purposes and goals are independent of institutional meddling.

It is the pitiable advocacy group whose leaders wake up one morning to discover that the group has changed its direction markedly only to qualify for funding, rather than because of a need the group perceived.

The other problem is that members of special groups are loyal only in an ad hoc way. The same people and institutions that help one group today may turn up working in opposition to that group tomorrow.

The best way for groups to use specialists is to interview them carefully, even if they are volunteering. No matter how well-known or knowledgeable the person is, if the person does not want to work within the group's decision-making structure, he or she should not be employed.

Second, the group should write out an agreement with the expert. It needn't be formal—it will serve essentially as a job description. It should spell out what the expert is expected to do, for how long, in what way and for what, if any, compensation. In this way, the specialist knows the advocacy group is boss.

Experts may make better teachers and consultants than actual participants in activities. Groups can use lobbyists, scientists, negotiators, lawyers and others to teach and advise them, rather than carry out activities. In that way, constituents gain skills they can use again.

Process Experts: Attorneys, Consultants and Lobbyists

Sometimes groups need the services of a process expert, usually an attorney or public policy consultant.

An article in one issue of *Everybody's Backyard* from CCHW begins by quoting Chico Marx: "When ya gotta trouble, getta lawyer. Then ya gotta more trouble but a least ya gotta lawyer."

The article suggests groups should hire lawyers for some purposes— taking specific legal actions—but not for others for which they have no training or experience.

Using lawyers can have drawbacks: "A large chunk of your membership may leave, thinking, 'Now we've got a lawyer to handle our problem for us.'

"Most lawyers have opinions about group strategy. If your lawyer says 'Don't protest,' at least a few of your members are going to agree and the internal fights begin."

Ron Simon, special counsel to CCHW, who also has a regular column in *Everybody's Backyard*, echoes the advice of many advocacy experts in discussing a key to every element of issues work: "BE CLEAR ABOUT YOUR GOALS. Some big problems with lawyers are not necessarily caused by the lawyers themselves, but by what people expect from lawyers and how they deal with them."

Later Simon says, "The most common mistake I have seen is that people believe they can hire a lawyer and stop all the work . . . that has brought the cause along. Too many times hiring the lawyer is the death knell to all other activities—a terrible mistake."

If a group is considering hiring a lawyer, Lois Gibbs says it should first ask itself why. Lawyers are useful for filing lawsuits and for other legal actions, but they are needed only after the group decides that taking court action is the best strategy to meet the goal at hand.

Will Collette concludes his article about lawyers in *Everybody's Backyard* by saying, "Don't hire a lawyer unless you have to. Dealing with problems . . . takes a mixed approach. You can minimize [difficulties] and maximize the benefits by keeping the lawyer's role secondary to "the overall activities of the group. Have a clear 'contract' with the lawyer," Collette advises, "and hold your lawyer accountable to the group."

Sometimes advocacy groups hire lobbyists to help with legislative campaigns. In general, this is a good idea and shows the professional determination of the group to get legislation passed. Some very good advocates who used to work for non-profit advocacy groups are becoming independent consultants these days, and groups can use them.

There are two main pitfalls to avoid when hiring lobbyists. First, some lobbyists, like lawyers, do not recognize—or have forgotten—the importance of group decision-making and activity. They can tend to be "lone rangers" who try to impress by pulling strings behind closed doors to magically save the day for the group. Unfortunately, it usually doesn't work and the strategy fails.

Lobbyists, like lawyers, come into the picture when a group has already decided what strategy to pursue. Although lawyers are required for court cases, professional lobbyists aren't required to carry out legislation.

A good lobbyist always includes the group in making major decisions. Problems with lawyers and lobbyists are that they are each heavily invested in pursuing a particular strategy. If, along the way, the group suggests other strategies, they are likely to be against them. Like lawyers and other experts, lobbyists often want to take over the activity. Good advocacy groups don't let them. Public policy consultants can come in at any stage of a policy campaign— the earlier the better—to help groups go through the five steps.

Content Experts

Advocates are in some of the same dangers with technical experts— scientists, medical doctors and others—as with lawyers. The group should not abdicate its authority or commitment to work just because it has become affiliated with one or two of these content experts.

Collette offers "a profile of a good expert" in one issue of CCHW's *Everybody's Backyard.* A good expert "has the right credentials to get respect . . . , charges a price you can afford, has the right experience, doesn't interfere by giving advice outside his or her expertise, builds your self-confidence . . . keeps commitments, helps you learn . . . , is honest . . . , doesn't dominate or take over the group."

It's almost impossible for a member of an advocacy group to become a lawyer or a banker to help the cause, but in the case of technical experts, often a person in the group learns enough to become one. Then the pitfalls are the same as when the group uses outside experts, except the person works for a lot less money and a lot of assured commitment to the cause.

Will Collette offers some wise observations in another issue of *Everybody's Backyard*. "Self-taught experts can be the very best kind," he says, "but the group will have to keep the leader from becoming a data fanatic."

Chapter Thirteen

The Challenge of Change

Even though advocacy has been compared to war, in actual practice, we are trying to convince people on a very peaceful level.

— Betsy Reifsnider

Without issues action, it's not advocacy. It's that simple. Working with a group because there's a problem isn't enough. If the group does not go on, consistently waging policy change campaigns, it's not an advocacy group.

If a group came together to correct a particular problem and succeeded, it may be better to disband than to hang around with nothing to do. Have a victory or farewell party instead.

No one ever said changing public policy is easy, but advocates report that the time and effort pay off in currencies of empowerment and change for the better.

Groups at the Helm

A policy campaign cannot be conducted without a group. Anyone who claims to be able to get policy changed alone is misguided and eventually unsuccessful.

Members and other constituents of advocacy groups need to have authority at every step in every policy campaign. Although the entire membership may agree to have a smaller group or committee that actually manages a campaign from day to day, managers have to be sure they don't ever take the next big step before they go back to the larger group for input and for a final decision.

There are three good reasons for making sure campaigns are managed by members. First, there is always a danger that the management group gets isolated and off track. Checking in with the larger group helps prevent that.

Second, it is very important that the whole group own the process and the result. Each person is more likely to help, and each person will learn to feel empowered by working in a well-run policy campaign.

The most important reason for having a preset group decision-making process is that it makes campaigns less likely to get stalled by members who object to some aspect of the plan after it's under way. Again and again, when decisions are made only by a small group or in an hoc manner, someone jumps up partway through to ask, often indignantly, "Why are you doing it that way?" Or, "Who said you could do this?"

Advocacy groups that have an open, often-stated process for making decisions at every step of the policy change process can answer those questions. Groups that just muddle along without a stated process very often get stopped in their tracks as soon as any question is raised from the group or from anywhere else.

Who Chooses Issues to Work On?

The most critical advocacy question comes at Step 1 of a change campaign. Different advocacy groups employ a variety of methods for choosing issues ranging from very purposeful, step-by-step decision-making processes to haphazard gee-this-is-a-problem-I-think-we'll-work-on-it approaches. A happy medium between three years of study with consensus building among hundreds and having one or two people decide informally seems to work best. The size and scope of the issue are relevant, too.

Ideally, Step 1 of the process would include ways all members (or otherwise affiliated persons, such as recipients of services) could introduce issues and express themselves on which ones should get attention from the group. Some advocacy groups let members of the public suggest issues and encourage them to work on them, too.

The LWV pamphlet "The Politics of Change" suggests taking polls because they are "useful to identifying the aims and goals of the ordinary citizen. His or her views are important...."

When staff or even board members—no matter how well-intentioned— make initial decisions about major issues to pursue without seeking information and opinions from membership or constituents, they weaken themselves unnecessarily. The power of the larger group's participation is needed to inspire and carry out the group's actions on issues over the long haul.

Different Folks/Different Strokes

Advocates have different problems and advantages as they work for issues depending on which of the four basic constituent groups they are working with. It is very important for advocates to be completely aware of the pluses and minuses that go with different constituent groups.

Two groups—those who were born with an uncontrollable factor (race, sex, etc.) and those who developed problems later (illness, poverty, etc.)— have a particularly tough time advocating for policies that would improve things. The very problem they are trying to address affects how effectively they can carry out the advocacy campaign.

Dorothy Ridings remembered League efforts to try to keep the ERA in place in Kentucky after the legislature passed it in 1972. She put her personal feelings and her policy principles on the line simultaneously.

"Ridings said, "We fought [ERA] recision for years. In every legislature there was a recision bill up, and we had to go back up, and the ladies in pink dresses would come in against us.

"I remember clearly getting so frustrated one time when I was testifying before a committee. I said, 'I'm here for the League of Women Voters. The issue is ERA. You know that I've been here. Other League members have been here arguing for rights for the poor, equal access to education, equal rights for the handicapped, civil rights. We're here for the human issues for the under-represented, those who are powerless to speak for themselves, those with great needs. . . . But this time I'm here for me. The ERA is very personal, and, by golly, I want it!'

"It was the first time in my experience that I was there to say, 'This is something that's important to *me*. It's not only right for society and for the group of people who are women . . . but this time it's very personal, because it's me.'

Blacks fighting for voting rights ran into racism in the courts. People who are ill don't have the strength to lobby. Some government administrators think people are poor out of choice. It goes on and on (see the "Surmounting Barriers to Change," page 261 for more about prejudice).

Surprisingly, although they have an extra burden in some ways, people who suffer tough life conditions have a few advantages in the policy realm. Sometimes 501(c)(3) groups qualify for grants general membership organizations do not. And when they speak about problems, officials know it is from direct experience.

People connected by similar jobs in professional organizations are fortunate to have both resources and life experience on their sides when it comes to advocacy. More than other groups, however, they are sometimes accused of being "selfish" or "greedy" in their positions. Since all groups want policy change that will help members, the name-calling is silly.

The other two types of constitutents — people with local problems and those who have general concern with an issue — usually have more resources to do advocacy. They are less hampered by personal problems and prejudice when they take action and tend to have slightly more time and money.

On the down side, people who discover they have a local crisis on their hands often lack experience and knowledge when the problem first hits. They have to take more time than established organizations to put their groups together. And some have to overcome shock and disbelief that things could go so wrong.

People with general concern, though they may have education and resources, have the exact opposite problem of the other three types of constituents. They have trouble speaking from personal experience.

The Root of All Good

Although advocates have people power, most of them lack monetary equity with corporations. Carol Tucker Foreman points out "the heavy impact of money" on members of Congress. "A great many of them cannot be bought off under any circumstance, but there are others who can. We have to counter an awful lot of people who have money and not much else with citizen interest and citizen activism."

When asked on a questionnaire what their biggest concerns are, several advocates responded "Finances!" Tish Sommers said she was concerned with "raising enough money for the organization to grow and flourish." And Connie Spruill asked, "Where does one go to get money to do effective lobbying?"

Funding policy campaigns is very difficult. Foundations, private resources and others sometimes fund service delivery groups, but that money is usually not for policy change. Only the most progressive funders will give money to an issue campaign. A vast majority want to pay for direct services only. Even operating costs for non-profits are hard to fund. Membership and professional organizations have it easier; they can use dues to help foot the advocacy bill.

Barbara Reed, a former Children's Foundation staff member, recalled, "In a way we did have a constituency, but it was very often us, the advocates, determining the issues. We were funded for particular issues. In other words, we didn't go into a community and ask, 'What are your major problems?'"

A major advance for advocacy would be to convince the many foundations that donate for direct services to give to policy change campaigns run by constituents. One obvious selling point is that in so many cases, if policy were different, the services wouldn't be needed so much. Foundations need to encourage change of root causes of social problems, not just the superficial results.

Keeping in Step

Following the five steps in a policy change campaign is difficult. Intentionally or by accident, some advocacy groups go to extremes, overemphasizing some activities and ignoring others. Without a balanced approach to all five steps, success is more elusive than it has to be.

A good rule of thumb is that if a group spends more than 50 percent or less than 10 percent of its energy and time on any one step of the process, activities are dangerously unbalanced and need to be adjusted.

Most advocacy groups portray each campaign as though it were completely unique. Their materials list advocacy activities in no particular order. Although every policy campaign feels special and in some ways is, they all go through the five steps in a process that is anything but random.

Going through those steps requires perspective and awareness in order to not get bogged down in details. The ability to create change depends on persistence. Success also, paradoxically, requires advocates to make definite decisions at each step but remain flexible enough to recognize when something isn't working and go back and make another choice.

Some reasons advocates and groups get stuck or skip steps are subtle. Fear of failure—and, surprisingly enough, of success—hinders progress sometimes. Except for sports and elections, there is probably no endeavor with more obvious wins and losses in our society than a policy change campaign.

Insecure groups resist following the straight step-by-step process because in every campaign there is a final score. The faint-hearted may feel unconsciously reluctant to go through the whole game for fear of learning a definite outcome. More secure, determined advocates know they can handle a win or a loss and come back another day.

As pointed out in Chapter Twelve, troublesome group members and other groups always hinder progress. Specialization is a factor. Some advocates have more interest and skills in some campaign activities than others, so they carry out those activities and ignore the others.

Although the process for changing policy is presented in a five-step chronology, those steps are more like spokes in an advocacy wheel that is constantly turning. As soon as advocates begin to follow through on issues campaigns, they begin to look further at the issues and discover more. As process after process rolls along, with each step in sequence, the entire policy cart rolls forward. Each step has different pitfalls advocates can fall into:

In Step 1, identifying issues, some groups discover problems and decide what to work on in a very informal, haphazard manner. Others have strict processes for seeking and officially identifying issues to work on that take months—even years—to complete.

It's also easy to get stuck in Step 2, research. How much information is enough? One way to see if there's been enough research is to go to the next step and begin planning.

Everyone has bumped into groups and individuals that are fixated on complaining. They articulate what's wrong very well and in detail, sometimes using data from polls, surveys and research. They also articulate how things should be, but they stop right there. They don't feel confident or responsible or educated enough to realize that they can and should take the big leap forward to try to effect change.

At the other extreme, some groups actually skip research. They go straight from discovering a problem to "solving" it, before they muster enough information and people to persuade government to change.

Many advocates skip Step 3, reviewing and planning, as a do-nothing activity, but it's actually a critical stage because at this point the goal is articulated, the strategy for achieving it refined and the group gets itself and its resources geared up for action. Trouble occurs when decisions are made accidentally, leaving the campaign disorganized and unfocused.

It's easy to get lost in Step 4, carrying out strategies. Education—along with legislation, litigation or negotiation—is so filled with details and people, it's easy to lose sight of the goal. This is the stage where managers have to have a plan and an outline of specific activities that lead to realization of the goal.

Step 5, following through, is also crucial. Even though you make contact with the ball in tennis, if you don't follow through you lose the point. The same is true in advocacy. Yet follow-through is the most ignored step in the policy change process. Getting a policy change is worthless if it isn't nailed down publicly, then thoroughly monitored through implementation.

Groups ignore this step out of inexperience. It's amazing how many groups finally score the apparent victory or loss and then just drift away from the campaign at that point. They are probably exhausted, and they mistakenly think they are done at the end of Step 4.

Balancing Acts

It's no accident that education and the legislation strategy take up much more space in the direct strategies chapter of this book than the negotiation and litigation sections (see chapters Nine and Ten). With a few notable exceptions, most advocates concentrate on education and legislation to bring about change.

Overall, advocates probably do the right amount of education — especially general education — in their efforts to attain improved policy. Lots of organizations list "public education" as one of two or three purposes for existing. It makes sense to devote a lot of time and energy to letting people inside and outside the group know about the issues in general and about problems and goals in specific campaigns. Change won't occur unless community awareness on the subject is heightened and people know about efforts for change. Monetary and other support are easier to find for education than the other strategies.

But education is not enough. One pitfall advocates fall into — especially with the current emphasis on media attention — is to believe that once the problem is documented in the daily newspaper, they can just sit by, and it will be solved. That doesn't happen.

Too Much Legislation

At Step 3, advocacy groups choose to go the legislative route much more often than they choose negotiation or litigation. Most advocates seem hot for getting new laws on the books as the best way to achieve policy change. Exceptions are the Civil Liberties Union, some local issues groups and occasional forays into the courtroom by the League of Women Voters.

Many advocacy groups even use terms like "taking action" or "issue campaign" to refer only to legislated change. But legislation is one of three equal actions or campaigns to choose for solid public policy improvement.

There are a lot of drawbacks to legislative campaigns. Legislation takes a long time, a lot of people power and a lot of resources to deal with a large number of officials in a complicated, uncontrolled arena where the law of averages shows there is a strong chance of losing.

Betsy Reifsnider described the typically erratic legislative process in California: "A bill that we [Sierra Club] think is good may be terribly compromised by the time it reaches the governor's desk. It may have a few good points, but it's very diluted. Some of the horrible bills we can stop, even if nothing good makes it through. If we can't stop the terrible thing from going through, we can challenge it in the courts."

One state representative has called the messy legislative process "more like mud wrestling" than an orderly process. Policy victories in legislatures are very hard to come by. Legislation does have some advantages. A law on the books or taken off the books is recognized as official change — usually.

Advocates, with no special training, often exhibit a knee-jerk reaction: we need a change, we go to the legislative branch. When that happens, the strategy choice is more of a gamble than a conscious decision. Sometimes — depending on the goal — legislation is the most appropriate, efficient choice.

A sure sign that a switch in strategy is needed is if a law doesn't make it for two sessions in a row. Advocates, no matter how legislation-centered they are, have to try another strategy, unless there is a drastic change in the status quo in the legislature. Some advocates and groups go back year after year to legislatures where there is almost no hope, when they could approach the executive or judicial branches with significantly greater chances of success.

Legislation is used so often simply because it is the best-known strategy. High school civics courses and many state governments, for example, present "how a bill becomes a law" lessons routinely. How a public interest court case is won or how a regulation comes into being — although they, too, are very important to policy-making — are not taught or highlighted.

When it's chosen only by virtue of familiarity, legislation is not the best strategy. Negotiation with administrators or a lawsuit might work much better.

More Negotiation and Litigation

Government regulations are critical to the implementation of laws, and negotiation is the strategy advocates need to use to affect them. If advocates pay little attention to these administrative decisions, they ignore some of the most important policy being made.

Negotiation with administrators is inexpensive and doesn't usually drag on for years. The entire advocacy group is consulted by its negotiating team, but members don't have to follow ornate process entanglements involving hundreds of people, nor do they have to be skilled in a variety of sophisticated communication methods.

Negotiation requires a whole array of methods practiced skillfully now by union representatives, diplomats, managers and others. Many grassroots local issues advocates know a great deal about negotiating for change, too. Negotiation techniques are taught in some colleges, but usually as they apply to business, not public policy. In the future, advocates would be wise to bring in experts in negotiation — not to conduct negotiations themselves, but to teach some of the basic skills involved.

At first glance, litigation might seem a really tough strategy to pursue because of legal costs and the unfamiliar courtroom terrain. But there are many ways to fund those costs; creative advocates can avoid big bills relatively easily by getting pro bono donations of skills and grants for public interest litigation.

Groups need to ask lawyers not to be stand-ins for policy advocates but to assume expanded, long-term advocacy roles as teachers who know the legal system and how courts can be used to affect policy. Then groups would be able to decide if and how to pursue a litigation strategy based on what they have learned from the attorneys.

A big advantage both negotiation and litigation have over legislation is that they are less regulated. The tax code clearly limits advocacy efforts of non-profit organizations as their work pertains to legislation. Although regulations that would have limited advocates' court actions in a small way were promulgated recently, they never went into effect.

If advocates learned more about the processes and methods involved in negotiation and litigation and educated members and constituents about them, too, they might be able to use those strategies to score more successes in terms of real policy change.

At the very least, all three strategies, like all three branches of government, should be given balanced attention and use. When advocates talk about "taking action" and "issues campaigns" they will then be referring to all three major strategies, not just difficult, "frustrating" legislation.

Communication for Change

Communication with government is a difficult enterprise. "I think the most frustrating thing is trying to see the elected member of Congress knows the strength of constituent opinion," Dorothy Ridings said. "Sometimes the issues are so complex that the member may not think his or her constituents have an opinion. On broad issues I have a high regard for the ability of citizens to make up their minds about how they feel on some very complex issues. Even if they can't discuss the ins and outs of the MX missile system they can know how they feel about the broader issue. Sometimes I feel a bit frustrated when I'm convinced that a particular member's constituents have a certain opinion and it's trying to translate that that is difficult."

Janet Ferone said one of her main concerns as an advocate is that she "can present facts and research, well-thought-out arguments and statistics on constituency support and yet not see any change."

From the Head and Heart: The Old One-Two

An argument that should not be an argument occasionally arises in advocacy circles. Which is better for persuasion, general facts or personal experience? Should we be subjective or objective? Should we appeal to heads or hearts? Compassion or intellect?

The answer is both—about 50/50. Generally, when dealing with the public or specific government bodies, the case needs to be presented both subjectively and objectively. Successful issue campaigns have to contain both personal and factual elements working in tandem.

"For the most effective meeting" with a legislator, OWL advises, "one person should be the main spokesperson, but the others might be those who can corroborate points made through their personal experience. When giving testimony, OWL says, once again, one person acts as objective spokesperson and three others testify to corroborate.

Carol Tucker Foreman said, "By and large, members of Congress are influenced first by data, and second—maybe first—by the interests of their constituents. I can go and see a staff person and present a good argument, but somebody I work for [asbestos poisoning victims] comes from Alabama and goes to Senator Heflin [Alabama] with the same information—or takes me along to argue the specifics, if they don't feel they can—they are much more effective than I am."

Janet Diamond suggested that welfare recipients who lobby, "say in her own words what the legislation would do for her. That's what the legislator wants to hear. Compassion has a place in public policy change. It's a time-honored, traditional thing, and I don't think we should abandon it."

But, Diamond added, "You have to be able to analyze a budget. You have to be able to speak in fiscal arguments if for no other reason than even a compassionate person might have to promote your legislation to people who aren't going to buy hearts and flowers. You've got to give members information to take to the floor."

Advocates accent facts or experience only if past education has been extreme, i.e. purely emotional or academic. Then a balance is struck by providing different information. Of course, advocates know that particular bodies and individuals may be more affected by one type or the other. Most administrators want more facts than anecdotes when it comes to writing regulations, for example. Generally, elected officials need both statistics and examples—especially from their home districts—to convince them to change.

Any advocate or group that uses only half of the one-two technique is going to have lots of trouble achieving change. Just the facts are not enough. And personal anecdotes by themselves won't do it, either.

"Marketing" Change

Advocates who become aware of techniques needed to educate the public and government about issues can get discouraged sometimes. Janet

Diamond said of CBHN's design of a welfare campaign strategy, "In a way what we have to do is market people's poverty. It's a horrible idea, and it's a shame we have to do it, but if there was one rule we had at CBHN it was "Use what works." And if you have to compromise what you feel and on your values, we compromise, because those people [welfare recipients] would rather have that check than they would have you feel delicate about their feelings."

Although "marketing" may sound inappropriate when connected to public issues, anyone who watches an election campaign knows that candidates use marketing techniques to sell themselves. And in essence, though they may not say so, advocates use devices that make issues and solutions easy for people to understand. Good marketing is informational and correct, and has varying degrees of depth, depending on time and audience.

The best information campaigns are layers, from easy to complicated. As many advocates and groups point out, problems and goals are always stated in brief, simple terms before a campaign passes Step 3 and gets carried out. Obviously, the campaign has other more in-depth statements it makes on fact sheets, in testimony, etc. But the material has to be designed to communicate just the right amount and must be written especially to who is going to take it in—from the general public to a congressional committee.

Just Picture It

Whether the issue or its symbols can be easily photographed actually influences the ease with which it can be resolved. And who the constituents for the issue are is also relevant. Advocates are conscious of these factors as they work for change.

When welfare recipients wanted an increase in benefits in Massachusetts, advocates carefully and consciously devised a picture for legislators—children's boots. Rather than ask for an increase, advocates asked for a children's clothing allowance. Because it was fall, they further translated what might have still seemed abstract to legislators, into a pair of little boots.

Welfare benefits cannot be photographed. Freedom of speech is not tangible. Health care is invisible. It's more difficult for the public and its representatives to be in favor of something they cannot see or touch. A hungry child, thin with a starvation-extended stomach, will bring people to attention. An eroded field has a strong impact. Some child nutrition and environmental programs, for example, can be communicated with pictures. Clean air is harder.

No matter what the issue, advocates have to come up with pictures — real or described in words — to communicate the problem or the solution. Second best, they can produce a person who describes or typifies a need. Different issues require varying amounts of imagination in creating real pictures for people to focus on.

The Legal Limits: Warming Up from the Chills

As advocacy becomes a more powerful force in this country, more representatives of "the powers that be" try to limit or negate its effects. Laws and regulations designed to keep a rein on advocacy efforts are suggested regularly. Some advocacy barriers have entered law books and some have not. In addition, a pattern of more informal yet troublesome methods of attacking and intimidating advocates and advocacy groups has been developed by some officials over the years.

Activities intended to influence legislation and other public policy decision-making in the executive and judicial branches are a sensitive and controversial subject, not only from government's point of view, but also within advocacy itself. Unfortunately, myth and pressure sometimes win out over information, and advocates unnecessarily limit their activities or limit the wrong ones. The confusion results directly in a chilling effect on advocacy work.

In the past, lawmakers and others often directed their laws and regulations at lobbying. Nowadays, they sometimes use the broader term "policy advocacy." No matter the term, these activities — especially regarding legislation — are regulated. But how, exactly?

A lot depends on what sort of advocate affiliated with what sort of non-profit organization is doing the lobbying (see Chapter Four for more about various non-profits).

One way to understand federal advocacy laws and regulations — models for many state laws — is to examine how a specific issue — asbestos poisoning victims compensation — might be handled in the U.S. Congress by different groups.

Registered Lobbyist

First, this is the way the issue was actually handled. Carol Tucker Foreman, former executive director of the Consumer Federation of America and former assistant secretary of the Department of Agriculture, is a public policy consultant with a registered lobbying firm in Washington, D.C.

Foreman and her firm are required to register with the government and file quarterly reports detailing their activities and finances. Lobbyists and lobbying firms—sometimes called "public policy consultants," and "legislative agents"—have been overseen this way since abuses, mostly involving railroad barons bribing legislators, were uncovered at the beginning of this century.

In April 1983 Foreman said, "I represent a group of attorneys whose clients are victims of asbestos-related diseases. There are 20,000 asbestos-related cases against the Manville Coroporation right now, and these attorneys all have suits against that corporation. Last summer, the Manville Corporation filed for bankruptcy, by their own admission to avoid paying future claims or to set a ceiling on how much they would pay out to victims.

"A bill which would change the bankruptcy law has provisions that would resolve most of my clients' problems. Congress should act to see that other companies don't do the same thing as the Manville Corporation."

Carol Tucker Foreman, lobbyist, up against other lobbyists hired by corporations, worked on a complex piece of legislation which would eventually help asbestos victims and, possibly, victims of other diseases.

Non-profit Organizations

If the group of lawyers had not employed Foreman to work on the bankruptcy legislation, any one of several types of non-profit organizations described in the federal tax code might have taken up the cause. These non-profit organizations, exempt from paying taxes, are restricted in their lobbying efforts in various ways.

If a 501(c)(3) worked for the bankruptcy legislation for disease victims, only 20 percent of the organization's total efforts could go into trying to influence laws. The other 80 percent would have to go toward other activities, such as offering direct services to the victims, research about the illness and education, to quote the law, "on subjects useful to the individual and beneficial to the community."

Furthermore, only 25 percent of the 20 percent could be used to "exhort the general public" to influence their representatives to vote for the legislation. The 501(c)(3)s are allowed to lobby for their own existence; i.e., for funding or other support.

According to the tax code, a 501(c)(4)—sometimes called a membership or citizens group—is a nonprofit organization "operated exclusively for the promotion of social welfare."

A 501(c)(4) could work on behalf of legislation for asbestos victims 100 percent of the time if it chose to. The catches are that donors to 501(c)(4)s cannot deduct their contributions, no revenue can come from government, and less would probably come from private foundations.

To form a 501(c)(4) to deal specifically with asbestos disease or with any narrow issue with a small constituency would be unwise. The group could, however, affiliate itself with a larger organization which could combine their issue along with similar ones, e.g. victims of all kinds of workplace toxicity.

The 501(c)(5) designation refers to non-profit unions and professional organizations. Because 501(c)(5)s exist for the betterment of members' working conditions and products, this type of nonprofit would be technically appropriate for asbestos workers. Unfortunately, the same problem exists as with 501(c)(4)s: all money comes from non-deductible contributions, usually in the form of membership fees. The Boston Teachers Union and the Association of Business and Professional Women in Construction are 501(c)(5)s. Again, asbestos disease sufferers probably could not support a 501(c)(5) by themselves.

Some issues work out well when two organizational set-ups are used in combination. One common pair is a 501(c)(3) and a 501(c)(4). In another type of highly successful combination, advocates who are affiliated with 501(c)(3)s form and belong to 501(c)(5)s. Asbestos disease victims could not take advantage of a combination, but others can.

Charlotte Tropp, former director of the Humboldt County (California) RSVP, described the plight of a typical advocate affiliated with a 501(c)(3). "I run a program for older Americans which is primarily funded with federal money, plus a little from the state. I am forbidden to do any kind of advocacy with that money except for things which have directly to do with my organization. If my program is in jeopardy, I may act. Otherwise, I may not act at all. That's a real problem.

"Our rent in this building and our telephone are being paid for by the federal government, so we are not supposed to use them for advocacy activities at all. What that does is make us impotent. Our job is to work on behalf of older Americans to make life better for them. I think that if we can't be advocates for legislation for the people we serve, we shouldn't be in the business at all."

Tropp employed two methods for staying within the law and still expressing the needs of seniors she and RSVP served. First, she expressed herself as an individual citizen, and second, she joined a professional organization.

"I work through an advisory council at RSVP," Tropp explained. "Depending on the issue, I send letters off [to legislators] without using letterhead stationery, and I put my own stamp on them, and I sign them 'Charlotte Tropp' without a title.

"It's really a very tricky situation," she added. "We have a telephone tree locally with all senior providers. We are supposed to be able to call each other when a piece of legislation comes up which will adversely or positively affect senior programming. We call each other so we can send telegrams or write letters. I don't know if that's legal or illegal."

Tropp described how she and others also used a 501(c)(5) professional organization to do advocacy her 501(c)(3) may not be able to do. "This is another way we do advocacy. I think this is pretty typical for senior programming. I belong to the California State Association of RSVP Directors. I also belong to the national association. We have a lobbyist. That's the way we get around the advocacy restrictions. We pay our association dues which are private. Then, through our national dues, we hire a portion of a Washington lobbyist's time."

Government-Employed Advocate or Agency

Contrary to popular myth, people employed by government, and government agencies themselves, can advocate policy change whenever and wherever they want. The Supreme Court said so in 1978.

If asbestos disease victims had a government agency or official on their side, those people could work all they wanted on the bankruptcy law that would help them.

Occasionally, persons affiliated with government say they are "forbidden by law" to advocate for policies. It's not true, and it's sad if the person believes that. Two real reasons a government employee might choose not to advocate are fear of political repercussions and orders from the boss.

Government employees are not supposed to work for candidates as part of their employment. And, although not forbidden by law, it is unethical for government employees to say they *represent* a group such as asbestos disease victims if the victims have not had input into the position (see Chapter Eleven).

Foiled Attempts to "Gag" 501(c)(3)s

In case advocates become, in the eyes of some, too "warm," government periodically comes up with new regulations, called "gag rules," to try to further restrict 501(c)(3)s' communications about legislative issues. Just putting out the proposed regulations for comment — even ones that never make it — often has a chilling effect on advocacy.

In January 1983 and again in November 1987, the Executive Office of Management and Budget (OMB) proposed new regulations which would have done what advocates fear most. They would have severely restricted 501(c)(3)s from doing any policy advocacy whatsoever, specifically disallowing legal actions as a friend of the court (1983); influencing public opinion in any fashion (1983); contributing dues to other organizations (1983); commenting during regulatory or legislative processes (1983); fund raising or advertising that mentions legislation (1987); most communications with elected officials, even when not about pending legislation (1987); activities that pertain to pending legislation, even if not attempting to influence it (1987); newsletters, conferences and workshops that address legislative proposals if they reach people who "share a common view," even if no position is advocated (1987); and nonpartisan research if its presentation favors one side or another "in any manner," even if no view is expressed (1987).

Under the proposed 1987 regulations 501(c)(3)s would have had a painfully narrow, almost impossible-to-use escape hatch; if, and only if, the organizatons set up completely separate offices and staffs for their allowed 20 percent advocacy work, could they continue to do any substantial influencing of legislation. OMB then went on to expand the traditional definition of lobbying in 1987 to try to bring more activities under its 1976 regulations.

After another massive campaign, spearheaded by a group called "OMB Watch," the 1987 proposed regulations were withdrawn. No substitute regulations were ever offered. Fortunately, 501(c)(3)s and their friends were able to stop the regulations from going into effect both times. When the gag rules were promulgated by OMB, they received a great deal of media attention, and news traveled quickly by word of mouth. The OMB and both sets of proposed regulations were drowned in a sea of negative comments from all sorts of people and groups, including the Girl Scouts.

Advocacy on behalf of advocacy is ironic. In this case, by commenting during a government process, non-profit organizations killed the regulations that would have prohibited them from commenting in the future.

Unfortunately, even though the proposed regulations never went into effect, and 501(c)(3)s won two important victories, the results were not publicized nearly as much as the proposed regulations—a classic case of lack of follow-up. OMB got much of the chilling effect it desired—a self-imposed curtailment of lobbying activities by many advocates and groups.

Myths and incomplete memories sometimes rule advocacy. For example, a lawyer attending a seminar to organize advocates to fight the 1987 gag attempts stood up and gave the following incorrect advice: "If you are asked to give testimony before a federal or state legislative body be sure to get it in writing; your testimony should be based on readily obtainable information because OMB does not want you to spend a lot of money on research that could contribute to a lobbying effort." He was speaking—or at least he was heard by advocates present—as though the proposed regulations were already on the books.

The best cure for the chill of confusion is to know the law. Advocates cannot rely on their common sense, popular perceptions or information from lawyers who are not very experienced and knowledgeable in this realm.

No doubt the federal government will promulgate more regulations to curtail advocacy in the future. So far, none of their threats has gone on the books, thanks to the vigilance of many non-profit groups. Advocates and their friends and attorneys will have to maintain that vigilance and continue to respond to the proposed regs as they come out.

To prevent chilling effects, advocates need to do a better job of letting people know when restrictive regulations are *not* enacted. Advocates need to avoid underinformed scaredy-cat types from the legal profession and from other groups. An effective technique is to ask attorneys for precedents, examples of advocacy groups actually penalized for breaking the rules. Actually, there are very few, and the penalties have been extremely mild.

Surmounting Barriers to Change

Many people have ambivalent attitudes toward change—especially when it is thrust on them. Even when they are included in the decision process, change can be extremely frightening to people who are reaping (or think they are reaping) benefits from the status quo.

One good advocacy motto is never to underestimate the paranoia of government. Those holding government office and other powerful positions often perceive suggestions of policy and program change as bothersome at best and a threat at worst.

Overcoming Prejudice

At the forefront of debate on public issues, advocates are convenient targets of prejudice. Being female or being a member of a minority group both seem to make for extra trouble for advocates today. Many feel that they get extra examination and questioning when they do their jobs because of human conditions over which they have no control. But they've learned how to handle prejudice.

Being female: In defending the ERA, Dorothy Ridings said, "I got caught up in the frustration of hearing them [legislators] saying: 'Why are you really here? Do your people really think this is right? Does your group really want this? You're a nice lady. You're well-educated. You've got a husband to take care of. You've got a lovely home. You don't have any material wants. So why should you want this?'"

"That sort of attitude! So paternalistic! And a sexist attitude. It just really ticked me off. In the ERA campaign I've seen some of the most blatant sexist attitudes."

Ridings said she confronted prejudice against women in working with other issues as well. "We're aligned with a lot of different groups, and many of them are traditional male organizations. Old habits are hard to break, even by people who try hard to break them. And it's not just men either. . . .

"It's unfortunate that a lot of lobbying is still done in places women don't have access to," Ridings remarked. "I'm not just talking about male bathrooms, although in some state legislatures that's where a lot of the work is done. But I mean the clubs the women can't go into, can't be members of. And that's still true."

Carol Tucker Foreman had to work inside the male-dominated Department of Agriculture. Although she thinks she had a positive influence, "this isn't to say that I didn't lose something because I wasn't someone they felt comfortable moseying off to the bar with," mused Foreman.

"They certainly viewed me as being an oddball and not a good old boy," Foreman remembered. "Although in some speeches I made early on I joked about it at the Department of Agriculture, I really wasn't sufficiently sensitive to how upsetting it was to the long-time constituency of that department to have to deal with a woman."

Practical solutions also work. Foreman said when she worked in the Department of Agriculture, she "would always have my male deputy with me in the office, because the meat packers found that it was much more comfortable to look at him and talk to me. They would try to persuade me to change a policy, but they found it so much easier to look at the man who worked for me than it was to look at me."

When asked what their concerns are as women, a majority of advocates asked repeated that "being taken seriously" is or was a major concern.

Kathy Kelley, a lobbyist for the Massachusetts Teachers Union, wrote, "Women are generally not accepted as lobbyists. It is still considered to be a 'man's world.' Women are expected not to be too tough [unladylike] or too weak [ineffective]."

Marlene Sciascia observed that as an advocate, "I always felt that in order to be really strategic I had to walk a fine line when I was in primarily male settings between being one of the boys and also still being female."

Norma Wilson said that "as a woman I am taken less seriously by those in political power" and "within organizations I am a part of this is also a problem."

Wilson's goal is "to have women advocates redefine power by the way they go about their jobs so as not to just model male advocates."

According to Dorothy Ridings, officials often questioned the League of Women Voters about why a women's organization would be interested in pursuing national security issues. Ridings reported, "People are asking . . . 'Well, how come you all are interested in this? And are you people really interested in it?' Well, if they weren't they wouldn't have voted for it at the convention and we wouldn't be having the tremendously high response to the first round of consensus."

Nancy Sylvester commented that she works "to make women's concerns a serious part of every policy decision." And Janet Diamond agreed she wants to "make women's issues and women's perspective on all issues a priority."

Eleanor Josaitis said she used to worry about "being taken seriously" but doesn't anymore. All of her work brought her to the point that she really didn't care if she was taken seriously by others. She takes herself seriously, and she says that's enough.

Being a member of a minority group: Kattie Portis, who is black, said she has had to deal with all levels of prejudice. "It used to be very lonely 'cause I had to convince people. I can remember when I first started running this program. We weren't black enough, we weren't white enough, we weren't gay enough, and 'Lord, they all women.'"

Portis said hers was the only drug rehab agency whose books the government examined. They did it twice. "The next time they did it I was prepared. I said, 'Why are we talking about that? Don't you ever call me up and ask me to come down again. You are not going to intimidate me. I can't be running down every day. I got a woman ready to deliver."

Eventually, "the research and demonstration money came straight to Women, Inc.," Portis reported. "Nobody was taking anything off the top. The state could have got five percent or ten percent off that for administration. Now they think I'm one of their best agencies."

After confronting prejudice frequently, Portis said, "I made a decision. It sounds simple, but it takes different people different amounts of time to say this: 'I'm not here to please the people out there.' I hope our job is to help some of these women get it together. And that's how I dealt with prejudice."

Martha Cotera, a Mexican American, reported, "A lot of people complain that minority women haven't moved beyond certain levels. It's because we have to keep constantly reinforcing the accomplishments we make. The issues are never in because we don't have any power. We have power in numbers. But now we have five administrators. As we become more a part of institutional life, they can handle most of it. They only need us some of the time.

"We know what we want to do," Cotera said of Mexican American women. "When minority women move in, we are a threat, because we are very strong. We have to be to get even halfway up the ladder."

Dealing with Negative Responses

Instantaneous, totally negative responses from officials to policy change suggestions result from fear. The actual content of these attacks or dodges is usually meaningless, no matter how specific, vicious or superficially reasonable. Rather than take the specific attack or avoidance seriously, advocates consider the fact the officials are even bothering to go after them as an indication of the degree of fear.

Lois Gibbs's Citizens Clearinghouse for Hazardous Wastes outlines some tactics in one issue of *Everybody's Backyard* and adds to them in the Leadership Handbook on Hazardous Wastes. Other advocates have a lot to say from experience, too.

Advocates have heard the same types of negative responses to their actions — regardless of the issue — again and again all over the country. People who want to block change either try to avoid the issue or else attack the issue and or the advocates.

"The men and women who represent government or industry have thought through how they will deal with you at least as well as you've thought through how you will deal with them," Lois Gibbs points out in the CCHW handbook. "In fact, some of them have even been given formal training in how to handle public participation."

"Basically," Gibbs adds, "they think they've seen it all before. . . . Keep reminding yourself of this fundamental fact, and you can turn their smugness to your advantage."

It's difficult for a government official or anyone else to freeze experienced advocates or groups in their work. Smart advocates know exactly what they can and can't do and have learned over the years not to take irrational responses to their efforts — especially personal ones — very seriously.

Avoiding the Issue

Officials are adept at feigning agreement to placate advocates. They will agree to something easy, saying "We'll take that under consideration" or "We'll set up a study/advisory committee" — or they'll promise to give you some information, rather than action.

Will Collette writes that they give "symbolic satisfaction: Public officials know how to smile, nod, use body language and words to give the impression of agreement, when in reality, they have no intention of conceding. Get agreements in writing, on the spot, so that everyone knows exactly what has been accomplished." When talking with legislators, it's a good idea to write to them later, confirming what they said.

One of the worst avoidance techniques is for officials only to pretend to agree to take action when they are face-to-face. Advocates can see through this if the official says something like, "I'll look into this" or "Let's set up a committee," or promises to get more information instead of take a stand, according to CCHW's Leadership Handbook.

A contrasting tactic to evading a problem is to deny there is one. Officials who deny say one or all of the following: "You don't have the big picture"; "If there were a problem I would have heard about it already"; "There is a problem, but you need to try another branch of government"; "You don't have all the information and I do."

Other officials have excuses for avoiding change, according to CCHW. They say, "We don't have the money"; "We have the money, but don't look to us"; "We tried it already, and it didn't work"; "I agree with you completely, but my hands are tied"; "We need more information." Or they try to change the subject to some area they are not responsible for.

Government officials know how hard it is to form groups and coalitions to deal with issues, and they may try to create or emphasize differences to divide one advocacy group or to pit one group against another. As long as advocates are fighting each other, they're using up energy they might use on the issue. And, the officials hope, maybe they won't have to change at all or just a little for one faction.

Typical tactics, according to CCHW, include trying to say one group can get something and not the other, and the groups have to decide who. Sometimes they pit neighborhood against neighborhood or race against race. And when advocacy groups for the same issue have not communicated before going public with goals, officials can constantly point out differences in the goals, causing strife in the groups and in the change process efforts.

Gibbs says officials also try to "buy off leaders; All of a sudden the strongest leaders are appointed to 75 boards, committees and commissions and are made to feel like big shots while for all practical purposes, they are being made to work for the opposition. Sometimes, the buy-off takes the form of job offers, putting the organization in the bad spot of now having to fight against its old friends and leaders. Or, offering individuals attractive individual solutions to their problems. . . ."

Outright Attacks

Sometimes advocates must take direct assaults — some of which are personally aimed. Brenda LaBlanc related a below-the-belt attack on housing protesters that was designed to shut them up. "When we were fighting against the housing inspection we just got terrible things said about us in the paper. I remember one editorial that said that the people who were opposing this housing inspection were people who simply didn't want to fix up their own homes. I consider this almost defamatory because that was not our concern at all."

Will Collette of CCHW calls this the "There's something wrong with you" category. "In this category, there are a hundred little put-downs and insults that they will try to shake your confidence. . . ."

They might say, according to Collette, "'You don't have all the information we have; and if you did, either you'd agree with us, or if you didn't agree, that means you don't understand it.'"

Name-calling generally takes two forms: political and personal. Political labels officials may use or imply are radical, communist, socialist, outside agitator, etc. Personal adjectives often impugn the advocates' mental stability. Advocates watch out for "too" and "un-" in front of these slams designed to shut them up. "You're upset." "You're too emotional." "You're unreasonable." "You're crazy." "You've naive." "You're out of control. Come back when you've calmed down."

Some name-calling is just plain mean and designed to intimidate. A state representative in Massachusetts, for example, called welfare mothers visiting his office "deadbeats" right to their faces, Janet Diamond reported.

"We should have known about this guy from his record on the rent supplement bill or emergency assistance for the homeless. He sat back and said, 'Seems to me anybody who can't pay their bills is a deadbeat. Why should I bail out deadbeats?' And we didn't know what to say except to think about the children. And then he said, 'Why should I pay for somebody else's bastards?' It was at that point where we said, 'Good-bye, Representative So-and-so,' but feeling totally destroyed and taking it very personally.

"A more experienced advocate taught us not to take it [negative responses and name-calling] personally," Diamond said. "Forget that you are or have been a welfare mother at this point. Forget that some of your best friends have been insulted by this man. Consider the source. Consider the goal and not your own personal interaction. You just want to further your goal. So somebody's not buying. You find somebody who will buy it. You find somebody else who can put political pressure on this guy."

Carol Tucker Foreman told how presidential candidate Ronald Reagan attacked her when she was in the Department of Agriculture. "I was supposed to be in favor of a cheap food policy. I don't know. What's a cheap food policy? When the price of food went up thirty percent in four years, I kept saying to the Carter administration, 'We're going to be in trouble because food prices are going up.'"

She was right and wrong. They were in trouble, but not with consumers. "In nineteen eighty [then the soon-to-be] President Ronald Reagan went to Texas and made a promise to a group of farmers that he would end the Carter administration's 'cheap food policy.' And that we had a cheap food policy because Carol Tucker Foreman was in the Department of Agriculture. And he promised to fire me. I was a symbol.

"In the late nineteen seventies Earl Butz [first secretary of agriculture under Reagan] made a great deal of money making speeches. He later went to prison for failure to pay income taxes of some two hundred thousand dollars to three hundred thousand dollars, but he was making three or four speeches a week then. And always the same speech. Each one of the speeches said, 'They've put in the Department of Agriculture the woman who led the meat boycott in 1973,' and so every place I would go, the farmers were sure that they were meeting the person who had led the meat boycott.

"Of course, I didn't even work in the Consumer Federation in those days, and the Consumer Federation did not participate in the boycott. But I just became the symbol of what farmers didn't like about Jimmy Carter's farm program."

After a while, advocates almost feel a sense of pride when unreasonable people attack them. Sandra Kurjiaka recalled the "moment I knew I was doing my job right."

"I'd had this job for a year and made a speech in response to President Carter's Human Rights Day. I was furious at Carter painting this wonderful picture of human rights here, when we have political prisoners in the state of Arkansas, and I made a speech about this at our Human Rights Day here. There was an entire column in the *Arkansas Democrat* devoted to attacking me. It's a very right-wing newspaper."

Betsy Reifsnider chuckled at an article in *Business Week* saying "how terrible groups like the Sierra Club are." "They are jealous," Reifsnider said, "because we have found out their tactics. We know how to get our agendas before legislators and get things accomplished. Now we can compete.

"The article said we are getting involved in issues we shouldn't be involved in—urban issues, dumping trash in parks, hazardous wastes, things of that nature. I think they've gotten to the point where they'll agree with us on one issue, sometimes. They see us as having too much political savvy now."

Personal questions are another tactic. "Who are you?"; "Who do you really represent?"; "Who's your daddy?" (actually asked of each member of a committee that visited a representative in Arkansas); "How old are you?"; "What do you do all day anyway?"; "What's in this for you?"

These questions are designed to rattle advocates, to shake their confidence, to intimidate them. Wise advocates answer briefly and factually once and never answer again. If the question is too personal and irrelevant to the issue at hand ("Are you married?"; "What does your husband do?"), advocates may politely refuse to answer at all.

Bullies go beyond name-calling when they resist change; they issue confrontational statements and veiled threats. They say things like "You are not going to stop us"; "You'll be sorry"; "Wake up and smell the coffee. You're going to get in trouble with [some powerful person or group] if you keep this up"; "We're going to take you to court." Sometimes bullies even scream or swear.

In the face of bullying, most advocates know better than to be afraid. Like bullies from childhood, adults who try to stop change with threats don't really mean it. Wise advocates ignore their threats and continue about their business.

Another means used in attempts to silence advocates is trying to diminish their numbers. Sandra Kurjiaka talked about the Arkansas legislature. "The session before this we beat back a fifty-page anti-abortion bill. Bella [Abzug] came for the Take Back the Night march. We did big actions up there. We had big rallies of two hundred fifty to three hundred women in the capital. They always underestimate us greatly but we have sign-up sheets so we know. After that, one of the members of the House wanted to pass a law that no more than twenty people could go into a committee for a hearing.

"They were very upset about all those women coming out. They had all this important business and all of a sudden there were all these 'hysterical' women." The Arkansas legislators went on to ask Kurjiaka to remove her group.

Kurjiaka replied, "I don't control that. Women are angry and they're going to be here."

So-called "progressive" officials have patronizing criticism down pat: "You haven't organized well enough," is one of their responses. And, as a spin-off, they say or imply, "If you were doing a good job, you wouldn't need my help." They will also say, "I agree with you, but I don't approve of your tactics," and try to distract advocates by critiquing strategy and methods instead of their positions on issues.

Standing Up to the Tactics

"I know our lobbyist must be doing a wonderful job, because the folks at ACTION, which oversees RSVP, wanted us to get rid of her," Charlotte Tropp laughed about government's attitude toward the Washington, lobbyist her professional organization employed. "She is very responsive to the needs of the program and she is very effective. She keeps us informed. She lets us know when it's time to take action with our congressmen."

Negative responses, it is helpful to realize, actually reflect a successful advocacy campaign. Officials don't waste their time criticizing and trying to distract ineffective people. Advocates take note of, then basically ignore, negative responses.

When persuading an official seems hopeless, advocates like Diamond and her group simply go elsewhere. When they are attacked, they ignore it. It's the don't-get-mad-or-upset, get-even-by-succeeding policy. It works well for morale and the issues, too.

More than anything else, exposure to the negative tactics used against them has influenced advocates to be nonconfrontational in their methods. Diplomacy and openness work so much better.

Advocacy for public policy is one of the most difficult jobs around. The hours are bad; the pay is worse. Getting people and policies to change is one of the most difficult enterprises in human experience.

Nevertheless, thousands of people around the country spend major parts of their lives working on issues important to them and to the public.

Afterword

A follow-up questionnaire sent in January 1989 to the advocates interviewed in this book revealed that most were still continuing the advocacy work they described in interviews in 1982 and 1983.

Betsy Reifsnider: "After working for the Sierra Club for six years, I then went to work as a legislative aide to Ruth Galanter, an environmentally minded L.A. City Council member. Working inside government has been invaluable. Dealing with good and bad lobbyists has given me better tips and stratagems for approaching elected officials, staff and bureaucrats. However, I missed working directly on wilderness and park issues, so I found a job as associate director of the Mono Lake Committee, protecting one of the oldest lakes in North America. It's been heartening the past few years to see an environmental ethic creep into the public consciousness."

Carol Tucker Foreman is now a partner in the lobbying firm Foreman and Heidepriem. She also works as a volunteer and board member with Public Voice and Food Research and Action Center FRAC working on the issues of food safety, food assistance, and women's rights.

Brenda LaBlanc is the chairman of the boards of directors of both the Iowa and Des Moines Citizens for Community Improvement organizations. "We are working on reinvestment by getting banks to lend for mortgages in low/middle income neighborhoods. We are working on our third bank. We have over $7 million committed in Des Moines. Also we are monitoring a utility assistance bill pilot project. I attended a conference on housing recently in Chicago with other groups from across the country. We are going to make a big push to be included in policy-making via congressional hearings, etc. But we need more people involved with the knowledge and desire to achieve improvement."

Carol Garvin is now the president of the National Mental Health Association "working on educating the public into the true nature of mental illness; building a mental health system comparable, in capacity and scope, to that of other illnesses. I'm still on my soapbox."

Lotta Chi is "one of the ten board members for the Minority Business Enterprise Advisory Board for the state of Virginia. We meet once a month to discuss how to assist the minority contractors that work on highway construction jobs for Virginia. The big construction companies do not want to subcontract jobs to women and minority owners, and we try to use the law and other pressures to make them comply. As for my business, I'm still facing the same prejudices from men as before. It is still difficult for me to get jobs for my company. But I'm not giving up and have moved to a better office. I'm also on the board of directors for the Woodbury Heights Condo Association. We are trying to fight the developer whose intent is to get rid of the low-rent apartment to build more offices, in which case many Hispanics will be displaced. But the county board voted for the project anyway."

Kattie Portis is still "very involved" with Women, Inc., but in the last two years has been the director of a new umbrella organization which she founded called Women's AIDS Risk Network (WARN). This organization focuses on the new area of danger to women drug abusers and their children—that of contracting AIDS.

Barbara Reed observes, "Old advocates somehow find a way to keep on keepin' on. Because of funding problems more and more advocacy efforts are coming from direct service providers, which at best makes these efforts more fragmented. In the past two months two major advocacy organizations gave out. As president of the Georgia Child Development Association I work on maintaining and expanding affordable quality day care for low-income working poor. I'm also still a day care center director. I edit a newsletter and am a board member of Continuum: Alliance for Human Development which is an advocacy organization to improve AFDC and to expand healthcare programs for low-income pregnant women and young children."

Gini Laurie wrote, "Negative attitudes are more disabling than disability and should be attacked on all fronts. Through the International Ventilator Users Network (IVUN), we are working to ensure the carriage of batteries on airplanes. Through the International Polio Network (IPN) we are trying to educate polio survivors who are encountering the late effects of polio. Most of them have been 'passing' as nondisabled, denying their disabilities, and have had no previous contact with the world of disability."

The Gazette International Networking Institute (G.I.N.I.) sponsored the fifth International Polio and Independent Living Conference in June 1989 in St. Louis, Missouri, including a day-long session on independent living worldwide with representatives from Africa, Australia, Asia, Central, North, and South America, and Europe." Laurie died later that year.

Dorothy Ridings writes, "Within the last three months I have become the president and publisher of *The Herald* in Bradenton, Florida, a 50,000 circulation daily newspaper. This involved a move to a new community and new state, and I am just now 'reconnecting' myself to advocacy work. Much of my ongoing activities are on behalf of the League of Women Voters, the Benton Foundation (on whose board I serve) and several national task forces of other foundations. I expect to pick up the reins of direct personal involvement here in Bradenton, after the moving vans have left."

Kathleen Kelley responds, "I'm sorry it took so long for me to reply as I've been involved in a now three-week-old teacher's strike in Westport, Massachusetts. It's awful. The city actually has a surplus in their budget and they won't even negotiate. And I don't see a good year up on the Hill (Massachusetts Legislature) because of the budget deficit. That's why the Massachusetts Federation of Teachers (MFT) is a member of the Tax Equity Association of Massachusetts (TEAM), a huge coalition lobbying for tax increases."

Stefan Harvey writes, "And yet our work will continue. It was a disappointing presidential campaign to say the least. Senator George Mitchell's election was sure a bit of good news. I have the same job at the Center on Budget and Policy Priorities working on child nutrition issues in particular with the Women, Infants, and Children's Supplemental Food Program, Inc. (WIC)."

Connie Spruill reports, "I spend many volunteer hours educating legislators and community organizations about how beneficial self-employment training can be for those who have been long-term welfare recipients or have struggled on below-poverty incomes. As a former welfare mother, I was able to become self-sufficient through becoming my own boss and starting my own business. I still work with the Association of Business and Professional Women in Construction and the Entrepreneur Development Institute for Training, Inc. Self-employment for the low-income person has not yet been accepted as an alternative solution to poverty. It is hard to get training dollars directed to this specific area because results can be managed only over a long-term period. Society is only ready to look at temporary quick fixes that fail in the end."

Kathleen Sheekey is still working for Common Cause and currently working on the issue of campaign finance reform. "I have been involved in advocacy work since the mid–1970s; first in the area of consumer protection as legislative director for the Consumer Federation of America, then as director of congressional relations at the Federal Trade Commission, and at Common Cause for the past seven years. Since the issues I have worked on — consumer protection, nuclear arms control, and campaign finance reform — are long-term, difficult issues, more and more of these efforts lend themselves to coalition building with other groups. Media advocacy and grassroots lobbying have taken on a greater importance as well."

Janet Diamond recently moved to Santa Cruz, California, to work in an employment and training program for the welfare department. "Working on behalf of welfare moms is a lifelong commitment for me and I have come to realize that I do it because it brings me great joy. The issue is not how do we get more welfare benefits but how do we create a system of supports. It continues to amaze me that 'welfare reform' still creates mandatory work programs. Welfare moms do not need to be forced to work; they need a chance to work at jobs that earn them enough money to support their families."

Lois Gibbs's organization, Citizens Clearinghouse for Hazardous Wastes, reports moving to a larger office to accommodate a trebled staff including five field organizers to cover different areas of the country.

Norma Wilson: "I am advocating tax reform in South Dakota as our funding for education is the lowest in the nation and one reason for this is a regressive tax structure. I am also working to protect and preserve our natural environment—probably the best thing about this state. Of particular concern to me is the strip mining for gold that is occurring in the Black Hills. I am working with Native American, black faculty and students to combat racism.

"In the November election, our reclamation and taxation initiatives, which were designed to place stricter regulations on the mining industry and to increase taxes on their gross products, were defeated. This was primarily due to the fact that the mining association spent 18 times the amount that we had in our Surface Mining Initiative Fund. Right now I am drafting a letter in response to a liquor distributor, who's also a big Democrat and who went around the state as a Mining Association advocate. He attacked me in letters that have been published in local papers, charging that a letter I had previously written was exaggerated, emotional, and immature. He said he hoped I teach fiction since I'm good at writing it. I'm recommending that he read *The Man Who Killed the Deer* and *Ceremony* so that he can begin to understand why I get emotional about the need to protect the earth. But I go on to suggest that if he's too immature to grasp the message of those novels, he might read some non-fiction like *Black Elk Speaks* and *The Unsettling of America*. My advocacy activities never end—they are part of my life. It gets depressing at times fighting the system; but it's the only way to stay alive and sane."

Martha Cotera still runs her business, Information Systems, not letting it interfere too much with her "forever job of keeping an eye on bilingual education. They keep trying to change it or water it down so it's meaningless."

Sally Mead has been the special assistant to the commissioner of health and social services for the state of Alaska for the last four years. "Since half the population of the state of Alaska lives in Anchorage, but the capital is in Juneau, the commissioner hired me as her liaison to health and social programs in Anchorage. I make the rounds to get their participation in all policy decisions. It's great!"

Dr. Carolyn Brown's libel lawsuit against a local anti-abortion group that had publicly accused her of being a murderer didn't work out so well. It was thrown out of court by the judge before it could get to trial because she was considered to be a public figure. Not only was she not given standing to sue but she was required to pay all the legal expenses for the anti-abortion group. "I guess it wasn't the right strategy to fight them through the courts. You never know who you are going to get as a judge."

Eleanor Josaitis reports, "Focus:HOPE gave out almost 70,000 pounds of food in January in our food prescription program. Our staff has increased by a third to 150. We now have bought and retooled 25 acres of abandoned factories in the city of Detroit. Many of these we have sold to minority owners who are retrained workers in that particular factory. We have a new program for highschool dropouts called Fastrack. If they remain drug-free for six weeks we train them in another six weeks for a job on the line. Then if they are successful for another six weeks we start them in special classes toward their G.E.D. We just started a day care center for our factory employees and Fastrack participants. I get calls from all over the country to come consult on starting any and all of these programs. I just went to Oklahoma recently. I still co-direct with Father Cunningham. All of my kids are off doing good things except for the youngest who is still at home."

Nancy Sylvester is still national co-director of NETWORK. The organization's membership now totals over 7,000 with a lobbying coordinator in each congressional district. This year NETWORK has committed itself to working on legislation to create affordable housing and to prevent and alleviate homelessness.

Glossary

accountability session a group meeting with an official where the official is asked to explain their stand and or behavior on an issue; can be used as a negotiation session or as a monitoring technique.

action (take action, action campaign, direct action) a policy campaign; sometimes narrowly used to mean a campaign using a legislative strategy but actually refers to the entire process, including any of three strategies.

actuality an interview taped by an advocacy group given to radio stations to use as part of news.

advocacy working with others on behalf of public policy change.

advocacy education training constituents in skills needed for advocacy; any number of courses that could be offered in high school, college or graduate school.

advocacy group a group that works together for public policy change; usually an incorporated non-profit or loosely organized group.

advocacy law tax code governing non-profit organizations' advocacy activities.

advocacy skills the variety of skills needs for managing groups and waging policy campaigns; generally learned on the job.

advocate a person who works with others for public policy.

amendment legislation added to a bill during the legislative process.

bargaining session negotiation session between advocates and administrators.

barriers to change reasons policy change may be blocked that have nothing to do with the policy; include prejudice, fear, etc. See **negative response**.

bill legislation that is going through the legislative process.

branches of government judicial, legislative, executive; where advocates press policy using litigation, legislation or negotiation; three branches usually exist at local and state levels as well as national level.

buttonhole to approach a legislator without an appointment to lobby for legislation.

bylaws rules that govern how an advocacy group functions.

canvass to survey a group or residents of an area thoroughly about issues.

carry out strategies Step 4 of policy campaign; involves education plus either negotiation, legislation or litigation.

case advocacy advocacy for one person about their particular problem(s) with policy.

chilling effect the result of regulations and laws proposed (and often not enacted) that would curtail advocacy by non-profit groups; often sought by government officials.

choosing issues second phase of Step 1 of a policy campaign; group decides which issues it will pursue.

coalition a temporary joining of two or more advocacy groups to work on a particular policy campaign.

comment on regulations respond to proposed regulations in person or in writing to the appropriate executive office or commission.

conference a gathering of members or representatives of one or more advocacy groups; possible purposes include education and decision-making.

conference committee a committee made up of representatives of both houses of a legislature that irons out differences in a bill.

confirm a constituent to get a constituent to commit theirself to a cause or group.

consensus agreement reached by members of an advocacy group.

constituent in electoral politics, a person the politician represents; in advocacy, a person with concern about an issue who may choose to be represented by an advocacy group.

constituent profile a description of typical constituents for an issue.

constituent types four general kinds depending on characteristics in common, useful to know when recruiting individuals. 1. constituents with common life experience; 2. constituents with common local problem; 3. constituents with common condition of birth; 4. constituents with general concern.

convention a gathering of members of an advocacy group, often to make decisions, share information, elect officers, do other group business.

co-opt to get someone's favor by offering him or her a position or other non-monetary reward.

court stripping bill legislation designed to negate a court ruling.

demonstration any public display supporting or opposing policy.

direct recruiting recruiting methods that ask the constituent to respond in a specific way. Indirect recruiting does not offer a response mechanism. See **hook.**

doorknocking going door to door in order to gather information about a problem and or to recruit constituents by offering information; used mostly for local problems, but may be used when a state or national issue has been "localized."

education effort to inform members, the public and government about issues in general and specific policies; one of the main purposes of many advocacy groups; a strategy of all policy campaigns; a policy change follow-through activity.

endorsement in electoral politics, formal support for a candidate; in a policy campaign, formal support for policy change.

evaluation part of Step 5, follow-through, in policy campaign.

expert person knowledgeable about process or content of an issue.

follow through Step 5 of policy campaign, involves evaluation, education and monitoring.

friend of the court a person or group that enters a court case on neither side; also amicus curae.

gag rule or regulation attempt by government to silence advocacy related to non-profit organizations. See **chilling effect.**

hearing session called by the executive branch regarding regulations, or by the legislative branch regarding laws, where people are asked to testify about pros and cons of policy proposals.

hook the mechanism used to recruit constituents that asks for a response; the mechanism used to ask constituents to take action about an issue.

identifying issues First phase of Step 1 in a policy campaign.

implementation carrying out policy decisions; legislation is implemented through the executive branch through regulations.

infighting conflict within a group or between related groups. See **strange bedfellows**.

involving constituents providing services for and receiving services from constituents/members.

lawyer a legal expert needed to carry out litigation or to advise on group legal matters; not the same as public policy advocate.

legislation the lawmaking process; proposed law; one of three possible change strategies.

legislative liaison usually an advocate employed by executive branch to communicate with legislative branch about policy.

letter (writing campaign, to the editor, to members, etc.) one of the most frequently used communication tools in advocacy.

litigation lawsuit or other court action; one of three ways to change policy; used in judicial branch.

lobby to try to influence legislators about legislation.

lobbyist a person who lobbies.

local issue an issue that pertains only to a specific location.

localized issue a larger issue that is dealt with at the local level.

media general term used to mean news media and staff.

member a confirmed constituent who belongs to a group.

membership organization informal term for a non-profit 501(c)(4).

model bill a bill that can be used as an example for drafting bills to submit to a variety of legislatures.

monitor to watch a government body or official for any of the following purposes: to check on officials, to discover problems, to research known problems, to follow through on a new policy.

negative response reaction of an official against a policy campaign, not

the policy; takes the form of dismissing the issue and or attacking the advocates. See **barriers to change**.

negotiation discussion with government officials in the executive branch with the goal of policy change; how regulations are formulated; one of three policy change strategies.

organizing a general term used to describe all advocacy activities, especially those that pertain to working with groups; sometimes used in combination with other words. (See more at the end of glossary).

petition a position statement about policy that constituents are asked to sign; used to recruit constituents and to show officials support for a policy.

policy campaign the five steps and many activities involved in a changing public policy.

policy campaign forum the government body or other official group that deals with the policy proposal.

policy campaign goal the exact policy change desired, stated briefly.

policy campaign management (coordination) taking a policy through the five-step process, overseeing the entire campaign, involving the advocacy groups and others.

policy campaign theme the reason for the policy change, stated briefly.

Political Action Committee (PAC) a group officially created to support candidates and donate funds to them.

poll same as canvass; can be done in person, by phone, in writing; used to solicit problems, choose issues and do research.

position statement a brief statement of the theme and goal of a policy campaign.

press advisory a statement issued to the media announcing an event.

press conference an event to which media are invited to listen to people on an issue.

press release a statement issued to the media about an event or issue.

pro bono without charge or at reduced charge, usually legally.

professional organization an informal name for a 501(c)(5) nonprofit; also a union.

promulgate to propose regulations for review and comment.

public policy consultant a professional freelance lobbyist or advocacy consultant.

public service announcement (PSA) a free announcement for non-profit groups.

recipient a person who receives services of a service group; also a constituent of policies that affect those services and the group.

record the stand an elected official has taken; the information management group keeps about the campaign.

recruit constituents to attract members through various activities.

referendum special legislation that is voted on directly by the public.

regulations policies made by the executive branch of government to implement a law or laws.

repeal take back or erase a law.

represent what an elected official does for constituents in his or her district; what advocates do for groups of people who give permission to the advocate to represent them.

representative democracy a system of government under which citizens do not usually vote directly on policy but for representatives to make and oversee implementation of policy.

research Step 2 in policy campaign; involves deciding who, what, where, when, why of the campaign.

service delivery organization usually a 501(c)(3) that delivers direct services to clients as its main goal; may also get involved in policy matters that affect clients and or services.

sign into law/veto what the head of the executive branch does with legislation after it has passed the legislature.

specialist an expert advocates work with in policy campaigns.

strange bedfellow a person or a group involved in advocacy that behaves in a way that may hamper change activities.

strategy plan for changing policy; education plus either negotiation, legislation or litigation carried out at Step 4 in a campaign.

sunshine laws Freedom of Information Act, Open Meeting Laws and others that allow citizens to find out what government is doing.

survey see **canvass** and **poll**.

targeting elections deciding what elections are important to work on to get public policy enacted in the future.

telephone tree or chain a system of rapid communication among members of a group.

testify to speak at an administrative or legislative hearing about a policy, often on behalf of a group; can be personal knowledge or objective data.

testimony oral and or written presentation at a hearing.

training education offered to members of advocacy groups in order to keep them involved.

turf war conflict between advocacy groups working on the same or similar issues.

visit meet in person with a legislator in order to get to know the person or try to persuade him or her about a piece of legislation.

volunteer organization a term sometimes used to describe 501(c)(3) nonprofits.

voter registration conducted by advocacy groups, especially for the purpose of building clout for constituents of the issues.

Tools of the Trade:
How-to Resources

The tools that advocates use are listed here, along with information about resources for learning more about them. These tools consist of specific methods, techniques and materials useful to all advocates. Some of the tools aid in putting together and maintaining groups, some are used to change policy and some are used, with different focuses, for both activities. For definitions of words and phrases below, see Glossary.

Although most of the how-to resources listed below talk about specific issues and groups, techniques they describe are applicable to any public policy or group.

The authors have found many excellent examples of the very important activities listed below, but they have been unable to locate complete materials that explain how to carry out all of them. The notation NF indicates "not enough found."

Listed below in alphabetical order are the names of the tools, the chapters they appear in and how the tool is used. Underneath each topic are names of materials that offer specific information on how to develop and use the tools. To obtain resources, write to addresses listed here and at the end of this section.

actualities (9) For public education. See: **media**.
  Media Means, CCHW.

advocacy law (4, 13) Legal information about nonprofits and activities.
  Should You Incorporate? CCHW.
  Facts on PACS, League of Women Voters of the U.S. (LWV). *Nonprofits' Handbook on Lobbying*, John T. Grupenhoff and James T. Murphy, Taft

Corporation, Washington, D.C., 1977. *OWL Organizing Manual. Lobbying and Political Activity for Nonprofits: What You Can and Can't Do Under Federal Law*, Children's Defense Fund, 1983. *Society for Nonprofit Organizations' Resource Center Catalog.*

advocacy roles (2, 11)
  Advocating Today: A Human Service Practitioner's Handbook, Family

Service of America, 1983. Books about organization leadership in Society for Nonprofit Organizations' Resource Center Catalog. NF

audio-visual materials (5, 9). To promote organization and or issues.
Projecting Your Image: How to Produce a Slide Show, LWV.

brochures (3, 4, 5, 9) To promote organization, issues, services. See **newsletters.**

budgets — government (7, 8, 10)
LWV: *The Citizen and the Budget Process.* See **Fund raising.**

bulletins (4, 9) To alert members about policy campaigns. See **newsletters.**

business — working with (3, 6, 7, 10, 11)
Lobbying the Corporation: Citizen Challenges to Business Authority, David Vogel, Basic Books Inc., 1979.

carry out strategies — Step 4 of policy campaign (8, 10, 13) See **education, negotiation, legislation, litigation.**

choosing issues (8) The second phase of Step 1. See **identifying issues, conventions, meetings, polls, surveys.**
In League, LWV. *Planning for a Change: A Citizen's Guide to Creative Planning and Program Development,* Dale Duane, Center for Organizational and Community Development, 1978. *Impact on Issues,* LWV.

coalitions (3, 4, 10, 12) Ad hoc advocacy groups that do policy campaigns.
How to Do an Advocacy Campaign, Sierra Club, Los Angeles, California, 1983. *OWL Organizing Manual. Getting It All Together* and *Campaign Handbook,* LWV. *Networking: A Trainer's Manual,* Joan M. Brandon and Asso-

ciates, Society for Non-profit Organizations. *Realizing the Potential of Interorganizational Cooperation,* Society for Non-profit Organizations. *Cutting Deals with Unlikely Allies,* Society for Non-profit Organizations.

comment on regulations (10, 13) See **regulations.**

conferences (4, 5, 8, 9) To attract members, promote group, make group decisions, educate about policy, offer services to members.
Making It Happen: Putting on a Leadership Development Conference, CCHW. *OWL Organizing Manual.* Society for Nonprofit Organizations' Resource Center Catalog.

demonstrations — including rallies, picketing motorcades, marches (9) See **Education.**
Leadership Handbook on Hazardous Wastes, CCHW.

doorknocking (5, 8, 11) To recruit constituents, discover problems.
OWL Organizing Manual, Leadership Handbook on Hazardous Wastes, CCHW. *Best of Organizing Toolbox,* CCHW.

education — public (5, 8, 9, 13) See **media.**
Reaching the Public, Mental Health Association of South Carolina, 1983. *Citizens: The Untapped Energy Source,* LWV. *LWV Media Kit: Reaching the Public, Setting up a Speakers Bureau Getting Into Print, Breaking Into Broadcasting, Projecting Your Image: How to Produce a Slide Show.*

elections — working in (6, 12)
All from LWV: *Getting Out the Vote. Election Check-up: Monitoring, Registration, Voting. How to Judge a Candidate. Endorsements: Pick a Candidate.*

How to Watch a Debate. Making a Difference.

evaluation (8, 13) At the end of a policy campaign. See **follow through**.
Changed Forever: The League and the ERA Campaign, LWV. *ACTION,* LWV. *Best of Organizing Toolbox,* CCHW. *OWL Organizing Manual.*

experts (6, 8, 10, 12) Help groups with process and content of policy campaigns.
Experts: A User's Guide, CCHW. *The Response of the Local Physicians and the Private Laboratories at Love Canal,* CCHW. *Beyond Experts: A Guide for Citizen Group Training,* Dale Duane, Center for Organizational and Community Training, 1979.

fact sheet (5, 9, 10, 13) To inform and recruit constituents, policy-makers and or media. See **education**.
Best of Organizing Toolbox, CCHW. *How to do Leaflets, Newsletters, and Newspapers,* Nancy Brigham, Vocations for Social Change, Boston, MA 02122.

flyers (5) Same as leaflets. See **education, fact, sheet, newsletters**.
Best of Organizing Toolbox, CCHW, *Media Means,* CCHW. *How to do Leaflets, Newsletters, and Newspapers,* Nancy Brigham, Vocations for Social Change, Boston, MA 02122.

follow through (8, 13) Step 5, of policy campaign. See **monitoring, education, and evaluation**.
The Implementation Game: What Happens After a Bill Becomes Law, Eugene Bardach, MIT Press, 1977.

friend of the court briefs (10) See **litigation**.

fund raising (4, 13) For group support and for policy campaigns.

OWL Organizing Manual. How to Raise and Manage Money, CCHW. *The Grassroots Fundraising Book,* Youth Project, Washington, D.C., 1980. *Lobbying on a Shoestring,* Massachusetts Poverty Law Center, Boston, MA, 1982. *Best of Organizing Toolbox,* CCHW. Society for Nonprofit Organizations' Resource Center Catalog.

grant writing (4) See **fund raising**.
The Rich Get Richer and the Poor Write Proposals, Nancy Mitiguy, CTIP, University of Massachusetts, Amherst, MA, 1983, *Grantseekers Guide,* Jill R. Shellow, Moyer Bell Ltd., Colonial Hill RFD 1, Mount Kisco, NY 10549.

identifying problems (8) Step 1, first phase of policy campaign. See **survey**.
Chapter Plan of Action, OWL. *Not an Act of God: The Story of Times Beach,* H. Karl Reko, c/o Lutheran Family and Children's Services, 4625 Lindell St., St. Louis, MO 63108. *OWL Organizing Manual. In League, Guidelines for League Boards,* LWV.

information booth (9) See **education**.
Reaching the Public, MHASC.

lawyers (6, 11, 12) To advise groups on status, conduct litigation.
User's Guide to Lawyers, CCHW. *Best of Legal Corner,* CCHW.

legislation strategy (8, 10, 13)
U.S. Congress
How Laws Happen, NETWORK. *Congress in Committee,* NETWORK. *The Dance of Legislation,* Eric Redman, Simon & Schuster, New York, 1973. *How to Win in Washington: Very Practical Advice about Lobbying the Grassroots and the Media,* Ernest Wittenberg, 1989, Blackwell, Basil, Inc. *Impact on Congress: A Grassroots Lobbying Hand-*

Amherst, MA, 1983. *Reaching the Public*, MHASC. *OWL Organizing Manual. LWV Media Kit: Breaking into Print, Breaking into Broadcasting. Leadership Handbook on Hazardous Wastes*, CCHW. *Best of Organizing Toolbox*, CCHW. Society for Nonprofit Organizations' Resource Center Catalog.

meetings—advocacy group (4)
Leadership Handbook on Hazardous Wastes, CCHW. *Chapter Plan of Action*, Carleen Joyce and Rita D'Ascenzo, OWL. *Putting Together a House Meeting*, Cathy A. Howell, Train Institute. *How to Deal with Trouble*, CCHW. *Best of Organizing Toolbox*, CCHW. *OWL Organizing Manual. Simplified Parliamentary Procedure*, LWV. Society for Nonprofit Organizations' Resource Center Catalog.

monitoring (6, 8) To keep track of officials or policy, to discover problems.
ACTION, LWV. *Planning Program*, LWV. *Going to Court in the Public Interest*, LWV. *In League*, LWV. *The Implementation Game: What Happens After a Bill Becomes Law*, Eugene Bardach, MIT Press, 1977.

needs assessment (5, 8)
Society for Nonprofit Organizations' Resource Center Catalog.

negotiation strategy (8, 10, 13)
Making a Difference, LWV. *Leadership Handbook on Hazardous Wastes*, CCHW. *How to Deal with Trouble*, CCHW. *Best of Organizing Toolbox*, CCHW. *User's Guide to Lawyers*, CCHW. *Breaking the Impasse: Consensual Approaches to Resolving Public Disputes*, Society for Non-profit Organizations. *Successful Negotiating in Local Government*, Nancy Huelsberg, William F. Lincoln, eds. Prac-

tical Management Series, 1985. *Negotiation for a Change*, Shel Trapp, National Training and Information Center. *The Implementation Game: What Happens After a Bill Becomes Law*, Eugene Bardach, MIT Press, 1977.

newsletters (3, 4, 9) To communicate with constituents.
Editing Your Newsletter: A Guide to Writing, Design and Production (Mark Beach, Coast to Coast Books), LWV. *How to do Leaflets, Newsletters, and Newspapers*, Nancy Brigham, Vocations for Social Change, Boston, MA 02122. Society for Nonprofit Organizations' Resource Center Catalog.

orientation—of new advocacy group members (4, 5)
OWL Organizing Manual. Membership Management, LWV.

pastoral messages (9) To inform the public about issues.
Parish Action Handbook, NETWORK. *Best of Organizing Toolbox*, CCHW.

petitions (5, 10) See **doorknocking.**
Leadership Handbook on Hazardous Wastes, CCHW.

picketing (9) See **demonstrations.**

Political Action Committees (PACs) (6)
Facts on PACs, LWV.

polls (5, 8) See **experts, research, surveys.**

position statements (8, 9, 10)
Leadership Handbook on Hazardous Wastes, CCHW. *Politics of Change, Planning Program, Campaign Handbook*, LWV. *OWL Organizing Manual.*

postcards (7, 10) See **letters.**

OWL Organizing Manual. Society for Nonprofit Organizations' Resource Center Catalog.

telegrams (10) See **legislation, letter writing.**

television (9) See **media.**
Breaking into Broadcasting, LWV.

testimony (6, 10) Written and oral at administrative and legislative hearings. *Anatomy of a Hearing,* LWV. *Experts: A User's Guide, Where to Find Them, How to Get Them, How to Pay for Them,* CCHW.

training (4, 9)
Putting on a Leadership Development Conference, CCHW. *Beyond Experts: A Guide for Citizen Group Training,* Dale Duane, Center for Organizational and Community Development, 1979.

trouble — **internal, legal, political** (11, 12, 13)
How to Deal with Trouble, CCHW. *Reaction to Collective Stress: Correleates of Active Citizen Participation at Love Canal,* Russel A. Stone and Adeline G. Levine, Dept. of Sociology, State University of New York at Buffalo, Spaulding Triangle, Buffalo, NY 14261.

voter registration (6) See **elections.**

visits to legislators (7, 10) See **legislation.**

writing a bill (10) See **legislation.**
OWL Model Bills.

workshops (5) See **training, conference.**

Addresses of Organizations That Publish Materials

A free catalog or list of inexpensive materials is available from many organizations. Some materials are usually available only to members and leaders but may be requested.

Citizens Clearinghouse for Hazardous
  Wastes (CCHW)
PO Box 926
Arlington, VA 22216

League of Women Voters of the U.S.A.
  (LWV)
1730 M Street, NW
Washington, DC 22036

Mental Health Association of South
  Carolina
1823 Gadsden Street
Columbia, SC 29201

National Training and Information
  Center
1123 W. Washington Boulevard
Chicago, IL 60607

NETWORK
827 Underwood NW
Washington, DC 20012

Older Women's League (OWL)
1325 G. Street, NW
Lower Level B
Washington, DC 20005

Society for Nonprofit Organizations'
  Resource Center Catalog
The Society for Nonprofit Organizations
6314 Odana Road, Suite 1
Madison, WI 53719
(Free catalog lists many books priced $10 and up).

Index